'What is this thing called growth and development? This book offers the best answers to date, based on a stunning integration of past and present realms of knowledge across disciplinary fields – not just subfields of psychology, but also literature, ancient mythology, and classic tales of human becoming. The book then moves to the realm of practice and application, seeking to distil how lives can be better lived. Guided by a profound humanism, it is hard to imagine a more valuable contribution than what these authors have assembled in this beautiful mosaic.'

—**Carol Ryff**, *Professor, University of Wisconsin-Madison*

'This is a beautiful and timely book, one which not only embodies the spirit of the new waves of development in positive psychology, but truly helps it take wing and soar in new directions. Its focus on development throughout the lifespan is very welcome, with invaluable lessons and insights spanning all steps and stages in our great existential journey. Moreover, the book breaks free of the self-limiting boundaries within which positive psychology sometimes finds itself hemmed, drawing on deep wells of thought and scholarship across myriad fields and topics, and bringing these together into a unique and generative synthesis. These not only include developmental and lifespan psychology, as one might hope and expect, but realms such as existential philosophy and psychotherapy, myth and metaphor, language and literature, and religion and spirituality. The authors' collective wisdom and expertise truly shine through across the pages, which are imbued with a generous caring spirit of truly wanting people to flower and become their best selves, something which this book will surely help make possible.'

—**Tim Lomas, Ph.D.**, *Honorary Reader –*
University of East London

'Positive and Existential Psychology complement each other. Finding the courage to say "yes" to this beautiful & painful life – that is the heart and soul of personal growth. This book will inspire you by providing theory, research, and practice within this positive-existential duo. Edited and co-authored by Piers Worth, one of the leading and courageous voices in positive psychology, this book invites you into your own Hero's or Heroine's Journey.'

—**Itai Ivtzan, Ph.D.**, *Director, School of Positive*
Transformation, Boulder, Colorado

Positive Psychology Across the Lifespan

Positive Psychology Across the Lifespan provides an insight into how we are affected by the different stages of adult development and gives us the opportunity to change through choice rather than leaving change to chance.

The science of positive psychology offers a wealth of research and evidence-based interventions and shares insights into which habits and behaviours contribute to how to live a flourishing life. This book aims to extend that knowledge by introducing and incorporating key aspects of existential and humanistic psychology and explores positive psychology with a lifespan perspective. It goes beyond theory to look at practical application, with insightful reflective questions. Whilst acknowledging the differences and disagreements between some of the key figures in the subject areas of the book, it seeks to highlight the areas where there is agreement and congruence which have been previously overlooked or ignored.

The book will be essential reading for students and practitioners of positive psychology as well as other mental health professionals.

Piers Worth, Ph.D., is Visiting Professor in Psychology at Buckinghamshire New University, a Chartered Psychologist and Accredited Psychotherapist. Piers' Ph.D. research focused on how creativity changes as we age, and how it may support positive ageing. His research and writing focus are on subjects and applications that may broaden the base of positive psychology.

Positive Psychology Across the Lifespan

An Existential Perspective

Edited by Piers Worth

Routledge
Taylor & Francis Group

LONDON AND NEW YORK

Cover Image Credit: From guiding-lights.art © Andrew Machon (2018)

First published 2022
by Routledge
2 Park Square, Milton Park, Abingdon, Oxon OX14 4RN

and by Routledge
605 Third Avenue, New York, NY 10158

Routledge is an imprint of the Taylor & Francis Group, an informa business

British Library Cataloguing-in-Publication Data
A catalogue record for this book is available from the British Library

Library of Congress Cataloging-in-Publication Data
A catalog record for this book has been requested

ISBN: 978-0-367-67719-0 (hbk)
ISBN: 978-0-367-67718-3 (pbk)
ISBN: 978-1-003-13253-0 (ebk)

DOI: 10.4324/9781003132530

Typeset in Times New Roman
by Apex CoVantage, LLC

Contents

Contributors

Diane Herbert, MSc

Diane is a part-time doctoral researcher at the Centre for Positive Psychology, Buckinghamshire New University. She is a graduate of BNU's MSc Applied Positive Psychology and holds a BA (Joint Hons) in French and Italian. Diane is a non-executive director and runs a consultancy business specialising in developing cultures that support creativity, innovation and change.

Lesley Lyle, MSc

Lesley Lyle MAPP – positive psychology practitioner trainer, author and clinical hypnotherapist. Her focus is helping create positive change through the application of science-based processes.

Andrew Machon, PhD

An experienced Coaching Supervisor, International Coach Trainer, Psychotherapist and Master Coach (ICF Certified) with three decades of experience working as a Change Specialist in Global Businesses and a Visiting Teaching Fellow on the MSC in Applied Positive Psychology at Buckinghamshire New University.

Lee Newitt, MSc

Lee Newitt is a MAPP graduate, transformational coach and psychology lecturer at Buckinghamshire New University, where he is developing a new master's programme in ecology, spirituality and psychology. Lee cares deeply about our wild and sacred spaces as an eco-mindfulness practitioner and 'earth protector'.

Piers Worth, PhD (Editor and Contributor)

Piers Worth, PhD, is Visiting Professor in Psychology at Buckinghamshire New University, a Chartered Psychologist and Accredited Psychotherapist. Piers' PhD research focused on how creativity changes as we age, and how it may support positive ageing. His research and writing focus are on subjects and applications that may broaden the base of positive psychology.

Foreword to Piers Worth's Positive Psychology Across the Lifespan textbook

Piers Worth's textbook on positive psychology represents a landmark publication because it heals the unfortunate divide between humanistic and positive psychology and demonstrates that an integration between these two schools can be done to advance the science of global well-being (Churchill, 2021; Kaufman, 2020; Wong, 2021a).

This book can be considered a worthy sequel to the ground-breaking textbook exploring a variety of topics considered relevant to Second Wave Positive Psychology (Ivtzan et al., 2016), which explores several aspects of the dark side of life and examines their role in our positive transformation. Worth, one of the co-authors of that textbook, has gone much further by integrating these topics within a coherent story of humanity's heroic struggles to survive and thrive in an often-hostile environment, as in the era of COVID-19.

An existential model of human development

There are several unique aspects of this textbook that are worthy of attention. First of all, it focuses on the process of change at different levels – from the unfolding of one's life to the dialectical process of achieving a goal in any lived context. Thus, the journey of life is conceptualised as different stages of development. Personal growth in each stage involves some struggles to resolve an existential crisis.

Here is my existential model (Figure 1) which is an extension and development of Erikson's (1958/1980, 1963) model and summarises the main thrust of this book. This model complements Erikson's stage model – life is a constant struggle at every stage of human development. How through overcoming the difficulties in our lives, can we achieve a healthy and happy psychological life?

The positive psychology of suffering

The second important aspect is its treatment of suffering as an inherent aspect of life. In a recent book review (Wong, 2020a), I mentioned that Compton and Hoffman's (2019) positive psychology textbook is the first one that devoted a whole section to the psychology of suffering in PP 2.0. I can hardly believe that the presence of suffering is weaved into every chapter of Worth's textbook.

An Existential Model of the 9 Stages of Life-Span Psychology, Tracing the Developmental Roots of Human Vulnerability, Frailty and Virtues.

◆Dr. Paul T. P. Wong

	Stage	Age	Existential Crisis	Main Task	Gains	Risks
1.	Infancy	Birth–2 years	Separation anxiety	Necessary gradual separation from mother	- Trust, faith, and hope - Secure attachment (love) - Enduring discomfort - Delayed gratification	- Dependency - Anxious/avoidant attachment - No frustration tolerance - Narcissism - Fear of abandonment
2.	Preschooler	3–4 years	Safety anxiety (Fear of getting hurt)	Testing limits of autonomy	- Obedience - Freedom and security within boundaries - Honesty and speaking the truth - Respect for rules and authority	- No respect for parents and authority - No impulse control - Exerting power through temper tantrums - Deception - Aggression
3.	Kindergarten to primary school	4–12 years	Social anxiety (Fear of not belonging)	School	- Sharing and belonging - Playing fair (justice) - Humility and forgiveness - Curiosity about the world	- Isolation/loneliness - Social anxiety - Fear of rejection - Bullying and cruelty - Poor self-esteem - Manipulation
4.	Adolescence	12–18 years	Identity crisis	- Puberty - Preparation for adulthood	- Self-knowledge - Self-awareness - Sexual orientation - Discovery of areas of strengths	- Role confusion - Dropping out of school - Low achievement motivation - Seeking pleasure and risky behaviour - Rebelliousness and antisocial behaviour
5.	Young adult or early career	19–25	Independence anxiety	- Love relationship - Entry into work force	- Courage - Hope - Purpose - Confidence in love relationship and work	- No meaning and purpose - Depression - Aggressiveness - Addiction - Loner - Making a living through illegal means
6.	Adult or mid-career	25–40	- Achievement anxiety (Fear of failure in career and marriage)	- Supporting a family - Parenting	- Responsibility - Resourcefulness - Perseverance - Career success - Happy marriage - A sense of actualization	- Getting stuck in a bad job or bad marriage - Divorce - Delinquent children - No close friends - Depression and addiction
7.	Mature adult or late career	40–60	Mid-life crisis	- Reflection on the first half of life - Ready for major change	- Generativity - Life satisfaction - Life transformation - Social conscience - Consolidating one's contributions - Redemption	- Stagnation - Regression to adolescence - Taking unwise risks - Taking early retirement - Giving up on life
8.	Early old age	60–75	Ultimate concerns about boredom and meaninglessness	Retirement	- Self-transcendence - Integrity - Spiritual growth - Enjoying life to the fullest - Volunteering - Grand-parenting	- Despair - Depression - Bitterness - Resentment - Blaming and complaining - Cranky old person
9.	Late old age	76–death	Worrying about unfinished business	Completing the race gracefully	- Letting go, facing death with gratitude and faith - Integration - Death acceptance - Legacy - Hope for immortality - Wisdom - Spiritual maturity - Mature happiness	- Regrets - Despair - Depression - Anger towards life - Suicide - Alienating adult children

Figure F.1 An existential model of the nine stages of lifespan psychology.

The problem of suffering was posed to Seligman shortly after launching PP in 1998. His answer in his 2003 Newsletter was 'More commonly we overcome troubles by doing end-runs around them, by deploying our highest strengths as buffers against the setbacks of life'.

However, it is very difficult if not impossible to manoeuvre around suffering, especially existential suffering, because it is an inherent part of life (Fowers et al., 2017).

No one is immune from it. It is inevitable that we will experience setbacks, obstacles, failures, losses, sickness and death. PP 2.0 is about how to respond to adversity in a positive and adaptive manner. From the perspective of lived experience, real resilience and life satisfaction come from eventual triumphs in the heroic struggles between life and death, good and evil and success and defeat.

Unlike cold statistics, such lived experiences fill the pages of Worth's book, giving readers an uplifting and realistic understanding of how to flourish in adversity.

The paradox of self-transcendence

Simply put, self-transcendence is the pathway of personal development and spiritual practice that can empower us to flourish through transcending our suffering and human limitations (Frey & Vogler, 2019; Worth & Smith, 2021). This approach can be described as going higher to fulfil one's aspirations by going deeper to sink one's roots in suffering; the result is to become what we were meant to be – making a unique contribution to humanity as illustrated in Figure 2.

ST is the least understood but most important breakthrough in psychology during the 21st century. The mental block could be due to the egoistic mindset in an

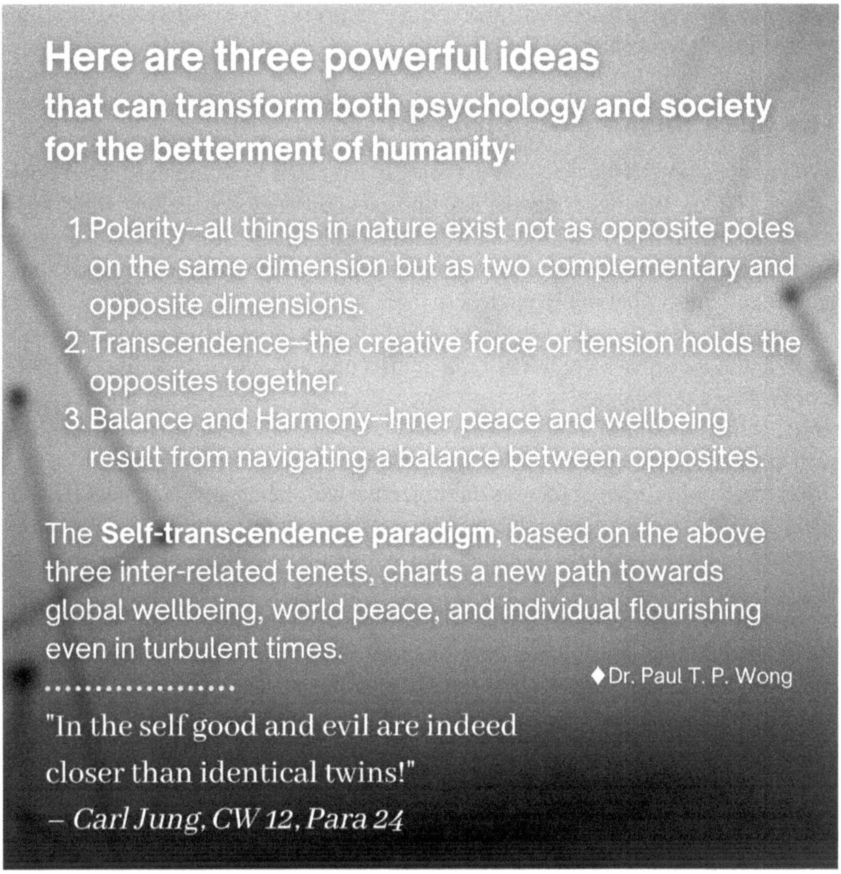

Here are three powerful ideas
that can transform both psychology and society
for the betterment of humanity:

1. Polarity--all things in nature exist not as opposite poles on the same dimension but as two complementary and opposite dimensions.
2. Transcendence--the creative force or tension holds the opposites together.
3. Balance and Harmony--Inner peace and wellbeing result from navigating a balance between opposites.

The **Self-transcendence paradigm**, based on the above three inter-related tenets, charts a new path towards global wellbeing, world peace, and individual flourishing even in turbulent times.

♦Dr. Paul T. P. Wong

"In the self good and evil are indeed closer than identical twins!"
– *Carl Jung, CW 12, Para 24*

Figure F.2 Towards a general theory of global well-being.

individualist and secular culture; a happiness-driven consumer culture wants us to avoid the subject of suffering to maintain our happy feelings and thoughts about life.

A less visible, but important, barrier in mainstream psychology is self-psychology (such as self-efficacy) from the last century, which dismisses self transcendence because it advocates selflessness (Yaden et al., 2017). Paradoxically, PP 2.0 emphasises that we need to confront and embrace suffering and death to find sustainable happiness and meaning in serving others. ST requires a mega shift to a more collectivistic and a more humanistic and existential mindset.

The new science of existential positive psychology was pioneered by Viktor Frankl and expanded by Paul Wong (2020b). Both began their search for meaning and well-being when they were at the bottom of a dark pit. They found their way out of the abyss through ST.

Maslow's (1971) concept of transcendence and Scott Barry Kaufman's (2020) expansion provide yet another pathway of how to lose oneself to serve something greater and awe-inspiring. The recent Frontiers in Psychology, special issue on existential positive psychology (Wong et al., in press), reveals the rapid development of this new science.

The need for an existential self

'Who am I really?' This question is typically triggered by some existential crisis (Wong, 2020c). Whenever people ask this question, they are seeking some existential understanding of selfhood beyond their self-image or objective characteristics, such as gender, occupation or marital status. This question demands some self-reflection on what really matters to them.

Worth's book shows that the discovery of an existential self is needed not only for living at a deeper level but also for transcending the horrors of life. Van Stee (2017) shows that Cognitive Neuroscience research is also looking into the existential selfhood, which used to belong to the domain of existential philosophers such as Søren Kierkegaard and Irvin D. Yalom.

Research on well-being focuses on subjective well-being and happiness (Diener et al., 2018). This is understandable: Who does not want to be positive? Who does not want to have more love, laughter and simple pleasures? But PP 2.0 proposes that the direct pursuit of happiness-enhancing activities as the final life goal may be counter-productive. It may lead to toxic positivity (Villines, 2021; Wibowo, 2020); furthermore, unexpected things happen and fate intrudes. Numerous unexpected undesirable events, such as life-threatening sickness, accidents, death of a loved one or the pandemic, can derail even the best evidence-based plans for happiness and success. That is why ST is the way to go beyond such egoistic concerns and to find enduring fulfilment (Wong, 2021b). True positivity is to discover the moon and stars in the darkest night.

There is also the all too familiar human phenomenon that successfully achieving one's cherished goal seldom leads to the kind of happiness as initially imagined or expected. Human beings are not very good in predicting their own happiness

(Gilbert, 2006). Happiness typically returns to the original 'set-point' for a variety of reasons such as the process of habituation and inescapable human suffering discussed earlier.

Humanistic–existential psychology founders, Carl Rogers, Abraham Maslow and Rollo May, were concerned about not only how to become self-actualised and how to live well but also the necessity of courage, anxiety and responsibility to live authentically even when life is full of uncertainties, suffering and mysteries. They inspire people to live fully, choosing one's own destiny and by accepting and experiencing the vicissitudes of life, no matter how difficult. Therefore, they offer a more realistic and helpful psychological and philosophical guide to living a good life, but they suffer from lacking a comprehensive empirical agenda based on quantitative research.

Through levels of processing, at the deepest level, all disciplines reach the same conclusion. Through the dialectical process of self-transcendence, at the highest level, all people can reach the same awe-inspiring mystery. Through selfless sacrifice, we can serve the greatest number of people. Through holistic integrative research, we can best approximate the ultimate truth of wellbeing.

Figure F.3 A summary of the main tenants of PP 2.0.

Worth shows that PP 2.0 can both deepen positive psychology with existential insights and strengthen the empirical base of humanistic–existential psychology. The most hopeful note is that we always have the freedom and possibility of creating a better future for ourselves and society, regardless of our circumstances.

Conclusion

The pandemic has shifted the focus on what is positive to a more realistic view of seeing the brightest stars in the darkest night – true positivity according to existential positive psychology. This shift is like changing the course of the Titanic towards a more balanced view of the good life.

The dominant narrative of positive psychology is to fill our lives with positive experiences and emotions to live the good life. An alternative vision is that life is a balancing act (Wong, 2011). The most fulfilling life is one of harmony when we learn to embrace and transcend its duality of the good and bad times, as represented by the ancient symbol of Yin–Yang (Carreno et al., 2021; Robbins, 2021). A truly positive person knows how to stay positive in negative and ambivalent situations. PP 2.0 encourages research on how such sustainable positivity is achieved through dialectical interactions between Yin and Yang.

The 'take-home' message of this textbook is that it is only through personal authenticity, struggle and fortitude can we discover our true existential self and grow as a person. More importantly, it is only through embracing life in its totality and wrestling with life's ultimate concerns that we can uplift the human spirit and improve the human condition even in the darkest moments. Figure 3 summarises the main tenants of PP 2.0. PP 2.0 says that happiness and suffering are inseparable; to become one's true self is to kindle one's light in darkness.

Dr. Paul T.P. Wong, Ph.D., C. Psych, Trent University

References

Carreno, D. F., Eisenbeck, N., Pérez-Escobar, J. A., & Garcia-Montes, J. M. (2021). Inner harmony as an essential facet of well-being: A multinational study during the COVID-19 pandemic. *Frontiers*. https://doi.org/10.3389/fpsyg.2021.648280

Churchill, S. (2021, August). *On the possibility of an existential positive psychology*. Keynote address presented at the 11th Biennial International Meaning Conference.

Diener, E., Lucas, R. E., & Oishi, S. (2018). Advances and open questions in the science of subjective well-being. *Collabra. Psychology*, *4*(1), 15. https://doi.org/10.1525/collabra.115

Erikson, E. H. (1958 / 1980). *Identity and the life cycle*. New York: Norton.

Erikson, E. H. (1963). *Childhood and society*. Second edition. New York: Norton.

Fowers, B. J., Richardson, F. C., & Slife, B. D. (2017). *Frailty, suffering, and vice: Flourishing in the face of human limitations*. American Psychological Association.

Frey, J. A., & Vogler, C. (2019). *Self-transcendence and virtue: Perspectives from philosophy, psychology, and theology*. Routledge.

Gilbert, D. (2006). *Stumbling on happiness*. Knopf.

Ivtzan, I., Lomas, T., Hefferon, K., & Worth, P. (2016). *Second wave positive psychology: Embracing the dark side of life*. Routledge.

Kaufman, S. B. (2020). *Transcend: The new science of self-actualization*. Tarcher Perigee.

Maslow, A. H. (1971). *The farther reaches of human nature*. Viking Press.

Robbins, B. D. (2021). The joyful life: An existential-humanistic approach to positive psychology in the time of a pandemic. *Frontiers*. https://doi.org/10.3389/fpsyg.2021.648600

Seligman, M. E. P. (2003). *Authentic happiness*. University of Pennsylvania. www.authentichappiness.sas.upenn.edu/newsletters/authentichappiness/suffering

van Stee, A. (2017). *Understanding existential self-understanding*. Universiteit Leiden. www.universiteitleiden.nl/en/research/research-output/humanities/understanding-existential-self-understanding?fbclid=IwAR2k0xL1-jn1UB8RjJRbT7fvHUKZOb-gwx-U9f2qXmvPNwdKmUiddl6gTgoc

Villines, Z. (2021, March 30). What to know about toxic positivity. *Medical News Today*. www.medicalnewstoday.com/articles/toxic-positivity Wibowo, Rahmadina. (2020).

Wibowo, R. S. (2020). *The answers are not always optimism: Overcoming toxic positivity during [ESSAY]*. www.researchgate.net/publication/349824345_The_Answers_Are_Not_Always_Optimism_Overcoming_Toxic_Positivity_During_ESSAY

Wong, P. T. P. (2011). Positive psychology 2.0: Towards a balanced interactive model of the good life. *Canadian Psychology/Psychologie Canadienne, 52*(2), 69–81. https://doi.org/10.1037/a0022511

Wong, P. T. P. (2020a). The maturing of positive psychology and the emerging PP 2.0 [Book review of positive psychology (3rd ed.) by William Compton and Edward Hoffman]. *International Journal on WellBeing, 10*(1). https://doi.org/10.5502/ijw.v10i1.885

Wong, P. T. P. (2020b). *Made for resilience and happiness: Effective coping with COVID-19 according to Viktor E. Frankl and Paul T. P. Wong*. INPM Press.

Wong, P. T. P. (2020c). Meaning and evil and a two-factor model of search for meaning [Review of the essay meaning and evolution, by R. Baumeister & W. von Hippel]. *Evolutionary Studies in Imaginative Culture, 4*(1), 63–67. doi:10.26613/esic/4.1.170

Wong, P. T. P. (2021a). Existential positive psychology (PP 2.0) and global wellbeing: Why it is necessary during the age of COVID-19. *International Journal of Existential Positive Psychology, 10*(1), 1–16.

Wong, P. T. P. (2021b, August). *Beyond happiness and success: The new science of self-transcendence*. Keynote address presented at the 11th Biennial International Meaning Conference.

Wong, P. T. P., Mayer, C.-H., & Arslan, G. (Eds.). (In press). Special issue: COVID-19 and existential positive psychology (PP 2.0): The new science of self-transcendence [Special Issue]. *Frontiers*.

Worth, P., & Smith, M. D. (2021). Clearing the pathways to self-transcendence. *Frontiers*. https://doi.org/10.3389/fpsyg.2021.648381

Yaden, D. B., Haidt, J., Hood, R. W., Vago, D. R., & Newberg, A. B. (2017). The varieties of self-transcendent experience. *Review of General Psychology, 21*(2), 143–160. https://doi.org/10.1037/gpr0000102

Foreword

Positive Psychology across the Lifespan is a stunning contribution, not only for students and practitioners in this field but also for anyone who wants to learn the deeper meanings of what human becoming is all about. Guided by the wise and thoughtful vision of Piers Worth, the reader embarks on a journey through distant lands that are so worthy of attention and careful consideration even though they are often neglected in contemporary views on positive human functioning. Those who aspire to be knowledgeable, however, need to know what different theorists from developmental psychology saw as the unfolding challenges and opportunities for the ever-expanding person traveling across the decades of life. It is also critical to take in the deep insights from humanistic and existential psychologists, past and present, who have grappled with articulating the unfolding journey of growth, change and ST, sometimes in the face of significant trauma and adversity. Adding further richness to this much-needed integration are chapters that bring symbolic, metaphoric and mythical stories to our understandings of varieties of human change. Thus, the adventures and transformations of mythical heroes and heroines from great literature offer further guidance and inspiration, including about what it means to strive for authenticity. Collectively, this exquisite mosaic embodies unprecedented scholarly scope that rarely, if ever, makes its way into a textbook – for the simple, sad reason that knowledge usually gets partitioned into disciplinary silos. This book defies all such implicit boundaries in weaving together its engaging content, drawn from diverse subfields of psychology as well as literature, philosophy and the humanities. This integration is, in itself, a spectacular achievement, but there is still more.

Building on the earlier, there is a concerted commitment to translate these rich ideas and imaginings to the world of practice, exemplified by programs now training applied positive psychologists. Here, the voice is that of the interventionist, the practitioner–researcher who is striving to help people achieve effective change in their own lives. Self-initiated change demands many things, but these authors are ahead of the game in emphasising basics, such as the importance of being alert, authentic, able, involved, empathic and compassionate – remarkably astute observations. Such messages are then combined with rich descriptions of behavioural change processes such as those involved in overcoming addictions, adhering to healthy lifestyles and dealing with financial difficulties. Of particular note is an amazing chapter by Andrew Machon on a profound topic: how we develop insight. Again, guidance is drawn from ancient mythology that is then combined with a compelling distillation of key points about the journey of becoming insightful – namely, that it involves understanding and accepting our own vulnerabilities as well as seeing the paradoxical nature of reality. Both require a reflective stance on living. These ideas have a bell-ringing clarity that is greatly needed in our troubled world, which is not helped by exclusive trumpeting about the positive in who we are.

As an educator who taught courses on Adult Development and Ageing and Personality Psychology over the course of her career, I have a deep affinity with much of the content in this book. But, I also wish to underscore key ways in which these authors have assembled something that goes notably beyond extant texts. As described earlier, the scope of what is covered is breathtakingly deep and wide, but there is also a commitment to help the reader actively engage with the ideas and apply them to his or her own life. Every chapter begins with thoughtfully distilled learning objectives that sketch what lies ahead. Every chapter also ends with discerning questions that encourage students to formulate their personal reactions to the topics covered as well as to reflect about the strengths and weaknesses of theories or research or practices that were covered. What one sees is pedagogy at its best in which students/recipients of this knowledge are not viewed as passive consumers, but as thinking, feeling, doing participants in human becoming. Stated otherwise, this is a book written by people who understand what great teaching requires – above all, it demands the active engagement of the learner.

The bridge on the cover of the book is inspired. It came from a dream of the editor, Piers Worth, who understands the power of imagery and metaphor. This collection truly is a beautiful bridge with its lights reflecting in the deep waters below, thereby symbolising the enormous breadth of the history and disciplinary domains covered. But, there is also the magnificence of the sky above, which captures the sense of endless possibility and the beauty of human striving to achieve a virtuous becoming. These aspirations need, however, another critical quality if human lives are to be beneficially impacted by future generations of applied positive psychologists: there is an authentic humanism that must be lived and enacted for others to see how it is done. That is the extraordinary gift of Piers Worth – he sees what is needed, and he lives it. We can all be grateful that he put his unique talents and beautiful personhood into this book. It is a remarkable exemplar of what it means to achieve the best that is within us.

Professor Carol D. Ryff,
University of Wisconsin-Madison

Acknowledgements

As Editor, I would wish to express my gratitude to the following people for their influence and contribution to this book:

Dr. Matthew Smith was the source of the idea and vision for this book in our team-teaching on the Journey of Change Module of the MAPP course at Buckinghamshire New University, and has played a key role in editing the final text.

Dr. Paul Wong has been the visionary and creative teacher and writer about the need for and the form of existential positive psychology. The work in this book draws from and builds on his ideas.

The contributors to this book, Diane Herbert, Lesley Lyle, Andrew Machon and Lee Newitt, who have committed themselves generously and creatively to develop the ideas expressed.

Andrew Machon, as an author of two chapters and co-author of a further three, has been a profound creative influence on the shape and depth of this book, the exploration and decisions made as part of this work and how it will support the reader.

Joanne Forshaw, Senior Editor at Routledge, has been generous, kind and supportive in the process of this book being proposed and coming into being.

The MAPP students on the Buckinghamshire New University course were a joy to work with and a source of ongoing learning in the interaction with them, particularly on the 'Journey of Change' module. Their influence is reflected in this book.

The preparation of this book has been an intense journey not unlike a doctorate albeit in a much shorter timescale. I would like to acknowledge and thank two individuals who shaped my understanding, my practices as a research psychologist and me as a person:

Professor George Vaillant, whose leadership of the Harvard Grant Study of Adult Development, and writing across five text books, has been a profound influence on my understanding of the adult lifespan and a role model in how as a researcher he aimed to write with precision, yet he did so with an extraordinary humanity and beauty that I can only call love.

Professor Carol Ryff of the University of Wisconsin – Madison. Her work in developing the model of 'Psychological Well-Being' (Ryff 1989) was, to me, a work of genius bringing together and synthesising aspects of theory and practice that had been overlooked or marginalised in mainstream psychology. The world class research work built on this theory, particularly in the 'MIDUS' study, has been a source of fascination and influence on me ever since.

Piers Worth, Ph.D.
Chartered Psychologist

Chapter 1

Introduction – positive psychology across the lifespan

An existential perspective

Piers Worth and Andrew Machon

Learning objectives: at the end of this chapter, you will:

Appreciate the context of this book, and how it extends the perspective and reach of positive psychology as a discipline.

Recognise, define and explore the nature of an Existentially Oriented Positive Psychology including specific examples of what its component parts may be and involve.

Possess an overview of the 'Third Wave Positive Psychology' and the way in which it broadens and unites aspects of the discipline.

Be able to use the overview of the book content to navigate your reading in support of your goals.

Introduction

Positive psychology as a discipline has given us the gift of focusing on aspects and characteristics of 'flourishing', 'the good life', the 'life worth living' – valued subjective experiences in the past, present and future for individuals, families and groups (Seligman & Csikszentmihalyi, 2000). Through research, PP is offering us the language and practises in a form that we may explore and incorporate them into our lives. Research and practice have been expanding, with a particular crucial contribution coming into and through what is called 'positive education' (e.g. Norrish, 2015) and positive psychology interventions (PPIs). Additionally, research and influence have spread into questions of mental health and health generally, providing new insights into the approach and treatment of specific conditions (e.g. Parks et al., 2015; Martin et al., 2015; Rashid & Howes, 2016; Rashid & Seligman, 2019). Wong (2011a), Ivtzan et al. (2016) and Lomas et al. (2020) have made key contributions in expanding the vision and framework of the discipline to encompass the dialectical nature of all of life which moves from the 'either or' of positive or negative aspects of life to the 'both and' perspective.

DOI: 10.4324/9781003132530-1

This book takes a step beyond the current map into two aspects of a bigger picture. First, the book is organised around an impactful teaching framework used in a module titled *The Journey of Change* for post-graduate students on an MSc in Applied Positive Psychology (MAPP). Positive Psychology, as it is now, emphasises 'content' of a good and healthy psychological life, emerging from empirical research. Yet, it sometimes lacks a framework of 'context' to help students, practitioners and readers understand many aspects of daily life which might influence the experience and implementation in which positive psychology contributions may be needed. This teaching structure of the module orients practitioners, professionals and interested parties to a deeper understanding of the lived context of our lives and positive psychology. The structure of this book reflects the subjects within the taught module and is mirrored in the chapter titles.

Yet, a second vision and intention emerged for the book – taking an existential perspective on Positive Psychology.

When we look more broadly than a specific aspect of life, such as characteristics of the 'good life' portrayed by PP, then, we are in the context of our wider 'existence' to broader experiences of living and being. When the frame of consideration or context of our work becomes wider, the content we are invited to explore becomes bigger. We are prompted to look inward as well as out and work more deeply. When we adopt an 'existential' perspective, the subjects considered and the frameworks explored will include our identity and how this adjusts over time; living authentically; how this influences the characteristics of happiness we experience and, in turn, orientates us to the meaning and purpose in life. In doing so, we extend the reach of positive psychology as a discipline. This book acts as an introduction and 'primer' for an existential perspective on Positive Psychology.

Overview of the book chapters

Each of the following chapters will offer:

– Learning objectives
– Reflective questions
– Summary of how chapter content illustrates an existential perspective
– Ideas for future research to broaden a lifespan knowledge base and contribution
– Resources for following up on chapter content

Chapter 2: Change in and over time: our journey of development

Author: Piers Worth

This chapter offers an exploration of five theories of human development, summarised separately, but when considered as a whole, they create a single story or overview of how we unfold within our lives. The unfolding has characteristics of time periods, stability and transition and our changing priorities and life focus over time. This content might be described as the 'what' of our lives and how we understand the structure, rhythm and periods of change within our lives over time. Chapter 3 moves this perspective on to explore the 'why' of how we unfold in and over time.

Chapter 3: Our unfolding journey of growth

Authors: Piers Worth and Andrew Machon

This chapter explores a number of ways in which 'psychology' suggests we grow and change over time to become who we truly are, the unfolding journey of our inner growth through time. This chapter will have the quality of a mosaic of ideas in which we may understand more of how we find ourselves at different times in our lives. A recurring theme in these ideas is the concept and experience of 'self-transcendence' as a process of how we become more of who we are. It suggests a paradox: in becoming more of who we truly are, we open to our links with others and often seek to be of service and support to others.

Chapter 4: The journey's hero: birth of an existential self

Author: Lee Newitt

This chapter moves beyond the research-based and theoretical contents of Chapters 2 and 3 to a symbolic, metaphoric and story-oriented perspective. The chapter builds on one included in the 'Second Wave Positive Psychology' text (Chapter 8) by using myth to illustrate through story and symbol a model of how we grow, unfold and change through time. The chapter offers a three-part model illustrating how the symbolic or metaphorical change can come about in our lives.

Chapter 5: Our symbolic journey – heroes or heroines?

Author: Diane Herbert

This chapter explores the gendered nature of the Hero's Journey and questions the extent to which the Hero's Journey and developmental psychology, more broadly, are reflective of contemporary women's lived experience. Much has changed for women since 1949 when Campbell wrote *The Hero with a Thousand Faces*. Contemporary women have more choices and opportunities than their post-war predecessors. However, those choices and opportunities present different challenges or 'trials' not least because the organisations in which women work and society more generally continue to be structured along patriarchal lines. With Campbell's suggestion that the Hero's Journey is a call to embark on an adventure to become more of who we truly are, there is an assumption that the journey towards authenticity is the same for men and women. The chapter will consider how the hero's journey may not capture some women's experience as they seek to reach their full potential and suggest characteristics of what the Heroine's Journey may represent in this context.

Chapter 6: The relational context of change

Author: Andrew Machon

This chapter, from the perspective of a 'practitioner–researcher', illustrates how the source of every aspect of our development is inextricably relational in nature. In taking a look at development from the 'inside out', the chapter explores relational markers in the evolution of our consciousness and how these inform the work of the positive psychology practitioner. These include the value of key capacities and qualities, an identification of our innate 'instruments' of practice when we deploy 'self as an instrument' and the essential roles that we play vital to the work of the positive psychology practitioner.

Chapter 7: An introduction to the trans-theoretical model of change

Author: Piers Worth

Positive Psychology Interventions (PPIs) are processes of change. Yet, the discipline does not offer new entrants or practitioners a wider context of change than the intervention itself. As an example of processes of change, this chapter offers a summary of the Trans-Theoretical Model (TTM) of change. The model has a research history of over 40 years portraying the way and realities in which 'successful self-changers' describe their change process. It will be considered in the context of Positive Psychology and what this discipline may enrich and bring to the TTM model.

Chapter 8: Developing insight

Author: Andrew Machon

This chapter illuminates a more subtle, less conflictual way of inner seeing than that of developing insight. The central premise is that we learn to see and expand our vision of reality from the inside out. Our perceptions of reality not only profoundly change in parallel to the evolution of our self-consciousness but, as we illustrate, can also profoundly impact if and how we develop. Throughout the chapter, we explore how we view beginnings and endings to illustrate how our perceptions remarkably change. Essentially, we examine three markedly different ways in which we can perceive reality: the first, seeing reality as duality; the second, seeing the paradoxical nature of reality and the third, a being 'at one with' reality. We begin by exploring how the self to which we automatically revert perceives reality as duality and how we can become caught in the conflict we unconsciously create and experience developmental dormancy.

Chapter 9: Existential positive psychology interventions in and over time

Authors: Piers Worth and Lesley Lyle

This chapter explores how positive psychology currently defines 'interventions' that may change and develop us as individuals and then propose how this may alter and grow when we explore the 'existential' perspective being added to this work and process. The chapter will summarise key areas we may experience in periods of stability and change over our lifespan and consider how existentially oriented PP 'interventions' may change and need to change when we consider age and time. The chapter will then outline examples of potential existential positive psychology interventions.

Chapter 10: Conclusions

Authors: Piers Worth, Andrew Machon and Lesley Lyle

What new have we learned in this exploration? What has the book told us both about positive psychology across the lifespan and about the existential perspective? The chapter draws out themes from each of the preceding chapters and propose some over-arching themes that have emerged in the book.

In teaching this content, we would always say to students look for what resonates to you, what moves you and what you care about. Ideas and writers that excite us and change us become part of our being and expressed, in turn, in who we are and how we work.

Diagrammatically, the book can be portrayed this way:

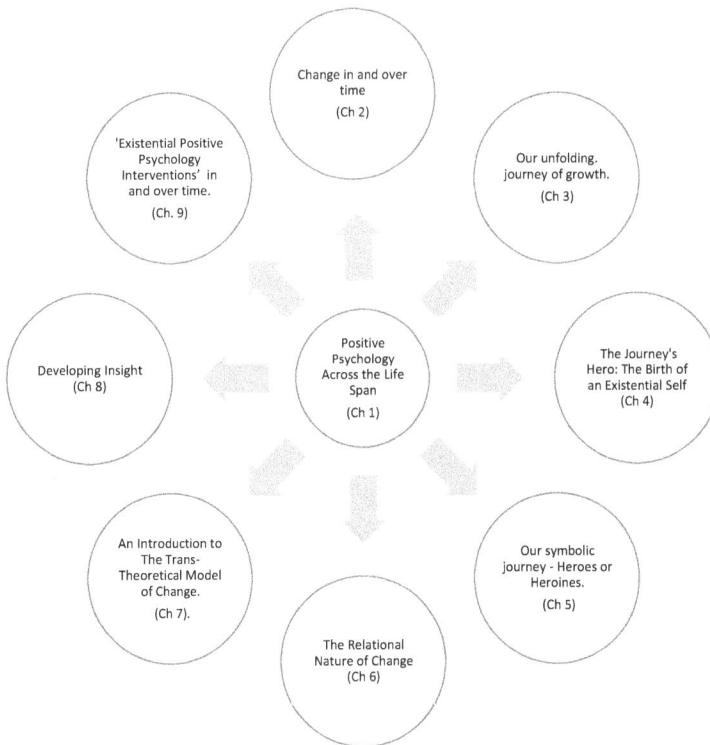

Figure 1.1 Diagrammatic overview of the book chapters.

At the time of writing the book proposal for this text, Piers Worth (editor and author) had a profound and memorable dream about 'building a bridge' while at the same time talking with four young men who were joyous at the task of expression through writing. The sense of this text representing a 'bridge' has recurred through the writing process, hence the picture on the book cover.

This book seeks to be a 'bridge':

• Encompassing a lifespan perspective of development, displaying not just localised events or time periods but the perspective of time (Chapter 2)
• Towards a perspective of personal development from the 'inside out' (Chapters 3, 4, 5 and 7)
• Linking the conscious with the unconscious – elucidating the nature of self-transcendence and informing its development (Chapters 3 and 8).
• Towards Practice – highlighting the key attributes and qualities in practitioners and a model of our key practice-based learnings (Chapter 6).

This introductory chapter starts the exploration from the visionary perspectives of Dr. Paul Wong, who proposes a definition and framework through which Existential Positive Psychology may be explored and then goes further, by incorporating key aspects of existential and humanistic psychology to enrich the framework through which we can perceive and experience 'existence', an existential perspective.

The 'why' and the 'what' of existential positive psychology

To link and orientate us to the gift of an existential perspective, a summary is offered of Dr. Paul Wong's theories, which make a case for Existential Positive Psychology (EPP) and what its nature should be. His proposals on EPP inform the exploration offered by this book. However, the authors aspire to go further and involve and work with a subject implied in Wong's writings (e.g. 2010) that we infer is also central to the underpinnings of this subject that this also returns us to the roots of existential and humanistic psychology. This section will summarise these topics.

Dr. Wong's ideas and writing (2004, 2010, 2011a, 2011b, 2016, 2021) were creative and deepening of the 'Second Wave' perspective introduced earlier and that of 'EPP'. Wong (2004) argues for a revisiting and redevelopment of 'existential psychology', a perspective of psychology originating over 40 years previously and used within the context of psychotherapy. He wrote: *By definition (Existential Psychology) is the psychology of human existence in all its complexity and paradoxes. Human existence is more than an abstract concept; it involves real people in concrete situations* (2004; p. 1). He proposed that Existential Psychology needed *to become the practical psychology of everyday living – how to survive and thrive in the midst of tensions between good and evil, hope and despair, love and hate, courage and safety, agency and community. It is about the high dramas of coping, dreaming and transformation* (2004; p. 1). He argued that the pressing questions facing psychology needed a broader perspective than single disciplines and that to achieve this kind of goal, Existential Psychology must value the phenomenologi-cal experience as well as the objective, observable and measurable (p. 2).

In 2010, in the first of what the chapter authors perceive as a 'trilogy' of articles on this subject over the following decade, Dr. Wong articulated the origin, structure and form of EPP. Wong (2010) proposed that positive psychology, without being accompanied by existential insights, was incomplete and lacking depth. He proposed that existential psychology and positive psychology deserved to be seen as a single domain – EPP. He believed that Positive Psychology brought rigorous research and a depth of insight on human strength and positive affect, whereas existential psychol-ogy brought both existential insight and a focus on phenomenological analysis.

He proposed that a mature PP could now *return to its existential–humanistic roots to discover the richness of lived experience* (p. 1). Wong proposed that Exis-tential Psychology broadens the definition of Positive Psychology to become: *the qualitative and quantitative study of what enables people to survive and flourish individually and collectively in the totality of life circumstances* (p. 2).

Wong outlined five key components of EPP:

1   Identity: We are grounded, rooted in our sense of identity, yet life generally, and in particular through transitions and change, involves a redefinition or a readjustment of ourselves over time (e.g. McAdams, 2015; McAdams & McLean, 2013; McLean et al., 2007). This ongoing shift and adjustment ask of us a conscious modification to stay connected, in a relationship, with who we are. A sense of 'identity crisis' is perhaps our way of knowing that the energy and wish for personal authenticity need adjustment.

2   The quest for authenticity: When we are truly grounded in our sense of iden-tity, then authenticity becomes possible. The need to adjust our identity is, Wong suggests, a form of 'crisis' we all face and necessary to stay connected to our authenticity. He proposes: *authentic people assume responsibility to live in a way which is consistent with their true nature and core values. They strive to become what they were made to be in spite of the anxiety and risks involved* (2010; p. 3). Wong goes further in emphasising authenticity will be fundamentally expressed as part of relationships and building community (2016). Yet being who we are, living our true nature and core values also involves facing the implications of ageing and death (May, 1983).

3   Authentic Happiness: Wong discerns different types of happiness. When we accept the existential nature of our lives, including the quest for authentic-ity, then an authentic happiness will emerge (May, 1983; Hartman & Zim-beroff, 2015). From a positive psychology perspective that would include knowing and expressing our strengths (e.g. Peterson & Seligman, 2004). Yet, Schumaker (2007) extends that perspective in proposing that we also live in a manner that reflects our need for social connection and relationships and spirituality. Wong (2010) suggests that this is a form of happiness that might be overlooked in research unless an existential perspective is adopted.

4   Mature Happiness: Wong (2010, 2016, 2021) proposes that this form of happi-ness occurs when we find a dynamic balance between the positive and negative

experiences in our lives. Wong defines further forms of happiness in his PP2.0 (2011) paper. Eudaimonic happiness is a broad term encompassing psychological well-being, virtue and living authentically. It will occur from being and seeking to be the best in us (e.g. Ryff, 1989), living a life rooted in virtue in and through our person and our deeds (Wong, 2011a, 2016). 'Chaironic' happiness emerges from the expression of our spiritual nature, a blessing or gift that is perceived and found in our circumstances and talents (Wong, 2010, 2016).

5 Meaning and Purpose in our lives: Writing from the perspective of existential psychotherapy, Frankl (1959/1992) proposed the central and critical role of meaning in our lives. He saw a health-giving aspect of connecting with our deep or core sense of meaning. He proposed that each person would have a sense of meaning unique to themselves and that its dynamic nature may fluctuate constantly with and through our circumstances. Viewing each of us as in relationship with our own lives, Frankl believed that our life circumstances were constantly asking us to find meaning within our lives. In this, he was communicating powerfully that he believed life questions us, and in the act of finding meaning, we are taking responsibility for our own lives (Frankl, 1955/1969). Delle Fave (2020) summarises how this process becomes a core component of mental health. Wong (1998, 2010) has given form and shape to the nature of meaning in his 'PURE' model: Purpose – Understanding – Responsible – Evaluation. Ryff (2014, 2018) articulates extensive research indicating the health and protective gains from 'purpose in life'.

The steps in this cycle imply two connected outcomes and implications: that of freedom to act as an expression of ourselves, accompanied by a responsibility, response-ability, for the choices we make and the consequences that accompany them.

Portrayed diagrammatically, this could be seen as:

Wong (2010 & 2016).

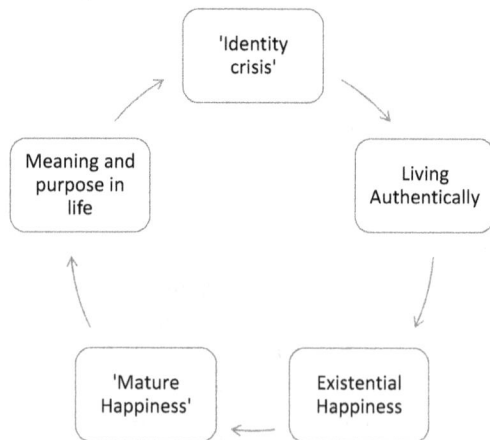

Figure 1.2 Wong's five component parts of 'Existential Positive Psychology'.

My perception (PW) as a writer and teacher, supported by MAPP students and wider audiences, is Wong's five elements are connected as a 'system' and potentially a cyclical system. For example, when we develop or adjust our sense of identity, this, in turn, creates a need for adjustment in our authentic living, which, in turn, alters our sense of existential authentic happiness and so on. The achievement of each step in the cycle creates an impact and a need to adjust to the one that follows.

Perhaps as an outcome from the changes to our sense of self, a way of living, a connection to meaning and purpose that these factors imply, Wong proposes (2010, 2016) that existentially a greater sense of freedom will emerge, and this, in turn, invokes a need to further responsibility within our lives.

A constant thread in Wong's writing (1998, 2004, 2010, 2011a, 2016, 2021) is the assertion of life as being fundamentally dialectical, involving polarities and the need to face and relate to all they may involve.

An essential example is how we as living beings are drawn to the expression of life yet must also relate to our accompanying mortality and eventual death (Yalom, 2008; Yalom & Yalom, 2021). Seen in this way, the positive aspects of life that we are drawn to are accompanied by a dark companion which points to the limits of time and experience, the presence of sorrow and suffering and that ultimately, we will die. Wong emphasised the argument for the understanding of the complexity of life as a whole and the paradoxical effect and interaction of the positives and negatives of our experiences. While a key motivation for PP as a discipline was to offer a language for a positive experience in life, the time had come to also create a language for the positive and negative interacting and, indeed, a more complete understanding of what we perceive as the 'negative'. Wong advocates the realisation that we can only truly relate to a positive experience in life when we have accepted the presence and possibility of its negative opposite. Investing our energy in the positive alone involves creating resistance to its opposite. When we can accept rather than resist the polarity, more energy occurs and becomes existentially available for all of life. Wong (2021) cites Ekman et al. (2005) in proposing mature happiness and flourishing occur from a mental balance based on an enduring trait giving insight into the dialectical nature of our lives.

The paragraphs earlier offer an outline of the potential construct and structure of EPP, each stage or step offering a possibility to either draw on existing research (e.g. the nature of identity and its change) to articulate its form or frame future research exploration. Also to consider how different approaches may marry together with the scientific perspective. Positive Psychology has a track record of emphasising quantitative and positivist research as establishing discipline in its findings. However, different sources and voices are arguing for a broader perspective to be taken, one which would be needed to deepen our understanding of the 'existential' experiences that are qualitative and phenomenological.

Rich (2017) argues that qualitative research is under-represented in positive psychology and should be seen as equal value to quantitative insights. Wong (2017) and Wong and Roy (2018) propose that wider research perspectives and methods are needed to understand the complexity and dialectics of human flourishing and that 'positive' perspectives alone risk being incomplete. Wong (2011a, 2017, 2021) adopts a change-oriented perspective in seeking a broader-based approach to research than the empirical alone, towards one that reflects the 'voice' of research participants, their subjective and experiential meanings, a recognition that we exist in multiple, socially constructed worlds and a combination of qualitative and quantitative research methods. In this, Wong also emphasises and asserts the need for rigorous research that implicitly may need further methodological development. These views are reflected in more recent proposals of Lomas et al. (2020) for a 'Third Wave' of Positive Psychology.

Wong (2021) proposes a range of research questions that are priorities for exploration and asserting the framework of EPP:

1 What does it mean to exist and live as a human being. . . . **What are our deepest yearnings and most cherished dreams? What are the highest riches of human aspirations?**
2 What does it mean to be authentic and fully alive? How can we discover our true identity? . . . How do we maintain a passion for living when things are not going well? **How can we function fully, develop our full potentials and remain optimistic in an oppressive or hostile environment?**
3 What are the givens of human existence? What is the structure of human existence in all its complexity and duality? What is the meaning of suffering, pain and death? What is the meaning of life in light of these negative givens? . . . **How can we integrate both the negative and positive givens to facilitate personal growth and community development?**

While effort has continued in the core of positive psychology as a discipline to articulate aspects of the good life, there is no doubt that researchers and practitioners have expanded their attention since Wong's paper to explore how positive psychology may sit alongside and contribute to challenging experiences in life. For example, Jeste and Palmer (2015), Parks et al. (2015), Martin et al. (2015), Rashid and Howes (2016) and Rashid and Seligman (2019).

The 'existential–humanistic roots' of EPP

While as authors we relate to Wong's definition of EPP and the construct of experiences he theorises as representative of it, quoted earlier, we believe that there is an opportunity to find and recognise additional value. Wong (2010) points us to the understanding that EPP *has its roots in existential and humanistic psychology origins*. What does this mean in practical terms and how does this influence our understanding of EPP?

We suggest that the focus of exploration that comes from Wong's definition described earlier can be broader in content and quality in a way that will illustrate this as a potential natural home for EPP as well as contribute to the development of material that may be created and potentially embraced within the proposed 'Third Wave Positive Psychology' (summarised later). This involves, at least, offering an overview understanding of the focus of existentialism and, in turn, existential psychology to draw out and bring about the best in existentially oriented positive psychology.

Existentialism, as a philosophy and a process of investigation, dates back to Greek philosophers over two millennia ago and the 18th- and 19th-century existentialist movement with such prominent figures as Kierkegaard and Nietzsche. These origins are vast and beyond the scope of this book. They include profound explorations of the nature of our experience of the world around us and the ways in which we can be fully ourselves, true to ourselves and take responsibility for living a full life that expresses our potential.

Humanistic psychology was originally considered the 'third wave' of the unfolding discipline of psychology in approximately the mid-20th century. In a response to the emergence of disciplines such as Freudian psychotherapy and Behaviourism, humanistic psychology has existential roots, in the manner in which it focused on the uniqueness of individuals, reflected, in turn, by the phenomenological quality of their world and their capacity and motive to identify and express their potential. It questioned the nature of reality and our experiences of it as individuals.

We propose that the existential–humanistic 'roots' of EPP inferred by Wong (2010, 2016) can be seen in the work of four key humanistic psychologists/ psychotherapists: Viktor Frankl, Rollo May, Carl Rogers, and Abraham Maslow. Key contributions from them are summarised in Figure 1.3.

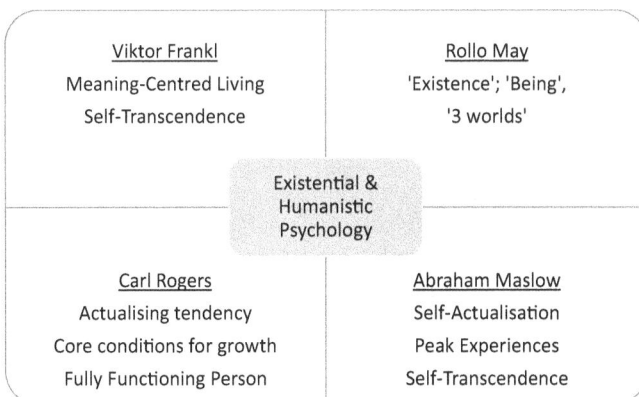

Viktor Frankl	Rollo May
Meaning-Centred Living	'Existence'; 'Being',
Self-Transcendence	'3 worlds'

Existential &
Humanistic
Psychology

Carl Rogers	Abraham Maslow
Actualising tendency	Self-Actualisation
Core conditions for growth	Peak Experiences
Fully Functioning Person	Self-Transcendence

Figure 1.3 Summary of key contributions from pioneers of existential and humanistic psychology.

An exploration of the literature on existential and humanistic psychology has what we would describe as certain 'key words' or key principles that recur within the classical writing. We infer that these are:

Existential Psychology: Key words

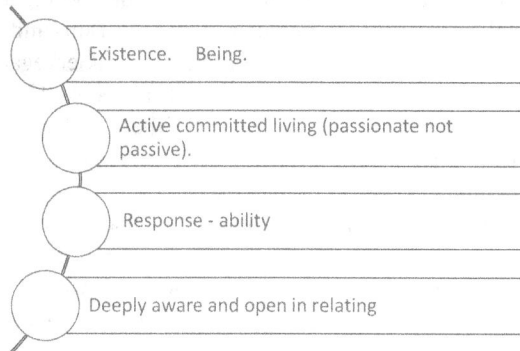

Figure 1.4 Existential and humanistic psychology 'key words and principles'.

These words and principles will be reflected upon in the chapters of this book.

Third wave positive psychology

The unfolding of positive psychology as a discipline described earlier is still occurring, and the recent proposal of 'Third Wave Positive Psychology' by Lomas et al. (2020) is a further development.

This article uses the metaphor of 'waves' to portray a phased, cumulative and organic development of positive psychology over time that is widening its area of focus and subjects included. By taking the step of portraying a 'Third Wave', the article authors remove some of the delineated, oppositional or questioning perspectives that may have entered with the emergence of 'Second Wave' or PP2.0 – to one of a dynamic response to change, one of the connected waves that draw on a core that is within an energetic foundational 'ocean' of the discipline overall. By creating this image, the article authors believe it provides a means by which researchers and practitioners might contribute to each of the foci of the individual 'waves'. This offers us a unifying concept or basis of understanding rather than one of the oppositional groups within PP overall.

The article authors propose that PP is developing through these waves via the process of 'thesis' (in the original conceptions of PP) – antithesis (in the PP2.0 and 'second wave' model which proposes life experience is dialectical, polarised and negative as well as positive) – to one of synthesis (expanding the focus of the discipline overall to look beyond individuals to groups, organisations, systems and cultures and multiple methodologies) to one that points towards an increasing complexity of this discipline.

Lomas and colleagues (2020) propose that the discipline is now developing further and via this complexity, and the focus of enquiry, the disciplines within the subject area widen to the consideration of culture and the involvement of new research methodologies. By this, they suggest that there is an epistemological broadening through which positive psychology may become more diverse, inclusive, complex and particularly hospitable in moving forward. The article authors propose that PP has maintained a largely individualistic focus, and in broadening scope, there are the means to consider systems and socio-cultural factors. In their attention to methodologies, they suggest that positive psychology has retained a substantially positivist quantitative approach to research and that the evolution of the work must involve qualitative epistemologies and methods such as the phenomenological, hermeneutic, constructionist and interpretivist. The work of this book reflects such a step.

The authors of this book believe that the exploration that follows has the qualities of each of the three 'waves' and particularly the broadening and complexity encapsulated in the 'Third Wave'. Yet, we believe that including and building on the perspective and context of existential psychology will add to the content and focus implied by Wong's (2010) definition summarised earlier and support ideas expressed in Lomas et al. (2020).

Reflections on the overall context of positive psychology and this book

So, existentially oriented positive psychology invites the aspiration to understand the whole of who we are and how we may learn to thrive and evolve in a world of apparent conflict. This creates the platform to ask and consider some of the most profound questions of our times – such as how do we make meaning of lives in the face of survival and death? How, when in times of crisis the temptation is to judge, can we open our minds to the gift of wisdom? What is the source of 'more than' in our lives in which we may place our faith? Who are we, as a self, and how do we fashion ourselves as practitioners and empty ourselves as an instrument (Worth, 2017) – to be fully in service of ourselves, others and, indeed, wider nature and the world in which we live? This book provides the opportunity and stage for us to conceive of the most important questions of our time and for them to be our conscious focus. Perhaps for the first time, maybe the profession has an all-encompassing reach – one necessary to understand and fully elucidate the vital mechanisms of how we develop and change and in that process discover our true place within the whole, whilst enhancing our capacity to relate and discovering our inextricable relatedness.

It is against this backdrop of the emergence of EPP that this book is written. Its goal is an aspiration towards wholeness and to offer new and deeper insight into how we change and develop. Our intent is to inform this new context, offering new and novel ideas and learning, pointing towards key aspects of future research of our evolving profession whilst equally considering how different approaches may marry with and complement the scientific. What we have learned in looking back in this way is the vital importance of *context* as well as the *content*. Context and change are intimately related and may offer new ways of seeing and making meaning of our lives and work. Maybe this context is now all embracing? And points towards the realisation that only when we seek a conception or perception of the whole can each and every part find place and meaning. The aspiration of this book is to give our full attention to this new emergent context and how this may more deeply inform our lives and work.

This chapter has

- Introduced the vision of the book to give positive psychology practitioners and students insight into patterns and processes of change in the human life. These include lifespan developmental psychology, ways in which we grow over time, processes by which we seek to change, the relational context of change and the paradoxes we face. Additionally, mythological, symbolic and story-based insights are explored via the hero's and heroine's journey.
- Introduced Dr. Paul Wong's theory of EPP and its links to existential and humanistic psychology.
- Summarised the nature and context of the newly proposed 'Third Wave Positive Psychology' and how this expands and changes the landscape of the discipline.

Further support for the contents of this book

This book is intended as a primer and introduction to a lifespan perspective of positive psychology and the possible nature and development of EPP. The contents of the book are 'free standing'. However, naturally, there are more ideas and possible developments of EPP than can be included in this book. Our intention is to offer support and additional material for the book on positivepsychologyonlinecourses.com/existential-positive-psychology

The nature of the content will evolve and change over time. We anticipate this including:

– Suggestions for 'EPP interventions'
– Podcasts, vlogs and interviews based on selected book content
– Recommended and suggested additional reading
– Updates on chapter content when they occur

Some of this content will be free for download and also shared on another sister website thepositivepsychologypeople.com and YouTube channel. Other more detailed aspects may involve a payment.

www.positivepsychologyonlinecourses.com is a relatively new website that is mainly of interest to those studying positive psychology academically.

References

Delle Fave, A. (2020). Meaning in Life: Structure, Sources, and Relations with Mental and Physical Health. *Acta Philosophica, 29*(1), 19–32. DOI: 10.19272/202000701002

Ekman, P., Davidson, R.J., Ricard, M., and Wallace, B.A. (2005). Buddhist and Psychoilogical Perspectives on Emotions and Well-Being. *Current Directions in Psychological Science, 14*, 59–63. https://doi.org/10.1111/j.0963-7214.2005.00335.x

Frankl, V. (1955 / 1969). *The Doctor and the Soul: From Psychotherapy to Logotherapy.* London, Souvenir Press. ISBN 13: 9780285637016

Frankl, V. (1959 / 1992). *Man's Search for Meaning.* London, Random House. ISBN: 9781846046384

Hartman, D., and Zimberoff, D. (2015). *Self-Transcendence and Ego Surrender.* Wellness Press. ISBN: 9780962272899

Ivtzan, I., Lomas, T., Hefferon, K., and Worth, P. (2016). *Second Wave Positive Psychology: Embracing the Dark Side of Life.* Abingdon, Oxon, Routledge.

Jeste, D.V., and Palmer, B.W. (Eds.). (2015). *Positive Psychiatry: A Clinical Handbook.* Washington, American Psychiatric Publishing. doi.org/10.1080/00332747.2017.1325677

Lomas, T., Waters, L., Williams, P., Oates, L.G., and Kern, M.L. (2020, August). Third Wave Positive Psychology: Broadening Towards Complexity. *Journal of Positive Psychology.* doi.org/10.1080/17439760.2020.1805501

Martin, A.S., Harmell, A.L., and Mausbach, B.T. (2015). Positive Psychology Traits. Chapter in: Jeste, D.V. and Palmer, B.W. (Eds.). *Positive Psychiatry: A Clinical Handbook.* Washington, American Psychiatric Publishing.

May, R., Allport, G., Feifel, H., Maslow, A., and Rogers, C. (Eds.). (1960). *Existential Psychology.* New York, Random House.

May, R. (1983). *The Discovery of Being.* New York, W. Norton.

McAdams, D.P. (2015). *The Art and Science of Personality Development.* London, Guildford Press. ISBN 9781462529322

McAdams, D.P., and McLean, K.C. (2013). Narrative Identity. *Current Directions in Psychological Science, 22*(3), 233–238. doi.org/10.1177/0963721413475622

McLean, K.C., Pasupathi, M., and Pals, J.L. (2007, August). Self Creating Stories, Creating Selves. *Personality and Social Psychology Review,* 11(3). doi.org/10.1177/1088868307301034

Norrish, J. (2015). *Positive Education: The Geelong Grammar School Journey.* Oxford, Oxford University Press.

Parks, A.C., Kleiman, E.M., Kashdan. T.B., Hausmann, L.R.M., Myer, P.S., Day, A.M., Spillane, N.S., and Kahler, C.W. (2015). Positive Psychotherapeutic and Behavioural Interventions. Chapter in: Jeste, D.V. and Palmer, B.W. (Eds.). *Positive Psychiatry: A Clinical Handbook.* Washington, American Psychiatric Publishing.

Peterson, P., and Seligman, M.E.P. (2004). *Character Strengths and Virtues: A Handbook and Classification*. Oxford, Oxford University Press.

Rashid, T., and Howes, R.N. (2016). Positive Psychotherapy: Clinical Applications of Positive Psychology. Chapter in: Wood, A.M. and Johnson, J. (Eds.). *The Wiley Handbook of Positive Clinical Psychology*. Chichester, John Wiley & Sons.

Rashid, T., and Seligman, M.E.P. (2019). *Positive Psychotherapy: Clinicians Manual*. Oxford, Oxford University Press. DOI: 10.1093/med-psych/9780195325386.001.0001

Rich, G.J. (2017). The Promise of Qualitative Inquiry for Positive Psychology: Diversifying Methods. *The Journal of Positive Psychology*, *12*(3), 220–231. DOI: 10.1080/17439760.2016.1225119

Ryff, C.D. (1989). Happiness Is Everything, or Is It? Explorations on the Meaning of Psychological Well-being. *Journal of Personality and Social Psychology*, *57*(6), 1069–1081. https://doi.org/10.1037/0022-3514.57.6.1069

Ryff, C.D. (2014). Psychological Well-Being Revisited: Advances in the Science and Practice of Eudaimonia. *Psychotherapy and Psychosomatics*, *83*, 10–28. DOI: 10.1159/000353263

Ryff, C.D. (2018). Eudaimonic Well-Being: Highlights from 25 Years of Inquiry. Chapter in: Shigemasu, K., Kuwano, S., Sato, T. and Matsuzawa, T. (Eds.). *Diversity in Harmony – Insights from Psychology: Proceedings of the 31st International Congress of Psychology*, 1st ed. Hoboken, NJ, John Wiley and Sons Ltd.

Schumaker, J.F. (2007). In Search of Happiness: Understanding an Endangered State of Mind. Praeger Paperback; cited in Wong, P.T.P. (2010, July). What Is Existential Positive Psychology? *International Journal of Existential Psychology and Psychotherapy*, *3*(1).

Seligman, M.E.P., and Csikszentmihalyi, M. (2000). Positive Psychology: An Introduction. *American Psychologist*, *55*(1), 5–14. https://doi.org/10.1037/0003-066X.55.1.5

Wong, P.T.P. (1998). Toward a Dual-Systems Model of What Makes Life Worth Living. Chapter in: Wong, P.T.P. (Ed.). *The Human Quest for Meaning: Theories, Research and Applications*, 2nd ed. London, Routledge. ISBN 9781138110823

Wong, P.T.P. (2004). Existential Psychology for the 21st Century. *International Journal of Existential Psychology and Psychotherapy*, *1*(1), 1–2.

Wong, P.T.P. (2010, July). What Is Existential Positive Psychology? *International Journal of Existential Psychology and Psychotherapy*, *3*(1).

Wong, P.T.P. (2011a). Positive Psychology 2.0: Towards a Balanced Interactive Model of the Good Life. *Canadian Psychology/Psychologie Canadienne*, *52*(2), 69–81. https://doi.org/10.1037/a0022511

Wong, P.T.P. (2011b, September). Reclaiming Positive Psychology: A Meaning Centred Approach to Sustainable Growth and Radical Empiricism. *Journal of Humanistic Psychology*, 408–412. doi.org/10.1177/0022167811408729

Wong, P.T.P. (2016, February). Existential Positive Psychology. *International Journal of Existential Psychology and Psychotherapy*, *6*(1).

Wong, P.T.P. (2017). Meaning-Centred Approach to Research and Therapy, Positive Psychology and the Future of Humanistic Psychology. *The Humanistic Psychologist*, *45*(3), 207–216. https://doi.org/10.1037/hum0000062

Wong, P.T.P. (2021). Existential Positive Psychology (PP 2.0) and Global Wellbeing: Why It Is Necessary During the Age of Covid-19. Posted by Paul Wong | Jan 5, 2021 | Existential Psychology, Positive Psychology, Writing. Available online at: http://www.drpaulwong.com

Wong, P.T.P., and Roy, S. (2018). Critique of Positive Psychology and Positive Interventions. Chapter in: Brown, N.L., Lomas, T., and Eiroa-Orosa, F.J. (Eds.). *The Routledge International Handbook of Critical Positive Psychology* (pp. 142–160). Abingdon, Oxon, Routledge.

Worth, P. (2017). Positive Psychology Interventions in Practice: The First Intervention Is Our Self. Chapter in: Proctor, C. (Ed.). *Positive Psychology Interventions in Practice.* Cham, Switzerland, Springer International Publishing AG.

Yalom, I.D. (2008). *Staring at the Sun: Overcoming the Dread of Death.* London, Piatkus Books.

Yalom, I.D., and Yalom, M. (2021). *A Matter of Death and Life.* London, Piatkus Books.

Chapter 2

Change in and over time

Our journey of development – lifespan developmental perspectives of change

Piers Worth

The 'what' and 'when' of change?

Learning objectives:

At the end of this chapter, you will

> *Understand* and explore five theories of adult development.
>
> *Recognise* and explore the interconnected model of five key developmental theories and how this may be related to and utilised in personal or client work.
>
> *Reflect* upon the unfolding patterns evident in the human lifespan and consider how this varies from your current understanding of the lifespan.
>
> *Understand* the strengths and limitations of this research, and how this subject can be further explored.

This chapter represents an updating, revision and extension of Worth's (2016) chapter titled *Positive Development – Our Journey of Growth*. Building on Chapter 2 of the original 'Second Wave Positive Psychology' book which presented four theories, on human development (Erikson, Levinson, Vaillant and McAdams) separately, this chapter will contain additional content and a perspective on each of these theories, and then be presented as a single model. Seen as a single model, this may support a depth of understanding and insight of our humanity over time. Lifespan developmental psychology is a theoretical perspective based on multi-disciplinary methodologies to portray characteristics of individual development over age and time (Baltes, 1987). These studies tend to be large and long-term. Alternative methods for studying lifespan development are considered at the end of the chapter.

Erik Erikson – the life cycle

Erikson's (1958/1980, 1963) theory of the life cycle is arguably the most comprehensive of the lifespan theories in covering childhood through to old age. His

DOI: 10.4324/9781003132530-2

theory was the first major whole-life developmental perspective offered in modern times and was a milestone in the history of psychology for that reason. Some may consider this dated, yet more recent work, for example, the Harvard Grant Study of Adult Development (Vaillant, 1977, 2002, 2012), has provided evidence of this structure empirically and finds it adds to our understanding of complex experience over time.

Erikson's theory originated through his psychoanalytic work and ethnographic work with healthy adolescents and the Sioux and Yurok American Indian tribes. It is a theory that is meant to encompass both sexes and to be cross-cultural.

Erikson saw the life cycle as containing eight discrete and sequential stages through which eight 'strengths' may emerge from a time-specific developmental experience and confrontation (Erikson, 1988). The timing of each stage was, according to Erikson, based on the earliest practical time it could be developmentally experienced and the latest moment it would need to give way or yield to the next 'crisis' and strength (Erikson, 1968). Each stage is characterised as a 'crisis' by Erikson that comes from the conflict of two opposing forces or trends at that time of life. This tension or pressure came from what he saw as polarised opposites. A positive outcome to the crisis led, in Erikson's view, to the development of a 'virtue' or 'strength' related to the time period and the growth applicable to it. This immediately offers an unexpected and unusual link to more recent theories of human strength in positive psychology and also reflects Wong's (2011) proposal that our discipline must involve a dialogue between positive and negative experiences. The resolution of the tension of the opposites is not 'either or' or a single outcome but a balance found between the experiences of the two.

Erikson's use of the word 'crisis' was intended to imply a turning point, an opportunity and that the resolution of the conflict of two polarised forces could direct individual development in positive or negative directions. The nature of the resolution achieved, or the failure to confront its needs, was proposed to affect each subsequent life stage. Erikson conceived of growth and development as occurring through an integration of the conflicting forces at each stage and not succumbing to alienation (Roazen, 1976). He believed that each person would interpret and experience this pattern through their own particular traits and character, a style unique to them.

A key practical part of this theory is that the individual faces holding the tension between the two opposing forces from that point on through life, with the goal being that the positive tendency or force, on balance, is primary. This illustrates to us how difficult experiences may bring about a change in our insight and understanding of the life that follows. Joan Erikson made clear that a failure to achieve balance, or the favouring of the negative tendency, could be redressed later in life (Erikson, 1988).

To summarise the stages and polarities:

The details of these stages are summarised in Worth (2016).

Life Cycle Stages	Stage 8: Old Age	• Ego Integrity vs. Despair **(Wisdom)** • 60 / 65 years +
	Stage 7: Adulthood	• Generativity vs. Stagnation **(Care)** • (40 – 60 / 65 years
	Stage 6: Young Adulthood	• Intimacy vs. Isolation **(Love)** • 19 / 20 – 40 years
	Stage 5: Adolescence	• Identity vs. Identity Confusion **(Fidelity)** • 13 – 18 years
	Stage 4: School Age	• Industry vs. Inferiority **(Competence)** • 6 - 12 years
	Stage 3: Play Age	• Initiative vs. Guilt **(Purpose)** • 3 – 5 years
	Stage 2: Early Childhood	• Autonomy vs. Shame **(Will)** • 12m – 3years
	Stage 1: Infancy	• Trust vs. Mistrust **(Hope)** • 0 – 12 months

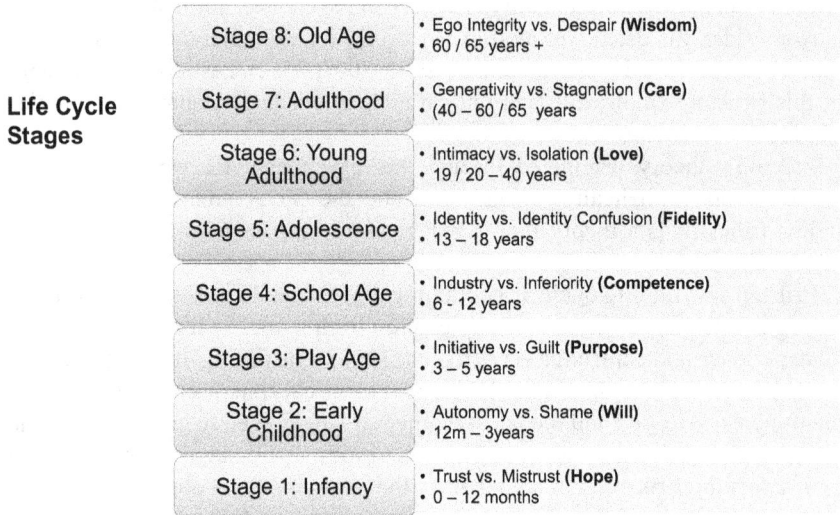

Figure 2.1 Erikson's life cycle stages.

It is important to consider the dynamics of these stages together. Erikson saw each stage as emerging from and dependent on its predecessor. Each stage is seen as 'grounded' in all the ones preceding it, and the achievement of the emerging developmental strength is expected to give new connotations or experiences to all the ones that had been experienced to date (Erikson, Erikson, & Kivnick, 1986; Stevens, 1983). It is as if all that had gone before becomes re-understood in the context of the polarity tension of the stage of the time. For example, the capacity for us to learn some skills when 'playing' (Stage 3) may, in turn, give us the confidence to learn further skills in school days (Stage 4). However, our ability to learn may be revisited and reshaped repeatedly over time. This suggests a process that is evident in Vaillant's findings: we continue to process and re-understand our experiences over time – this adds to our sense of awareness and who we are.

Acknowledging the extension to longevity experienced in both their lives (writing at the age of 97), Joan Erikson (Erikson & Erikson, 1997) described a ninth stage of the life cycle (which appears to have been ignored in modern psychology textbooks) as the experience of living a simple, sometimes limited life in the physical frailty of advanced years. This increased age brought with it new demands often characterised or influenced by the frailty, and it being impossible to know when loss of physical ability might occur. In contrast to the other eight stages, the ninth has the negative possibilities or outcomes assumed and placed first. She described a process of review again of each of the prior stages and a re-evaluating and experiencing their qualities through the perspective of physical frailties and limitations of advanced age. Her descriptions offer us, even now, a rare insight from someone living advanced years. These ideas are extended further in Chapter 3 through the work of Lars Tornstam.

Erikson's theories are hard to evaluate and have been criticised. The complexity and lifetime encompassed by Erikson's theory make it very hard to test. Erikson puts forward his theory as cross-cultural and universal; yet others (e.g. Perlmutter & Hall, 1992; Stevens, 1983) acknowledge that its focus on individualism makes it oriented to Western culture and the generality of the research which originated these theories makes such claims at best still unproven. This said, the work of the Harvard Grant Study of Adult Development and George Vaillant (discussed below), argues that these stages are seen in their empirically collected data.

In considering the applicability of these theories to women, there is questioning, for example, whether the stage of intimacy (the sixth stage) would precede the stage of identity (e.g. Stevens, 1983). Erikson discussed these questions in later life (e.g. Erikson & Erikson, 1981). His perspective remained that these theories were 'only a tool to think with, and cannot be a prescription to abide by' (Erikson, 1980) – therefore, not an absolute definition but a tool through which to explore.

G.E. Vaillant – Harvard Grant Study of Adult Development

The Harvard Grant Study of Adult Development is one of the longest prospective follow-up studies of adult development in the world. The study was initiated in 1938 and comprises 268 males recruited from Harvard University student cohorts between 1939 and 1944. The focus was to look at participants likely to be healthy and to live well. Over time, the study staff comprise psychiatrists, social investigators (exploring family context) and medical doctors on physical health as well as regular questionnaire feedback obtained from participants. Through this, multiple research perspectives of individual participants were accomplished. The first major write-up of their findings was contained in Vaillant (1977). The descriptions of this and in subsequent works are an eloquent and moving description of life stories and conclusions on what we may learn from them as well as scientific data (e.g. Vaillant, 2002, 2012).

In 1980, the study broadened to include two other prospective studies and cohorts. Four hundred and fifty-six males from working-class families were drawn from the 'Glueck study' which had commenced in 1939 and focused on delinquency. This group was the 'non-delinquent controls' of the overall study. Ninety women were also incorporated from the 'Terman Study' which had commenced in 1920. Vaillant (2002) acknowledges the cohorts, 814 participants in total, are drawn from a narrow sample of the wider population, yet the gift and the gain of following individuals over decades provide enthralling insights into life experiences into the early part of this century.

While academic output (176 journal publications and 11 textbooks listed in Vaillant, 2012) emerged from the study, there were three primary outcomes relevant to this particular writing.

First, Vaillant (1977, 2002) confirmed that the study had empirically validated the presence of the life cycle proposed by Erikson (1958/1980). He went further and suggested that Erikson's eight-stage model has, in fact, nine stages with an additional one that he saw as implied by Erikson yet differentiated within the experience of the seventh stage, the 'Generativity' phase that Vaillant named as 'The Keepers of Meaning'. While Generativity involved a care for a person, the Keeper of Meaning broadened that focus to that of care for the wisdom within a culture and the preservation of its products (2002).

Second, Vaillant identified within the study data empirical evidence for 'adaptive defence mechanisms' in the individual stories that acted as an unconscious adjustment to and coping with the experiences of life over time. These represented a process of adaptation to life (the title of Vaillant's 1977 text) and maturation of the individual ego over time. Vaillant echoed the work of Jane Loevinger (1969) in proposing that how we make sense of our experiences and absorb their implications is a core function of the ego and its development. Vaillant (2000, 2012) proposed that we cope consciously with life experiences and challenges via social support and cognitive coping strategies. However, he also acknowledged the presence of 'involuntary mental mechanisms' that adjust our internal and external perceptions as a means of reducing stress and distress. Additionally, these defences are believed to reduce the experience of conflict and cognitive dissonance during periods of sudden change and challenging life events. Vaillant proposed that the way in which these may appear is influenced by our physical and biological maturation over time, along with the internalised influence of positive role models encountered in our lives. He defined the ego, movingly, as a combination or integration of benign and positive role models experienced over time that becomes a form of identification for us (1977). As the study progressed and Vaillant reported further (1993, 2000, 2002, 2012), he expressed a moving and defining perspective on ageing; that we become a 'sum' of all those we have loved and that as we lose others through life changes, illness or death, we must seek new people to love, that this is a defining quality of our growth and capacity to grow.

The startling element of this reporting was these adaptive defence mechanisms, detected in the study data (1977, 1993, 2002), validated the defence mechanisms proposed initially by Freud (1894/1964) and subsequently by his daughter, Anna (1937).

Eighteen of these defences were identified in study life stories and data. However, five were considered positive and highly adaptive and represent ways in which study participants were seen to 'mature' and positively adapt over time. While these mechanisms are 'unconscious', Vaillant indicated that as participants became more mature and conscious in their behaviour with age, these also moved into conscious coping styles. The five mechanisms were altruism, sublimation, suppression, anticipation and humour. These are defined in the following way:

Mature Defences

Suppression	Postponing paying attention to the emotion.
Sublimation	Channelling the emotion into some other more acceptable form.
Altruism	Doing for others as we would wish to be 'done by'.
Anticipation	Taking or accepting our 'pain' in small doses.
Humour	Being able or determined to 'laugh' at our struggles.

Valllant 1993: p33 - 73

Figure 2.2 Vaillant's summary of the mature defences.

Vaillant positioned his description of these unconscious adaptive mechanisms in two quite startling ways. He suggested that they were a form of psychological 'immune system' in parallel to our physical one. Additionally, that this perspective offered a wider theoretical orientation or 'compass' and an expanded perspective on adult development.

Through the gift of following the cohorts into retirement, Vaillant was able to identify positive ways of participants' adjustment to an older age. These were summarised in his 2002 text as:

New social networks
The rediscovery of how to 'play'
Development of creativity
Continuing to learn

Daniel Levinson – the 'seasons' of a man's and woman's life

Levinson et al. (1978, Levinson & Levinson, 1996) conducted two qualitative research projects over a 25-year period (1969 to his death in 1994) into the adult development of men in the first and women in the second. The first study took ten years from its inception to the publication of results, and the second started in 1979 and was published in 1996. Levinson's works are different to those of Erikson's in that they were empirically (rather than clinically) derived; and at a point in time, unlike Vaillant who's research was prospective, through time. Researching and writing at the same time as George Vaillant's early work, his view and motivation at the time was understanding of the adult lifespan was limited and in need of development. He felt additional understanding was needed in its own right as well as to counter negative stereotypes existing in society at the time of decline with age.

The studies were based on 'intensive biographic interviews' conducted by a team of researchers. The focus was on the individual in society, relationships and roles, their involvement and engagement with the world around them, drawing on psychological, sociological, cultural and historical perspectives. In both studies, they involved approximately five to ten interviews per participant over a two-month period each of one to two hours duration to create a biography and draw generalisations from the group. In addition, there was a secondary sample of lives portrayed in published biographies. Levinson was explicit about the work being influenced by an intellectual tradition emerging from the work of Freud, Erikson and Jung. There were 40 male participants aged between 43 and 45, between 1969 and 1977 and 45 female participants aged between 35 and 45 years. The sample was drawn from diverse social class and ethnic backgrounds. While offering perspective on all of the adult lifespan, the focus and detail of their findings were on early adulthood, from the approximate age of 17 through to late middle adulthood at circa age 50. The findings nuance and add form and shape to those emerging from Erikson and Vaillant.

The following descriptions of adult development represent material from the men's and women's studies. Levinson presented three primary findings:

- *Four Eras* each of approximately 25 years, which form the underlying 'macro structure' of the human life course.
- *Developmental periods* which are the structure of each era, approximately ten years in length and comprising times of transition and stability.
- *The individual 'life structure'* within these eras and periods, based on the choices and priorities of the person.

The finding of eras within the human life, what Levinson described as a 'macro structure', was an underlying order within the life through which we would all pass. Reflecting the names of his books, they are 'Seasons'. This order, flow or sequence does, however, permit expression and variations that reflect what must be countless combinations of gender, race, culture and social context (Levinson & Levinson, 1996). Levinson and his colleagues saw the eras as lasting approximately 25 years. The eras overlap so as one ends the next is starting – and this ending and beginning are embraced in a transitionary period (Levinson et al., 1978). The eras are the broad structure of the life cycle and within them are contained developmental periods. Each era was seen as having its own biological, psychological and social character that added to the overall development in the life cycle (Levinson, 1996). The sequence was found to be the same for men and women.

Each era had within its developmental periods – an alternating pattern of periods of building and maintaining a life structure and periods of transition in which aspects of a life structure are terminated and individuals move towards a new one.

Levinson saw a further primary contribution of this work as providing a language and detail to the nature and structure of this experience and age in adulthood (Levinson & Levinson, 1996). Table 2.1 portrays the eras of the life cycle and the development periods

Levinson found that the eras and the developmental periods began at an average age (shown in Table 2.1), with a range of variation two years above and below this average. The era of childhood or 'pre-adulthood' was not covered as part of these studies.

The concept of the 'life structure' was also centrl to Levinson's findings, and he is credited with being the first person to propose it. He defined the life structure as the small number of key choices that form our lives over time (Levinson et al., 1978; Levinson & Levinson, 1996). He saw a person's life as having many components (e.g. occupation, relationships, marriage and family, relationship to self and roles in social contexts). The choices and decisions associated with these components and the balance between them change through time, reflecting the importance accorded to them by the individual. These components and the decisions about them formed the fabric of our lives and the relationships between the self and the surrounding world (Levinson et al., 1978). This concept mirrors or reflects ideas on 'meaning' subsequently described in Wong's (2012) portraying ways in which we give priorities to core aspects of our lives. Levinson proposed that those parts of our lives accorded the greatest priority are also the central components that will influence the unfolding of our lives (Levinson et al., 1978). When one or more components of the life structure are given priority Levinson argued, by implication, other aspects of life would not receive so much attention and may eventually be perceived as unfulfilled (Levinson & Levinson, 1996). The choices made, experiences of their effects and personal wishes for change or difference form the focus for any alteration to the life structure.

Levinson reports a core aspect and development of these phases as being the 'individuation' of the person. This is a concept found in Jungian psychology (Stein, 2006/2018) arguing we grow into the fullness of who we are. We draw more fully on our inner resources (desires, values, talents, archetypal potentials) and relate to aspects of our lives that may have become unconscious to us (Levinson & Levinson, 1996).

The descriptions provided earlier are generalised comments on the experiences of both men and women. There is a strong possibility in the lapse of time since Levinson's writing that his comments on the differences in the experiences of women may have been subject to social change. The writer has repeatedly presented these findings to undergraduate psychology students in the past five years to ask their views of the accuracy. Their opinion has always been divided; some saw society as very different now and others didn't.

Table 2.1 The eras of the life cycle and the developmental period within them

Era	Ages	Phase	Age
Early Adulthood	Approximately 17–45	Early adult transition	17–22
		Entry life structure for early adulthood: Exploring and tentative decisions on a provisional life structure and direction	Approximately 22–28
		Age 30 transition: A re-evaluation and possible revision of early adult decisions and directions.	Approximately 28–33
		Culminating life structure for early adulthood: In which individuals seek to establish and express decisions on life direction	
Middle Adulthood	Approximately 40–60	Midlife transition: Choices made *and not made* in the 20s are revisited. Life aspirations are contrasted with life as it is in reality	Approximately 40–45
		Entry life structure for middle adulthood: There may be similarities and differences to the 30s for relationship, job and community, with shifts and changes in priorities	Approximately 45–50
		Age 50 transition: The middle adulthood life structure is reappraised and may be changed	Approximately 50–55
		Culminating life structure for middle adulthood: with potential changes towards achieving the aspirations and goals of the era	Approximately 55–60
Late adulthood transition and life era were not researched by Levinson			

Levinson's work has obvious limitations. He is clear that his studies involved relatively small numbers of people in geographically defined areas and that they capture information at a point in time for the individuals and the culture in which they are found. While acknowledging his results must be seen in the context of their time, Levinson proposed a universality of these results. Levinson backed up the information from participants with data from biographies and questionnaires of many hundreds of people, so he will have considered other factors. It needs to be acknowledged, however, that the universality has not been much tested in other times and cultures. The work does, however, offer a level of detail on early and middle adulthood absent from Erikson's sixth and seventh stages covering the same period (Levinson & Levinson, 1996).

The work of Vaillant (1977, 2002, 2012) provides endorsement for Levinson's findings from different study groups, using different research methods. If, as Levinson asserts in the 1996 study, there are still comparatively few studies on adult development, then his work offers a language and a structure through which to anticipate and examine the experience of adulthood.

Dan P. McAdams – identity and life as 'story'

Dan McAdams has provided an increasing milestone contribution to psychology in his theoretical and research-based work on personality and identity as life 'story'. He (and Jeffrey Arnett in the section that follows) are a different, younger, generation from the theorists reviewed earlier and are using innovative methods and concepts that extend traditional psychology.

McAdams' innovation in the early 1980s was to associate 'identity' and 'narrative' (McAdams, 2018). He drew on Erik Erikson's definition of identity (Erikson, 1958/1980) which pointed to it comprising almost a mosaic of different aspects of the self, internal and socially situated. While most psychologists might see this mosaic as factors one tested or treated as aspects of theory, McAdams took the creative step of seeing them as characteristics of a story (e.g. 1985, 2018). McAdams (1985, 1993, 2001) draws on the fifth Eriksonian stage of development in which identity, an integrated sense of self, is believed to form for the first time. This argues the individual, in teenage years, is exploring their talents and strengths, social context, possible roles and motivation into a sense of self and direction in their adult world. It is at this stage that McAdams argues we begin to make sense of ourselves, our past, present and possible future through self-defining stories (2001). Implicitly, this making-sense-of-self task never stops and becomes revised through life. McAdams proposes that stories have multiple functions, including explanation, sense-making, entertainment, learning about morals and virtue and how to live what would be called a good life as well as creating autobiographical memory.

In the act of reflecting on and describing our biographical experience, we display and use the features of stories and their structure (McAdams, 2001). While research suggests this occurs from an early age, Erikson and McAdams argue that it is in the teenage years that this constitutes identity formation (McAdams, 2011; McAdams & Guo, 2015).

If life events are seen, made sense of, as stories, then it is a natural extension that individuals will infer causal links within these stories. This, in turn, may mean we explain our traits, talents and strengths, beliefs and attitudes via these stories (McAdams, 2001). Habermas and Bluck (2000) suggest these causal links go further to a sense of coherence in our sense of self in the areas of time, context and specific themes. As we form and re-form these stories over time, our identity is a life journey and potentially our biggest creative task (Csikszentmihalyi, 1996). By describing it in this way, Csikszentmihalyi links this act of 'identity creation' to our strengths, positive experiences and emotions, finding meaning and a meaningful life.

Having made an argument for the place and presence of personal story and life narrative, let us turn to *summarise* examples of the characteristics we may find within them. These are drawn from (with permission of Professor Dan McAdams) McAdams (1985, 1993, 2006a, 2006b) and Adler and Poulin (2009).

Story characteristic: thematic lines

These are the main 'themes' showing in the story, the motivational forces within the individuals and their *needs, drives and incentives*.

McAdams argues for two primary themes being apparent in stories: 'agency' and 'communion'. 'Power' and 'intimacy' are comparable words he uses.

References: McAdams (1985): pp. 70 and 71 and p. 73; McAdams (1985): p. 84 and p. 149; McAdams (1985): pp. 76 and 77 and p. 152.

Story characteristic: nuclear episodes

These 'episodes' comprise the core structure of our story. They are likely to be associated with our feelings at certain times. These episodes may be critical or formative, and which we experience as defining who we are. They may be positive or negative. They may have transformative qualities or act as confirming the stability or sameness in our lives.

The episodes may include early memories, peak or nadir or 'flow' experiences. Bear in mind that the feeling of these episodes may be our interpretation of events rather than their factual content.

References: McAdams (1985): pp 133–140 and p. 170.

Story characteristic: 'images' or characters

McAdams suggests that the characters that populate our lives reveal indications of our identity. He draws on the Jungian concepts of characters as 'archetypes', *patterns of behaving and experiencing* that may reflect polarities of experience within our lives. Within his earlier research, McAdams found that the characters in the stories of those motivated by power and agency or intimacy and communion with others commonly represented characteristics of those two states. They represented, to McAdams, *idealised and personified images* of the self the individual seeks to be.

References: McAdams (1985): pp. 176–178, pp. 183 and 185 and p. 210.

Story characteristic: setting

The setting of a story will often have a quality, reflective of an individual's culture, values and/or beliefs. The setting reflects a time and space of the individual's story and within which the actions find sense and meaning.

Reference: McAdams (1985): p. 215.

Story characteristic: narrative tone

McAdams proposes that the narrative tone of a story is both pervasive and reflective of a storyteller's view of their world. In more recent research and writing, McAdams describes two embracing tones within stories, those of redemption and contamination. Redemption is described as a capacity to find positive meaning, benefits and growth within difficult circumstances. Contamination is defined as being negatively affected by events, with an inability to control them.

Reference: McAdams (1993): p. 48; McAdams (2006): pp. 5–8.

Story characteristic: generativity

McAdams makes a startling development of Erikson's thinking of 'generativity' as a stage of development; he proposes that it is a larger aspect of our identity in which we form a view of our generative future. What are we going to do to have a generative future, to leave a legacy for others? What are we going to create, produce or institute in the future? McAdams sees this as a general sense we may have over time and then particularly in mature adulthood where this may be motivated in the care for others and a younger generation.

Reference: McAdams (1985): pp. 252–254

McAdams (2006, 2006a) has taken a major step in asserting that our stories and life narratives represent one of the primary ways in which we can reach an integrated understanding of personality and meaning. The readjusting or rethinking of our life stories over time may reflect the very act of responding to and reconsidering the full range of experiences of our lives, the 'light' and 'dark'.

Having established via research the presence of stories and their contribution to the understanding of self, McAdams has given us the gift of extending the ideas much further. He defines 'identity' as an integrative configuration of the self in the world (2001: pp. 102). The configuration brings together in present time roles and relationships in a culturally situated world. Further, that the stories allow us to understand and adjust to changes we have experienced over time.

The life story is internalised and evolving, focusing on reconstructed perspectives of the past and an imagined future which combined give qualities of focus and purpose in the present time (McAdams & McLean, 2013). McAdams argues that when achieved this allows the individual to be self-situated in a particular meaningful niche that has characteristics of unity and purpose. McAdams proposes, reflecting Eriksonian theory on the emergence of identity, that narrative identity, based on an internalised story, starts to occur in the late teens and onwards. McLean, Pasupathi, and Pals (2007) nuance the theory in saying the stories are adjusted and amended over time, based on experience and a changed understanding of ourselves (McAdams, 2015). The life experience supports the creation of a story. The story, in turn, influences subsequent experience, which then influences further amendments to the story. As McLean et al. suggest, *self creates stories, stories create selves* (2007).

Both Hammack (2008) and McAdams (2006b) take our understanding further still, in saying our individual stories will have characteristics of the cultures in which they are situated, that they may comprise a 'master narrative' which becomes reflected in the personal narration. This will include norms through which personal characteristics like 'traits' may be displayed; the content of personal goals and values and images and metaphors which may shape the telling of a story (McAdams, 2015). Our cultural context will be a powerful influence on the content and shape of personal narratives. Further, that when the stories display characteristics of 'redemption', problems in earlier life which involved a sensitivity to the experiences of others, in addition to a life path where the problems were overcome and a positive outcome experienced, they were more likely to display the 'generativity' (active care for future generations) theorised by Erikson (1950/1980, 1997) and well-being (Bauer, McAdams, & Pals, 2008).

In adding to and extending personality psychology, McAdams and Pals (2006) situate integrative life narratives as one of five key principles of personality psychology, along with the evolved design of human nature, dispositional traits, characteristic adaptations to our lives and the meaning systems and practices within our culture – all situated in the social ecology of everyday life. They portray this as an integrated system where all aspects of a system influence others.

Developing his concepts further, McAdams (2013, 2015) puts forward a new three-part model of the development of personality and the 'psychological self' based on the characteristics of 'actor, agent and author'.

- The social 'actor' is based on the traits, skills and roles that result in our actions and performance in the social context.
- The motivated 'agent' emerges at the end of childhood as important explorations are occurring and decisions are being made about life choices and goals. Through this, the individual develops motives, values, hopes and plans for the future.
- The autobiographical 'author' develops in emerging adulthood through the self-developed story that integrates the past, present and future.

McAdams (2013) emphasises these phases are not separate or autonomous but link, interact and change over time via experiences and shifts in the personally perceived story.

Jeffrey Jensen Arnett – the concept of 'emerging adulthood'

Over the past 20-plus years, Jeffrey Jensen Arnett has offered us a new concept of adult development. With a skilful and exciting 'weave' of interpreting demographically based changes in the experiences of young adults, researching his proposals and connecting them to Erikson's (1968) and Levinson et al.'s (1978) work, he gives us a backdrop of development in language that has become accessible to audiences beyond psychology or psychologists.[1]

Arnett focuses on a period from the late teens through the 20s, with a particular focus on the ages 18–25. He highlights how this period is a profound period of change and exploration for young people with particular foci on education, work, love and relationships. Arnett, Robinson, and Lachman (2020) argue that the characteristic timing of life events in any of these areas has changed significantly enough that adult development generally needs rethinking and reconceptualising. Arnett suggests this emerging adulthood period has five features that make it distinct: a focus on the self while explorations are made, the searching for identity, the instability of choices made, a sense of possibility, yet also feeling in a transitional state, of being in-between (Arnett, 2007, 2015). He argues that huge demographic changes in industrialised countries have moved this age range from a transition to a specific period of adult development in its own right (Arnett, 2000, 2007, 2015).

Arnett suggests that Western industrialised countries accept this age range as relatively independent from social roles and normative expectations (Arnett, 2000). Further, that it is a period of life where many different life choices can be explored and made by young people in the areas of education, work, relationships, love and worldviews. He notes that the timing of many of these events has changed significantly in recent decades. Exploring patterns researched in the United States, Arnett describes changes occurring in a residential location and increased post-school education and subsequent changes made within those choices and courses. Yet, Arnett (2000, 2004) highlights that this period is *subjectively* felt as different by young people who in research do not see themselves as adolescent *or yet adult*. It could be straightforward to assume young people would perceive themselves as adult if choices were emerging in the 'life structure' concept of Levinson et al. (1978) that reflected decisions based on education, work and relationship. Yet, Arnett proposes that it is quality of character (2000) that marks the felt transition to adulthood. He cites the top two offered in research as the accepting and taking responsibility for oneself and the shift to making independent decision-making. When these qualities become established, Arnett suggests that the young person moves from emerging adulthood to what is now being named (Arnett, Robinson, & Lachman, 2020) as 'established adult-hood' at the age 30.

Arnett (2000, 2007, and Arnett, Robinson, & Lachman, 2020) articulates in detail the exploration of possibilities that takes place in characteristics of identity in education, love, work and worldview. In experiences of love, he summarises adolescent exploration as tentative and transient. In emerging adulthood, this acquires a longer-term, relational quality, likely to have settled periods, yet still an exploration of love and intimacy. Reviewing education, he highlights choices of courses that become changed and occupational experimentation. Arnett suggests that these choices may not necessarily be motivated by a move towards more settled adult responsibilities but experientially oriented prior to making longer-term choices. He emphasises the extent to which these experiences are heterogeneous and individual. In this, he highlights and argues that this time period is sufficiently long and significant and detailed in its shaping quality that it is appropriate to see it as a discrete period of adult development, not merely a transition (2007).

Arnett (2000, 2007) makes an interesting link to earlier theorists in suggesting that both Erikson (1968) and Levinson et al. (1978) pointed towards this possible change and revised interpretation which subsequent social changes have heightened. Erikson commented on the extent to which adolescence could be perceived as prolonged which implicitly involved a psychosocial moratorium in which young people could explore and experiment in choices (Erikson, 1968). Levinson et al. (1978) reported the 20s as a period of provisional choices which could be rechecked and changed prior to a more settled period commencing at approximately 30 years old. An implication offered by Arnett of this newly proposed phase of adult development is adolescence as a discrete age range of 10–18 years, which then moves not in a transitionary way but to a new phase of adult development – 'emerging adulthood'. He takes a further step into theorised adult development more broadly in suggesting that this pattern of exploration and discovery in a new period of adult life may be a norm, in that any significantly new phase of adult life will call for similar qualities to make a transition from one time of life to another (Arnett, 2007). Arnett, Robinson, and Lachman (2020) special edition of the American Psychologist points to new directions of research needed to revise concepts of general adult development (Buhler & Nitkin, 2020; Diehl, Smyer, & Mehrotra, 2020; Mehta et al., 2020).

Weaving the five theories to a linked perspective?

Table 2.2 seeks to summarise key aspects of each theory, and in positioning them side by side, there is the opportunity to see patterns across them that potentially deepen our overall understanding of their work.

Summary of theories tabulated and presented in this chapter:

- There are discrete phases in adult life across the lifespan.
- The phases of adult life alternate between times of stability and transition. Stability seeks to maximise what we learn and develop in a phase. Transition

Table 2.2 Five lifespan developmental theories contrasted

Seek to read the theories from left to right, cumulatively: ⇒

Erikson	Vaillant	Levinson	McAdams	Arnett
Method? Psychoanalysis and ethnography	Method? Prospective study of adult development	Method? Qualitative interviews. Thematic analysis	Method? Qualitative and quantitative research	Method? Analysis of demographic trends, tested in qualitative and quantitative research
Phases of life across the entire lifespan	Empirically established Erikson phases from new data (Vaillant 1977)	Articulated the developmental structure of early and middle adulthood	Our personality is a narrative or 'story' We re-story, adjust our story, over time	Presents a detailed case for how demographic changes in the last three decades have changed the nature and timing of adult development phases
Polarity, positive or negative of potential experience and outcome	Added one new phase of the lifespan (Keeper of Meaning) between Erikson's seventh and eighth stages	Demonstrated life unfolds in phases of approximately a decade that reflect periods of stability and transition	Our story has recognisable themes, for example, nuclear episodes, settings, characters and narrative tone	Builds on Erikson (1968) and Levinson et al. (1978) to propose a phase of 'Emerging Adulthood' based on a substantial exploration occurring by young people in their teens and 20s in most characteristics of personal identity, particularly education, work, love and relationship
The positive outcome of the developmental 'crisis' in each phase creates a 'developmental strength' in addition to what positive psychology might label as character strengths	Identified empirically, through study data, the presence of unconscious adult defence mechanisms. With age and maturity, these mechanisms represent a positive adaptation to life stresses and experiences	Early adulthood involves the choice and formation of a 'life structure'. This is customarily 3 or 4 key decisions around which goals and life energy are focused	Motivational themes involve the tension of 'power' and 'love'. In some stories, these may be 'either or', one motivation or the other. In others, they are present together Healing and meaning go together	
The outcome of each phase is re-processed and re-understood in				

(Continued)

Table 2.2 (Continued)

Erikson	Vaillant	Levinson	McAdams	Arnett
each subsequent phase potentially as a way in which our self-awareness and self-story change over time	Broadly mirrors Erikson and Levinson Highlights the emergence of our 'inner voice' at around 40 years old Generativity and 'mature coping mechanisms' support healing and positive ageing Personality may be relatively static; 'character' matures and changes	A life structure decision made or chosen implies decisions not made or not chosen. Development over time involves reassessing and adjusting decisions made and decisions that could have been made The passage of time and age sees the need to live 'polarities' of experience, a positive and a negative, not 'either or'. For example, youthful in outlook while also accepting the implications of ageing	Our personality growth unfolds in a three-part content and structure: becoming the social 'actor', 'agent' and 'author'	More recently Arnett, Robinson, and Lachman (2020) suggests if Emerging Adulthood as a phase of adult development has changed in the way that it has, then subsequent phases of adult life need reconsideration

seeks to help us prepare for new times and eras in our lives and the choices we may make.

- Decisions we make about the shape of our lives imply a decision or choice made and not made. Choices not made may periodically resurface or revisit seeking to be reconsidered.
- Whatever theory is used, we might infer there is a polarity of experience, developmental strengths, to be resolved over time, ideally towards the positive.
- There are unconscious adaptive processes which we draw upon to manage stress and experience, ideally moving to a greater personal maturity.
- Over time, we increasingly perceive and process our lives as 'story'. The stories are likely to have predictable characteristics. A 'redemptive' story, one where difficulties may have been experienced yet still overcome, was indicative of likely well-being.
- The time period of 18–30 years old approximately is exploratory to identify and relate to aspects of love, relationship, education and work that will become reflections of your future life structure and identity.

Strengths and limitations of this research?

Erikson, Vaillant and Levinson each offer a detailed picture and language for adult development in the depth and detail of their work that we did not have prior to them and arguably have not yet replaced since them. However, they are all a previous generation and the time since their work raises questions on the extent of changes since. Additionally, while women were part of the research of each, their representation and voice were limited. This is a major gap needing to be filled.

The work of McAdams is unfolding, developing and active now. His work viewing the way identity is fundamentally grounded in 'story' and the use or focus of 'story' has face validity and accessibility for modern readers. He is a leading voice theorising the development and nature of identity.

Arnett, again, is another example of the current generation asserting major changes via research. Interestingly, his ideas appear to have been drawn on from a range of professions beyond psychology. Yet, Arnett Robinson, and Lachman (2020) make clear that the task of exploring and asserting new theories of adult development has a huge amount of work before becoming comparable to Erikson, Vaillant and Levinson in their volume and detail.

The resources listed later offer opportunities through which individual stories and voices can be seen in their contribution to development.

This chapter has

- Summarised five theories and research of lifespan development, each offering a different descriptive language of the experience of growth and ageing.
- The research, when considered together, portrays eras and phases of the human lifespan; alternating periods of stability and transition across time,

characterised by the life content of that age period and developmental strengths and life stories are grown and constructed by the processing of live experience over time.

Reflection?

Can you see the details of these theories reflected in your own life experience?

Are you drawn to one or more of these theories than others? Why?

Do one or more of these theories prompt you to understand new aspects of your life experience?

An existential perspective?

These theories and research point at the form and shape, the patterns that might be found in individual lives. These, in turn, may give us indications of the expressions and explorations of personal 'being' and 'existence' and how we gradually become who we are. Our invitation as individuals or practitioners is to become more conscious and aware of their implications and consider choices we would make as a result.

Research questions or possibilities?

Can you identify these patterns in specific populations that you work with?

What do these ideas 'miss' or not include about specific populations you work with?

Consider reading this chapter *and* Chapter 3 simultaneously and ask in what ways the expressions of individual existence are found in groups you work with?

Resources

References specifically related to the psychology, development and growth of women:

Arnold, K., Noble, K.D., and Subotnik, R.F. (1996). *Remarkable Women: Perspectives on Female Talent Development*. Cresskill, NJ, Hampton Press Inc.

Belenky, M., McVicker-Clinchy, B., Rule-Goldberger, N., and Mattck-Tarule, J. (1986 and 1997). *Women's Ways of Knowing*. New York, Basic Books.

Gilligan, C. (1982 and 1993). *In A Different Voice*. Harvard, Harvard University Press.

Gilligan, C. (2011). *Joining the Resistance*. Cambridge, Polity Press.

Jordan, J.V. 'et al'. (1991). *Women's Growth in Connection: Writings from the Stone Centre*. London, The Guildford Press.

Josselson, R. (2017). *Paths to Fulfilment: Women's Search for Meaning and Identity*. Oxford, Oxford University Press.

Note

1 In a 2007 paper Arnett highlights an apparent large range of interdisciplinary interest and use of the emerging adulthood concept, including psychiatry, sociology, education, epidemiology health sciences and more.

References

Adler, J.M., and Poulin, M.J. (2009). The Political Is Personal: Narrating 9/11 and Psychological Well-Being. *Journal of Personality*, Vol. 77, No. 4, 903–932.

Arnett, J.J. (2000). Emerging Adulthood: A Theory of Development from the Late Teens Through the Twenties. *American Psychologist*, Vol. 55, 469–480. https://doi.org/10.1037/0003-066X.55.5.469

Arnett, J.J. (2004). *Emerging Adulthood: The Winding Road from the Late Teens through the Twenties*. Oxford, Oxford University Press.

Arnett, J.J. (2007). Emerging Adulthood: What Is It, and What Is It Good for? *Child Development Perspectives*, Vol. 1, No. 2, 68–73. doi.org/10.1111/j.1750-8606.2007.00016.x

Arnett, J.J. (2015). *Emerging Adulthood* (2nd edition). Oxford, Oxford University Press.

Arnett, J.J., Robinson, O., and Lachman, M.E. (2020). Rethinking Adult Development: Introduction to the Special Issue. *American Psychologist*, Vol. 75, No. 4, 425–430. http://dx.doi.org/10.1037/amp0000633

Baltes, P.B. (1987). Theoretical Propositions of Life Span Developmental Psychology: On the Dynamics between Growth and Decline. *Developmental Psychology*, Vol. 23, No. 5, 611–626. https://doi.org/10.1037/0012-1649.23.5.611

Bauer, J.J., McAdams, D.P., and Pals, J.L. (2008). Narrative Identity and Eudaimonic Well-Being. *Journal of Happiness Studies*, Vol. 9, 81–104. DOI: 10.1007/ s10902-006-9021-6

Buhler, J.L., and Nitkin, J. (2020). Sociohistorical Context and Adult Social Development: New Directions for 21st Century Research. *American Psychologist*, Vol. 75, No. 4, 457–469. DOI: 10.1037/amp0000611

Csikszentmihalyi, M. (1996). *Creativity: Flow and the Psychology of Discovery and Invention*. London, Harper Collins.

Diehl, M., Smyer, M.A., and Mehrotra, C.M. (2020). Optimizing Aging: A Call for a New Narrative. *American Psychologist*, Vol. 75, No. 4, 577–589. doi.org/10.1037/amp0000598

Erikson, E.H. (1958/1980). *Identity and the Life Cycle*. New York, Norton.

Erikson, E.H. (1963). *Childhood and Society* (2nd edition). New York, Norton.

Erikson, E.H. (1968). The Human Life Cycle. Paper contained in Schlein, S. (Ed.). *A Way of Looking at Things: Selected Papers From 1930 to 1980*. New York, Norton.

Erikson, E.H. (1980). On the Generational Cycle: An Address. *International Journal of Psychoanalysis*, Vol. 61, 213–223.

Erikson, E.H., and Erikson, J.M. (1997). *The Life Cycle Completed* (Revised edition, by J.M. Erikson.). New York, Norton.

Erikson, J.M. (1988). *Wisdom and the Senses: The Way of Creativity*. New York, Norton.

Erikson, E.H., and Erikson, J.M. (1981). On Generativity and Identity: From a Conversation with Erik and Joan Erikson. *Harvard Educational Review*, Vol. 51, No. 2, 249–269. DOI: 10.17763/HAER.51.2.G211757U27732P67

Erikson, E.H., Erikson, J.M., and Kivnick, H.Q. (1986). *Vital Involvement in Old Age*. New York, Norton.

Freud, A. (1937). *Ego and the Mechanisms of Defence*. London, Hogarth Press.

Freud, S. (1894 / 1964). The Neuro-Psychoses of Defence. Chapter in: *The Complete Psychological Works of Sigmund Freud*. London, Hogarth Press.

Habermas, T., and Bluck, S. (2000). Getting A Life: The Emergence of Life Story in Adolescence. *Psychological Bulletin*, Vol. 126, No. 5, 748–769. doi: 10.1037/0033-2909. 126.5.748

Hammack, P.L. (2008). Narrative and the Cultural Psychology of Identity. *Personality and Social Psychology Review, 12*, 222–247. doi.org/10.1177/1088868308316892

Levinson, D.J., Darrow, C.N., Klein, E.B., Levinson, M.H., and McKee, B. (1978). *The Seasons of a Man's Life*. New York, Ballantine Books.

Levinson, D.J., and Levinson, J. (1996). *The Seasons of a Woman's Life*. New York, Alfred Knopf.

Loevinger, J. (1969). Theories of Ego Development. Chapter in: Breger, L. (Ed.). *Clinical Cognitive Psychology: Models and Integrations*. Hoboken, NJ, Prentice Hall.

McAdams, D.P. (1985). *Power, Intimacy and the Live Story: Personological Inquiries into Identity*. London, Guildford Press.

McAdams, D.P. (1993). *The Stories We Live By: Personal Myths and the Making of the Self*. London, Guildford Press.

McAdams, D.P. (2001). The Psychology of Life Stories. *Review of General Psychology*, Vol. 5, No. 2, 100–122. doi.org/10.1037/1089-2680.5.2.100

McAdams, D.P. (2006a). *The Person: A New Introduction to Personality Psychology* (4th edition). Chichester, John Wiley and Sons Inc.

McAdams, D.P. (2006b). *The Redemptive Self: Stories Americans' Live By*. Oxford, Oxford University Press.

McAdams, D.P. (2011). Narrative Identity. Chapter in: Schwartz, S.J. Luyckx, K. and Vignoles, V.L. (Eds.). *Handbook of Identity Theory and Research* (pp. 99–115). New York, Springer Science + Business Media. https://doi.org/10.1007/978-1-4419-7988-9_5

McAdams, D.P. (2013). The Psychological Self as Actor, Agent, and Author. *Perspectives on Psychological Science*, Vol. 8, No. 3, 272–295. doi.org/10.1177/1745691612464657

McAdams, D.P. (2015). *The Art and Science of Personality Development*. London, Guildford Press.

McAdams, D.P. (2018). Narrative Identity: What Is It? What Does It do? How Do You Measure It? *Imagination, Cognition and Personality: Consciousness in Theory, Research and Clinical Practice*, Vol. 37, No. 3, 359–372. doi.org/10.1177/0276236618756704

McAdams, D.P., and Guo, J. (2015). Narrating the Generative Life. *Psychological Science*, Vol. 26, No. 4, 475–483. doi.org/10.1177/0956797614568318

McAdams, D.P., and McLean, K.C. (2013). Narrative Identity. *Current Directions in Psychological Science*, Vol. 22, No. 3, 233–238. doi.org/10.1177/0963721413475622

McAdams, D.P., and Pals, J.L. (2006). A New Big Five: Fundamental Principles for an Integrative Science of Personality. *American Psychologist*, Vol. 61, No. 3, 204–217. Doi: 10.1037/0003-066X.61.3.204

McLean, K.C., Pasupathi, M., and Pals, J.L. (2007). Self Creating Stories, Creating Selves. *Personality and Social Psychology Review*, Vol. 11, No. 3, August. doi.org/ 10.1177/1088868307301034

Mehta, C.M., Arnett, J.J., Palmer, C.G., and Nelson, L.J. (2020). A New Conception of Ages 30–45. *American Psychologist*, Vol. 75, No. 4, 431–444. doi.org/10.1037/amp0000600

Perlmutter, M., and Hall, E. (1992). *Adult Development and Aging* (2nd edition). Chichester, John Wiley and Sons Inc.

Roazen, P. (1976). *Erik H. Erikson: The Power and Limits of a Vision*. New York, Free Press.

Stein, M. (2006/2018). *The Principle of Individuation: Toward the Development of Human Consciousness*. Ashville, NC, Chiron Publications.

Stevens, R. (1983). *Erik Erikson*. Milton Keynes, The Open University Press.

Vaillant, G.E. (1977). *Adaptation to Life*. Boston, Little, Brown and Co.

Vaillant, G.E. (1993). *Wisdom and the Ego*. Cambridge, Harvard University Press.

Vaillant, G.E. (2000). Adaptive Mental Mechanisms: Their Role in a Positive Psychology. *American Psychologist*, Vol. 55, No. 1, 89–98. DOI: 10.1037//0003–066x.55.1.89

Vaillant, G.E. (2002). *Aging Well*. Boston, Little Brown.

Vaillant, G.E. (2012). *Triumphs of Experience: The Men of the Harvard Grant Study*. Cambridge, The Belknap Press of Harvard University Press.

Wong, P.T.P. (2011). Positive Psychology 2.0: Towards a Balanced Interactive Model of the Good Life. *Canadian Psychology*, Vol. 52, No. 2, 69–81.

Wong, P.T.P. (2012). Towards a Dual System Model of What makes Life Worth Living. Chapter in: Wong, P.T.P. (Ed.). *The Human Quest for Meaning*. London, Routledge.

Worth, P.T.P. (2016). Positive Development – Our Journey of Growth. Chapter in: Ivtzan, I., Lomas, T., Hefferon, K. and Worth, P. (Eds.). *Second Wave Positive Psychology: Embracing the Dark Side of Life*. London, Routledge.

Chapter 3

Our unfolding journey of growth

Piers Worth and Andrew Machon

The learning objectives of this chapter are to

- Understand and interpret the theories of different researchers proposing the pattern of inner growth over the human lifespan.
- Compare and contrast the theoretical perspectives offered of 'transcendence' and form a view on which, as the reader, applies to your experience and practice.
- Analyse and distinguish ways through which we as individuals may approach the experience of transcendence.

Introduction

Chapter 2 lays out lifespan development descriptions of the structure, time-scales, and rhythms of stability and change within our lives. These ideas pick up the potential content and dynamics of our lives over time. They are the work of lifespan developmental researchers looking from an 'outside-in' perspective, learning the patterns of experience in others. The theories and research portrayed have a common theme implicit across the five main sources. Each, in some ways, describes an unfolding growth and evolution over time of our ego, our sense of self or consciousness. Yet, within this work, there are clues that something else is occurring. Something else is unfolding. We could call this the 'inside-out' perspective. What are we experiencing from the inside that is unfolding and shaping our experience of the outside world? What is it over time that allows us to become more of who we truly are? What is the journey we take to become less subject to the vicissitudes of the outside world, and more mature, choosing and responsive from the inside out to what is happening around us?

This chapter will focus on these processes that point towards the different ways the unfolding of who we truly are, our character and nature may take place over time. This journey will also illustrate a paradox that as we display and identify with who we most truly are, at the same time we may seek to go beyond it, to 'transcend' our ego in service of others.

DOI: 10.4324/9781003132530-3

We speculate that there is potentially an infinite number of ways in which we as individuals may grow.

These are complex questions on which philosophers and psychologists have expressed many views over time. This chapter explores leading theorists/researchers and their views on this experience to point towards many ways in which we grow, and ways you might recognise in yourself or those you work with as clients.

The chapter is hugely ambitious given the number of writers, researchers and concepts that contribute to this understanding. It is, by necessity, a summary of key ideas that we would encourage you as readers to explore in more detail for yourself, perhaps via the resources offered at the end of this chapter

These theorists commonly use different language and perspectives for what they propose and in places overtly disagree with each other. Yet, one term recurs in several descriptions: 'transcendence' or 'self-transcendence' (ST), apparently used interchangeably, over the course of our lifetime. This chapter will propose that we are not looking at how one theorist/researcher is 'correct' and others are not; these perspectives have a quality of 'both and', a 'mosaic', in being seen together rather than separate we obtain a broader perspective. And while key theorists were commonly quite a 'big picture' in their orientation, other theories point towards small steps that we as individuals might take to encounter this experience. Let us proceed to explain this journey.

Growth in the phases of our lives

In all of the theories explored, the indication is that this process of growth is inherent within us and occurs potentially normally, naturally, for the most part outside our awareness. Erikson and Erikson (1997), Vaillant (1977, 2002, 2012), Levinson et al. (1978, Levinson and Levinson, 1996) and McAdams (2013, 2015, 2018) each point to changes over time in our understanding, awareness, in a maturation of our 'ego' and consciousness that emerge from engagement with life, ageing, the interaction between our bio-psycho-social nature. Erikson inferred this was 'epigenetic' in our nature, found within us and engaged and brought into action by engagement in life.

For example, Erikson and Erikson (1997) propose that who we are is a combination of bio-psycho-social interaction. Over 8 or 9 phases of our lives, we engage with our inner and outer context, and we grow. He claims we re-process the developmental polarities and strengths of each phase of our lives every time we enter a new phase of our lifespan and, through this, our strengths and self-awareness will change. Vaillant (2002) empirically confirms the Erikson life cycle phases and the presence of unconscious adaptation and maturation processes that develop the ego over time. Further, that these processes become attuned to supporting others as we age and coping more positively with the challenges of our lives. Levinson et al. (1978, Levinson & Levinson, 1996) believed that our lives moved forward in periods of stability and transition alternately, and in both, we learn (grow) in different ways. He established within this research the process of 'individuation', of becoming more complete in ourselves, proposed by Carl Jung (1930), which occurs over time particularly when we revisit and re-evaluate at midlife and beyond our life choices made, and not made. McAdams (2013, 2015, 2018) reports that we experience our identity and life as 'story' and we adapt and develop this over time.

If we pause and look back, we can see that philosophers have offered insights on this for over 2,000 years. Norton (1976), in a classic text exploring this perspective, offered insight from them. He proposed that the imperatives emerging from Greek philosophers were that we should know ourselves and commit to who we are, as our destiny, and who we are to become. The inner self we were to discover was described as our inner 'Daimon', an aspect of ourselves that was inborn, from birth, and our innate potential, there to be discovered. Deep within these words are beliefs and assumptions of how we should each seek to live (Waterman, 2014). The recurring description of this process is 'eudaimonia', a concept that reaches as far back as Aristotle, and is a cluster of subjective experiences associated with virtue and excellence. The 'daimon' was originally conceived of as a guiding 'spirit' and then as internal, reflecting the potentialities of the person, shared with others and unique to themselves, where fulfilment and happiness were found in their expression. Aristotle argued that this virtue was expressed as a balance, rather than excess, yet still reflects the best thing that is us (Ryff, 2014). Norton (1976) argued that this would be a progressive actualisation of an innate potential and the living of a life that is truly our own. Waterman and Schwartz (2014) proposed this gradual self-creation reflects in the formation of our identity.

In these descriptions, we see aspects of Wong's (2010, 2016a) model of Existential Positive Psychology (EPP), concerned with committing to and expressing authentically our identity and happiness that may emerge from doing so. Yet, Quoidbach et al. (2013) suggest our personal perception may be different; while we may see and acknowledge a change in ourselves retrospectively, we do not anticipate changing significantly in the future – at any point in time, we seem to believe we have become the person we will be in the future. Maybe this points towards an ongoing 'blindness' we have of the changes that will come to us as we age.

Growth through role models and mentors

May (1953), Machon (Chapter 6) and Worth (2000) highlight how we change and grow in the 'mirror' of those with whom we relate. The role of the other, the mirror, may vary considerably, yet mentors, teachers and comparable influential adults become a way of another person seeing in us what might yet become manifest, and for us to be drawn to the radiant positive in others that we may be unconscious of in ourselves. Carl Rogers (1957) highlighted 'core conditions for growth' received from and modelled by another were central for the emergence of a stronger sense of who we are; they are 'empathy', unconditional positive regard and congruence in this other person. Through interactions of this kind, we become more than we may have thought we were. Vaillant (2002) highlights that our ego comprises those we have loved in this way.

Growth (and self-transcendence) as a normal aspect of daily reflection and consciousness

Rollo May (1960, 1983), from the discipline of existential psychology and psychotherapy, arguably takes a first step within the literature on the process of growth and self-transcendence (ST) by focusing on the human being, with an emphasis on 'being'. It is important to note here the meaning and priority given to the term 'being' within existential psychology. It implies an energy and a direction of growth where we will seek to become all we are and to express and grow these characteristics (Hartmann & Zimberoff, 2015).

May defines 'being' as the propensities within us that are continually emerging and becoming that will stand out in time. May (1953) argued that the central need in life is to fulfil our potential. For May (1983), from an existential psychology perspective, the focus on 'being' and our engagement with our being was crucial in our unfolding. This way of describing 'being' becomes a focus and process for our 'becoming' expressed in the words of Norton (1976) earlier. May describes this as an emergent evolution (1983). He proposes that our natural self-awareness and reflexiveness as human beings expand the range of our consciousness and thereby create the situation in which we may perceive, transcend and go beyond our immediate circumstances. He argues that, further, our self-consciousness or self-awareness makes the capacity for this development and ST as inseparable through the way in which we might reflectively stand outside a situation and consider both its content and characteristics as well as choices for the future. In exploring both the characteristics of psychological existence and highlighting the vibrancy with which we come into 'being' as a constant process, May has pointed towards the presence of personal development and unfolding, and ST in a manner that is built upon by subsequent writers.

Growth through a spectrum of 'self-transcendent' experiences

David Yaden and colleagues (2017) propose that experiences where we lose or relax our sense of self and find a sense of connectedness with others or our surroundings are representative of ST. They offer us the insight from their research of a spectrum of intensity through experiences and actions, from concentration in the act of reading or listening to music to meditation or a sense of awe as examples of ST and through which 'growth' may incrementally occur.

Growth through the experience of 'flow'

Csikszentmihalyi's (1993) book takes a wide view of human nature and the evolution of the self. Csikszentmihalyi proposes that human evolution ('growth' in the terms of this chapter) would be a function of increasing complexity in consciousness. He emphasises that consciousness is not only intelligence, knowledge or cognitive traits but also personal feelings and actions together with an awareness and development of our unique potential. Csikszentmihalyi acknowledges that the 'self' is reflected in the nature of our consciousness and shaped by our patterns and habits of attention, what and how we pay attention. This, in turn, is influenced by our context and traits. Further, that our patterns of attention are who we are. He proposes that 'goals' become a means by which what enters our attention is prioritised and that a hierarchy of goals will mirror the nature of the self.

Commenting on the development of the self through time, Csikszentmihalyi observes that developmental theorists such as Maslow (1968), Loevinger (1976) and Fowler (1981) see a pattern of dialectical motion as core to our growth. This occurs in the presence of differentiation (from what we were before) and integration (of what we learn and change), an inner focus of attention then turning to an outer one, self and then the wider community. He proposes that this creates an ascending spiral pattern in our development or growth. Csikszentmihalyi believes that this pattern is observable cross-culturally.

It is against this backdrop that Csikszentmihalyi places the experience of 'flow' as a key contribution. His writing and research over time (e.g. 1975, 1993) point towards flow occurring when we accept an opportunity and challenge to act that is on the edge of our current expertise. The challenges we are oriented towards will reflect our innate talent and strengths. If the current skill and challenge are balanced, then the opportunity and outcome are for growth of skill. The task needs focus and attention that is likely to absorb our capacity for attention, which, in turn, results in a decrease in awareness of self and absorption in time. This is a form of transcendence – the boundaries of the self-relax and we become absorbed in an outer experience. Csikszentmihalyi sees polarities occurring in these experiences: moving from the known to the currently unknown, focusing attention on the outer experience which decreases inner awareness of self and time. He proposes that if there is a willingness to enter this state of growth and development, over time, we incrementally develop our uniqueness and, in the transcendence, become oriented towards the outer goals that contribute to others.

Csikszentmihalyi asks the question whether this development is an inner focus, on skill and self-development, before that of an external contribution to others. His conclusion is that this must be development on 'all fronts' at the same time, a 'both and' perspective rather than an 'either or'. The inner skill and outer challenge must be encountered in awareness, simultaneously. In turn, the gradual development that takes place will begin to also develop qualities of wisdom and potential spirituality. He concludes that this gradual development of being willing to engage with skills on the edge of our ability and ongoing learning also leads to a willingness to accept the unknown and uncertain more regularly and willingly, which could be inferred as a quality of the transcendent self.

Growth through 'self-actualisation'

Abraham Maslow (e.g. 1968, 1970) is primarily known as a humanistic sychologist and the originator of the theory of the hierarchy of needs and 'self-actualisation'. Self-actualisation offered a new vision of psychology in its time and reflected Maslow's motivation to study, via today what would be called qualitative research, the healthiest of people.

Maslow proposed that if a specific sequence or hierarchy of needs was met (e.g. physical needs, safety, belonging and love and esteem), then a process became initiated through which we developed progressively to who we are. Self-actualisation (SA), at the peak of this hierarchy of needs, is released to unfold and evolve when these needs are met (Hoffman, 1999). Maslow (1968) defined SA in four parts that may represent a focus of our unfolding over time: the actualisation of our talents, capacities and potential; which then enabled fulfilment of what we may perceive or choose as our 'calling'; which, in turn, creates a deeper sense of meaning and understanding of our own nature and then a trend in which we move towards personal integration and unity.

Maslow described SA as synonymous with other concepts such as individuation, self-realisation, and self-development. He implied that the fulfilment of our basic needs was not constant or achieved only once and would require actions and adjustment over time. He saw SA as an ongoing process, not an end-state, actualising our potential at any time. Further, that the expression of potential would vary considerably between individuals (Worth & Smith, 2021).

Maslow (1968), preceding May (1983), emphasised that we are always in a state of becoming and that one's inner core consists merely of potentialities, yet to be formed. These potentialities may be subtle and over-ridden by fear of disapproval or contextual or cultural expectations. May (1983), unlike other psychologists who perceived the 'unconscious' as a place of repression and negativity, saw our potential and development coming through what was latent and emerging in our unconscious minds.

Maslow also expressed surprise in this work at the presence of 'transcendence' in 'self-actualisers'. Perceiving the effort that was invested into developing their own potential, he acknowledged that they then, in turn, invested time in the support of others. He proposed that self-actualisers were commonly invested in a cause outside or beyond themselves. This could be interpreted as ST although these were not words he used in this instance.

It was in his qualitative case studies of SA that Maslow's awareness of ST emerged. The reports came from self-actualising individuals of what were described as 'peak experiences'. He defined them as wonderful experiences and happy, rapturous, ecstatic moments (1968, p. 71). In these experiences, individuals would appear to become self-forgetful, unselfish and ego transcending (1964).

In a later paper, yet included in the same 1971 text, Maslow apparently stepped away from self-actualisation and his focus on learning from healthy individuals, and accepted he saw the presence of transcendence in some self-actualising *as well as* non-healthy people, and non-self-actualisers. Through this insight, the concept becomes more widespread and arguably more 'democratic' in its presence.

Maslow (1971) built on his findings of peak experiences in addressing ST directly. In summary, he defined ST as a loss of self-consciousness and self-awareness, a self-forgetfulness that comes from a profound sense of absorption. In this state, the sense of a loss of self may involve a transcendence of time, culture, basic needs, polarities and any sense of our own weaknesses. In turn, it includes love, unselfishness and a wide identification with others. He highlighted that this also means to 'surpass' and exceed what we otherwise believed we could do, and in this, there comes a transcendence of effort and striving.

A simplistic reading of Maslow's work would point towards ST being experienced by those reaching the higher levels of self-development. However, his insights, reached over time, point towards ST being present and experienced in different groups:

- As a new sixth level of the 'hierarchy of needs', a step beyond that of self-actualisation
- In 'peak experiences', which may or may not reflect self-actualisation
- In non-healthy and non-self-actualising individuals

A comment that recurs in Maslow's writing likens those displaying ST as showing the 'Bodhisattva' state, oriented to support and serve those beyond themselves in difficulty or confusion (Hoffman, 1999). This reflects a paradox in those individuals who invest in or are motivated by the development of their potential, in becoming a healthy and strong 'ego', in turn, then seek to let go of this state to merge with causes and the need to support other individuals or causes (Maslow, 1971). Kaufman (2020) proposes that self-actualisation acts as a 'bridge' to self-transcendent states, values, and motivation and that it is in these states we may see some profound possibilities for human development. Maslow and Kaufman refer to this as a form of 'meta-motivation' that takes an individual's focus beyond fulfilment of the self and a commitment to a calling outside one's self. This is a state involving a transcendence of polarities or dichotomies. Kaufman reflects and summarises this as a form of 'ego development', wisdom and creating a synthesis of what is, otherwise, described as positive and negative aspects of life into a more integrated or whole sense of self. Maslow (1964) proposed that in resolving and transcending polarities and dichotomies in life experience, we open to a broader and more accepting perception of ourselves and the world around us. The potential paradox of this claim is it involves an acceptance and integration of what might, otherwise, be seen as darker aspects of ourselves as part of our whole being. In turn, this could involve a redefinition of 'symptoms' of difficulty as a reflection of our whole, rather than something that needs to be taken away from us by medication or something similar (Kaufman, 2020).

Growth through psychological well-being

Ryff (1989) proposed an astonishingly creative development to describe the structure and characteristics of psychological well-being by integrating theories of seven major psychologists in two categories and offering a means by which this may be measured.

In summary:

- Psychological functioning:

    - Self-actualisation (Maslow, 1968)
    - The Fully Functioning Person (Rogers, 1961)
    - Individuation (Jung, 1933)
    - Maturity (Allport, 1961)

- Lifespan developmental perspectives:

    - Psychosocial stages (Erikson, 1959)
    - Fulfilment of life (Buhler, 1935)
    - Positive criteria of mental health (Jahoda, 1958)

Ryff asserted that integration of mental health, clinical and lifespan developmental theories pointed towards multiple congregating aspects of positive psychological functioning. All of these theories, in Ryff's view, lacked a strong empirical basis established at the time. A central motive of her work and theory was to devise ways in which these six factors could be measured and assessed. Ryff identified core dimensions from within these theories as a parsimonious summary in six dimensions of PWB via:

Self-acceptance
Positive relations with others
Autonomy
Environmental mastery
Purpose in life
Personal growth

Ryff's motivation was to propose an innovative structure of PWB that explicitly involved the self-realisation and development of the individual (Ryff & Singer, 2008) and ensure it was empirically validated and justified via psychometric measurement. This has occurred subsequently over nearly a 30-year period (e.g. Ryff, 2018).

The theory encompasses lifespan development and an unfolding human flourishing via the actualisation of the six factors. It is an evolving act of living in a value-driven and holistically focused manner (Ryan & Deci, 2001).

Growth through finding and expressing 'meaning' in life

Frankl (1946, 1959, 1966) and Wong (2016a, 2016b, 2017) offer us perspectives on personal growth and ST coming from meaning-seeking and meaning-making. Notably, this is an example of ST being defined in a different way to Maslow and others. Frankl defines ST (1959, 1966) in a manner subsequently mirrored by May (1983). He proposes that ST is a natural part of being human in that our cognition, attention and focus are always directed outside ourselves and to something other than the self, and that this aspect, this quality of our existence is often overlooked or neglected.

Building on this, Frankl draws on and accepts the work of Buhler (1965) in portraying this external focus as involving intentionality and, in turn, has the quality of seeking purpose and meaning. He suggests that we have a 'will to meaning', a goal in which we seek a fulfilment of meaning in an overt contrast to Maslow's suggestion of self-actualisation or a focus on the development of the self. Frankl portrays us as driven by our attention and being 'pulled' towards meaning (1966). Frankl goes further in suggesting the centrality of the cognition of our attention creating a polarity between the external object and the subject, the person. Frankl sees humankind living in dimensions of a somatic, mental and spiritual world (1969/2004) and argues that our existence is not authentic unless it involves the self-transcendent quality of this form of attention, beyond ourselves and towards meaning. He believed that this was the primary motivational force of human beings. Note the two aspects of ST proposed: attention focused beyond ourselves and being drawn and pulled towards meaning. He believed that this is a central essence of our existence that energetically draws us forward.

Writing from the perspective of existential psychotherapy, Frankl (1959/1992) believed 'existential' had three parts. First, existence as the unique human way of being, second the meaning of our existence and third the striving to find our specific meaning as individuals (something he also described as our 'will to meaning'). He described 'logotherapy' (meaning therapy) as focused on making a patient connect with what he or she longs for in the core and depth of their being. Understood in this way, Frankl is communicating the criticality of meaning to human existence and the health-giving aspect of connecting with our deep or core sense of meaning. He articulated that each person would have a sense of meaning unique to themselves and that its dynamic nature may fluctuate constantly with our circumstances. Viewing each of us as in relationship with our own lives, Frankl believed that our life circumstances were constantly asking us to find meaning within our lives. In this, he was communicating powerfully that life questions us, and in the act of finding meaning, we are taking responsibility for our own lives.

Frankl proposed that we find meaning in our lives in three possible ways (1959/1992). First, in the creation of work or a deed or action. Second, through the experience of something or someone. Third, by the attitude we choose to adopt when we face unavoidable suffering (which he defines as 'fate'). Movingly, he argues that we can only understand the depth or core of another person through love, a love broader in nature than romance. His writing conveys his insight into the dynamic nature and energy of life, where we find meaning experientially and in all contexts. His writing proposes suffering is only one of three possible sources of meaning, yet unsurprisingly given the intensity of his own wartime experiences he offers profound examples (1946, 1950) of how this may occur through a transformation of a situation or the perception or attitude we hold towards the circumstance (1959/1992). Frankl was specific that we have a spiritual dimension as part of our being, that it may be theistic or non-theistic, and in our finding personal meaning or supporting others doing so, this dimension warranted recognition and that its presence and development reflected our wholeness as individuals (1969/2004).

Frankl was emphatic in his writing that any circumstance could be transformed or reframed and in which we could and would find meaning (1959/1992). He believed that human beings were self-determining within the limits of the environment and their own capabilities. He wrote that the potential in us was made real, actualised, via our decisions, not our conditions. The capacity and skill to make these decisions, in his view, were a fundamental reflection of our own development (1969/2004). Frankl wrote of his belief that if we can relate to our lives and life experience, mindfully and find meaning, this act (as well as being health-giving) not only changes us but also the environment in which we exist (1946/2020). He proposed that we could not only ask questions about the meaning in our lives but that life and life experience would ask questions of us in which we had to determine meaning, to force us to reflect upon something we did not choose. Frankl argued that part of the meaning in life was the profound uniqueness in each individual and our opportunity to respond to our life experience. Our uniqueness is also reflected in the extent to which we live out our own unique 'meaning'; he saw this as an act of love within our own lives and love towards others when we can see and witness their own uniqueness and individuality (1946/2020).

Growth through self-transcendence

Wong has offered us significant support in understanding the concept of ST by summarising and building upon Viktor Frankl's works, including translating the ideas into a three-step model.

Wong (2016b) proposes meaning-seeking and ST are a fundamental expression of our spiritual nature and through this influence our healing and well-being. Mirroring Frankl, he asserts that meaning is to be found in our relationship with the external world, rather than internally to us as human beings, as if this gain was a 'closed system' within us. Wong suggests that the more we 'forget ourselves' in the act of giving ourselves to a cause, service or love, the more human we become and, in turn, actualise who we truly are.

Wong (2016b) describes humankind as fundamentally motivated by meaning-seeking and meaning-making as we work to understand the world around us and seek value and meaning in our life experience. In the act of focusing beyond ourselves and seeking meaning, we transcend ourselves and, in turn, become more fully human through this experience.

Wong proposes three levels of ST (and growth) that offer readers a sequenced, unfolding focus on what this might involve.

1   Seeking Situational Meaning: This involves looking beyond our personal or situational constraints to values, which may be spiritual. To do this, we would rely on mindfulness of the present moment in our inner and outer experiences, and the need to maintain an attitude of 'openness, curiosity and compassion'.
2   Seeking Our Calling: Through this, we seek and pursue and engage with a higher purpose, mission or vocation connected to or serving a greater good. This may have the characteristics of concrete meaning or life goals in the direct service of others. Wong proposes that calling is not only about work or career, but how we respond to the demands of life itself. Our expression or response to our calling would draw upon the uniqueness of our talents, our personal temperament or experiences.
3   Seeking Ultimate Meaning: To look beyond the current context, the physical limitations we experience, and time and space, to a transcendental realm. It is here Wong helpfully recognises that not everyone focuses on a religiously oriented spirituality and defines what non-theistic seekers might consider, such as experiences of goodness, truth and beauty. This level of transcendence will reflect an individual's assumptions about the world, philosophy, views and beliefs.

Wong (2016b) reviews a wide range of empirical evidence for the well-being outcomes that may occur at each of these levels. He suggests that ST at each of these levels will involve a continuous process of personal improvement to expand our potential. He emphasises that this improvement process is not based on self-reference but based on service to others.

Growth across the lifespan to self-transcendence

This section offers an overview of different theorists and researchers focusing on our growth over the lifespan. As suggested earlier in the chapter, a recurring theme being suggested is transcendence or ST.

Of the many different theories of ST, perhaps the most common and well represented are those proposing that this happens as a result of ageing and the internal processes that are part of maturation and ageing.

This section will summarise the work of Erik and Joan Erikson, Pamela Reed, Lars Tornstam and Carl Jung.

Erik and Joan Erikson

Erik Erikson's work, summarised in Chapter 2, gave us the gift of the insight, ground-breaking at the time, of the life cycle of development. Offered in 1950 and after, this theory of development was original and revolutionary in its time in covering all life, from birth to death, being bio-psycho-social in its nature, not simply psychological, conceptualising eight discrete stages of varying length, the way in which each stage had a developmental strength that it sought to bring about, and the tension between two potential polarity outcomes that may result in each stage. Further, that when we entered any new stage, we seek not only to relate to its polarity, but the outcomes of each earlier stage would also be cumulatively revisited, reviewed, through time. This cumulative incorporation of all developmental strengths meant that they adjusted to the bio-psycho-social context of each developmental phase. Erikson inferred that each stage developed a characteristic of our ego that integrated the phase of organic development with the surrounding social experiences, context and institutions (Erikson & Erikson, 1997). Erikson was clear in his writing that the individual and environmental interaction would reflect the qualities of the culture, history and events of the time period of the individual. These stages communicated how an individual may live and age.

The portrayal of the life stages and the engagement of the ego or self with two opposing tensions characteristic of the development of the time illustrated a mediating process occurring in growth, the finding of an appropriate and dynamic balance of the polarities of each life period (Kivnick & Wells, 2013) to reach the emergent developmental strength. The mediating process was both

Life Cycle Stages

Stage 8: Old Age	• Ego Integrity vs. Despair **(Wisdom)** • 60 / 65 years +
Stage 7: Adulthood	• Generativity vs. Stagnation **(Care)** • (40 – 60 / 65 years
Stage 6: Young Adulthood	• Intimacy vs. Isolation **(Love)** • 19 / 20 – 40 years
Stage 5: Adolescence	• Identity vs. Identity Confusion **(Fidelity)** • 13 – 18 years
Stage 4: School Age	• Industry vs. Inferiority **(Competence)** • 6 - 12 years
Stage 3: Play Age	• Initiative vs. Guilt **(Purpose)** • 3 – 5 years
Stage 2: Early Childhood	• Autonomy vs. Shame **(Will)** • 12m – 3years
Stage 1: Infancy	• Trust vs. Mistrust **(Hope)** • 0 – 12 months

Figure 3.1 Erikson's life cycle stages of development.

within our being and between us and the environment. This process was also proposed as a reflection of the meaningful engagement between the individual and the surrounding environment, what Erikson and colleagues called a 'vital involvement' (Erikson, et al. 1986).

Yet, there is a cumulative growth-oriented quality to this work that continues with age as the developmental tension of each stage is re-experienced, reworked, reviewed, refaced and renewed in each time period (Erikson & Erikson, 1997). This conveys how an individual may adjust, change, deepen their sense of self and life perception repeatedly through life, an interpretation put forward by Erikson, and reflecting McAdams' (2013, 2015, 2018) research that we construct and adjust our sense of life story through time.

We propose that this has the quality of a transcendence of an earlier sense of self and a finding of a new sense (Kivnick & Wells, 2013; Erikson et al., 1986; Erikson & Erikson, 1997; McAdams, 2013, 2018). Joan Erikson (in Erikson & Erikson, 1997), proposing and reviewing the ninth stage of life cycle development to account for the experiences of advanced ageing, implied how challenging this could be, and how the polarity of integrity and despair in the eighth stage of the life cycle, was, in fact, the potential to arrive at despair in the ninth, in the face of advanced ageing. Joan Erikson also related the experiences she was writing about to those of 'gerotranscendence' portrayed by Tornstam, reviewed below.

Lars Tornstam – gerotranscendence

Lars Tornstam has been researching for over 30 years, reformulating and deepening our understanding of the experience of ageing. In an area of knowledge perhaps customarily driven by the positivistic and the quantitative, he offers profound qualitative work and insights that encounter the phenomenology of ageing on the terms of those experiencing it, rather than projections or assumptions about the experience from those younger. In this way, he described his work (2011) as like a grounded theory approach.

He described himself as formulating ideas and theories inspired by other theorists and practitioners, including Jung (1930) and Chinen (1985, 1986). His data gathering comprises 50 interviews and 3,773 participants providing information via questionnaires in two postal surveys gaining insight on how they perceived their lives and the dynamics within them (1997, 1999, 2005, 2011). The age ranges were 20 years to 100+ years. He proposed that the data collected challenged and contrasted with negative perceptions of ageing from academics, and practitioners who he proposed were projecting interpretations and values in life on the elderly, often negative (2005, 2011).

Tornstam (2011) proposes a theory and experience of 'gerotranscendence', one in which it becomes apparent that beyond the losses of ageing, there remains a capacity for and presence of learning, change and psychological growth and that individuals may redefine themselves and their relationships and change their understanding of core existential questions. His definition is summarised:

> *Ageing is a natural and continuous process involving maturation and wis-dom, of which 'Gerotranscendence' is the final stage.*
>
> *In gerotranscendence we will re-evaluate our world, and our place within in it.*
>
> *The re-evaluation of our place in the world involves a large scale or 'meta' perspective shift, broader, cosmic, and transcendent in quality, that influences experiences of life satisfaction.*
>
> *This new perspective allows changes in which we define 'reality' and our-selves in this experience of ageing.*

Tornstam describes three dimensions to the data he calls gerotranscendence – the transcending of 'borders and barriers' of earlier life experiences. The dimensions are the cosmic, the self and social and personal relationships (1997, 2005, 2011).

Within the cosmic dimension, the experience of time has changed dramatically, and seemingly earlier times, like childhood, also exist in present time contexts that permits new perceptions, understanding and changes in ways that are often healing and helpful. This occurs in parallel or maybe because of an increased sense of connection to earlier, previous generations. The sense of cross-generational connections and being part of a wider flow of life led to becoming less afraid of death. This weave of experience also appeared to create a stronger sense of the mysteries of life (1997, 2005, 2011).

In the dimension of the self, the individual is looking back on the self he or she once was, and perceiving and learning more, an awareness that included shadow or negative aspects of their being. This increased self-awareness also resulted in a reduction of a willingness to judge others and any sense of being self-centred. The relationship with their own body shifted towards caring while at the same not being obsessive in concerns. The passage of time had led to a transcending of concerns about personal needs towards an increasing attention to the needs of others, particularly children. This involved a renewed or increased sense of wholeness and acceptance of one's life, the life that has been lived (1997, 2005, 2011).

The meaning attached to social and personal relationships had also changed, with a withdrawal from superficial socialising and a focus on meaningful friendships and contemplative solitude. Previous roles were transcended, and there was an increased sense of authenticity or genuineness. This was also characterised by a transcending of restrictive conventions towards freedom of self-expression (1997, 2005, 2011).

Tornstam (e.g. 2005) and Joan Erikson (in Erikson & Erikson, 1997), see elements of the other's work in their own.

In both theories, the experience of ageing is viewed as a developmental process which seeks or works towards a higher state of personal maturity. In Erikson's work, this is called ego-integrity; in Tornstam, it is named gerotranscendence. In Erikson's work, the ego-integrity comes from a revisiting and revised encounter with the polarities of development at this older age, where a realistic balance of perception and experience is sought of the retrospective life reviewed. In this, the individual may find an acceptance of, and peace with, the life lived. This process as described, a retrospective re-exploration, could be described as a backwards integration of earlier experiences to reach a sense of the ego-integrity proposed by Erikson. The process of gerotranscendence defined earlier by Tornstam implies a focus more in the present time and relationship with future time, ways of perceiving the self, experiencing, relating and behaving (1997, 2005, 2011).

Pamela Reed: theory of self-transcendence

Hartman and Zimberoff (2015) propose that Reed's articulation and structure of ST make it one of the clearest and most useful concepts to explore and apply. Reed (2008) defines ST as an expansion of our boundaries of ourselves:

- Intra-personally (towards a greater awareness of our inner state, values and dreams)
- Interpersonally (supporting the way in which we relate to others and our environment).
- Temporally (through which we integrate our sense of past and future that alters meaning in our present).
- Trans-personally (through which we connect to dimensions beyond the discernible world).

Reed parallels May's (1983) proposal in suggesting that ST is a state accessible to all of us as we age, and one which influences our well-being. For Reed, ST is linked to lifespan development and may facilitate an acceptance and integration of conflicting experiences in the way we live, age and die. This integration, she asserts, supports the individual in organising what may be challenged into some kind of meaningful system. Core to Reed's theory is that we are integrally connected to our environments and that the experience of ST connects us to ourselves, others and our environment.

Research exploring ST was originally oriented to elder individuals and those coping with an approaching end of life. The presence of ST correlated with the quality of mental health. In a literature search on ST for this chapter, research based on Reed's theory was the largest single presence in search results.

Carl Jung – growth through the 'transcendent function'

The concept of the 'transcendent function' is found in the work of psychiatrist Carl Jung (e.g. 1930). Jung's psychological theories are vast in number and nature and as such beyond the scope of this chapter. Jung proposed that our 'ego' and consciousness were but one aspect of our being and an incomplete one and that our passage of life involved a progressive opening to and awareness of the self that is 'more than' just ego. As a forerunner of psychotherapists such as Rollo May (1960, 1983), Jung saw the 'unconscious' as an unacknowledged aspect of our being and wholeness. The completeness of our lives, according to Jung, came from the acceptance that our conscious and unconscious represented our whole, and for the sake of our growth, they needed to come into a relationship. Another central aspect of Jung's theories was polarities or opposites within our conscious and unconscious worlds. Therefore, any move to an acceptance of the wholeness of the two would involve a reconciliation of opposites. This was a process in which unconscious content, and conscious content, would relate and come together. The aspect of our being, engaged or initiated by this intention, is our 'transcendent function'. If seen as a means by which the conscious and unconscious come together, it has a quality of a 'bridge' between the two and which, within Jung's theories, had an awareness beyond that we attribute to our ego or consciousness. Further, in the reconciliation of polarities or opposites, a third perspective, rather than one or the other, would emerge. He proposed the existence of the 'transcendent function' as a key, ultimate reflection and step of personal growth and wholeness implying that if unconscious content that represented more of who we are and our potential becomes part of our whole, then we, in turn, have grown (Stein, 1998/2015, 2006/2018).

Conclusion

This review was intentionally a sense-making process (Worth & Smith, 2021). The review suggests that while we appear to believe we are as we are now, we can't help but grow further. This will happen inside and outside our awareness.

The opportunity for growth is in all of life – the large phases and the small events.

We have an inherent potential within us to actualise and express. And a drive to grow. These will be unique to us as individuals as well as reflecting the bio-psycho-social nature of each phase. We reassess and relearn from our lives as we age and grow. We adjust and re-story our lives as we age. As we learn and grow, we integrate our new knowledge and awareness. As we take the next step in our learning, into uncertainty, we differentiate again. Stability and transition (Levinson et al., 1978; Levinson & Levinson, 1996). I (PW) have always conceived of these periods of transition as 'growth spurts' in our development and nature. We seek meaning and the transcendence of self all our lives (Tornstam, 2005, 2011). This appears to become stronger as we age.

Growth through transcendence is broad and strong in its gifts. The opportunity to look beyond ourselves (May, 1983). To give of ourselves (Frankl, e.g. 1959). To find meaning. To see ourselves as one with others and the world around us, not separate (Tornstam, 2005, 2011). Unique in ourselves and one with others and all

(Tornstam, 2005; Worth, 2016). Transcendence is a thread from the small step to gain perspective (Yaden et al., 2017), to let go into what we enjoy and growing our abilities as a result (Csikszentmihalyi, 1993), to bigger steps when the boundary of self is often and willingly let go, (e.g. Reed, 2008; Tornstam, 2011). Arguably, transcendence becomes the common thread or process, the heart of our unfolding journey of growth. And in depth, beyond the types of experience transcendence brings together, bridges our conscious and unconscious nature, all that we consciously are, its opposite and what we are still to become in our unconscious nature – and open to the influence that is 'more than' our conscious mind alone.

This chapter summarises

- Growth in phases of life and across the lifespan: Our growth is 'grounded' in phases of life that are bio-psycho-social in nature. Our age, our social and cultural context will influence the content and possibility of growth at any point in time.
- An inherent lure or process of growth occurs largely outside consciousness awareness: Maslow (e.g. 1968) proposed that we all have a hierarchy of needs which when met take us to point where we will seek to actualise our potential. Maslow implies that in the appropriate conditions, we will experience a natural move or expression towards our growth and potential.
- A natural, reflective aspect of our consciousness creates the opportunity of increasing self-awareness: May (1983) proposed that a normal aspect of the processing of our experience was to see beyond ourselves, to see ourselves within a wider context and to learn from that perception.
- Growth through naturally seeking 'meaning' in the processes of our lives: Frankl (1959/1992) and Wong (2016b) both assert that humankind will naturally seek a perspective of meaning in our life experiences and that this orientates us to growth and well-being. Both Frankl and Wong assert this occurs independently of any potential or actualising potential within us – that it is the seeking of meaning that draws us into a wholeness.
- Growth through 'transcending' ourselves: Different theorists, for example, Csikszentmihalyi (1993), Maslow (1968), Frankl (e.g. 1959) and Wong (e.g. 2016a, 2016b) all assert that in the act of letting ourselves go beyond the known, to extend and develop our skills, our awareness and ourselves will grow. Theorists suggest that this can occur simply, in everyday activities, through giving of ourselves to others. Or that transcendence of self occurs in a bigger context when we have developed more of our overall potential. There is an 'either or' quality in these writers. The authors of this chapter view the potential as 'both and', a quality occurring throughout our lives (Worth & Smith, 2021).
- Growth and transcendence as a natural quality of our ageing: Tornstam (e.g. 1997, 2005, 2011) argues that we have a capacity, under supportive conditions, to find a transcendent perspective through much of our lives, increasing as we age.

This 'both/and' perspective is also apparent in recognising ST can be experienced and observed as a localised outcome of our approach to a task (e.g. as in 'flow') or small acts that become cumulative and developmental over time, *and* as a process of cognition at a time of life in illness and approaching death (as in the contexts pertinent to the work of Reed). Self-transcendent experiences exist on a spectrum of possibility, intensity and choice (Yaden et al., 2017).

Links to existentially oriented positive psychology

These perspectives of our unfolding growth point towards the qualities and characteristics of our personal existence and 'being' throughout our lifespan. The theories presented here do not argue for one pathway but multiple opportunities in which we may grow and unfold. Within Wong's (2010, 2016a, 2021) model, these connect to our sense of identity, how these change over time and how we may seek and express meaning.

Research possibilities and questions

Many of the theories presented in this chapter connect to existing research exploration (e.g. Frankl, 1969/2004; Wong & Reilly, 2017). Additional possibilities for exploration include

- Extending the work of Quoidbach et al. (2013) on the 'End of History Illusion' to prospectively explore how the sense of personal change expresses itself and why, in turn, this may not have been anticipated.
- Exploring the qualitative and quantitative work of Tornstam (e.g. 1997, 2005, 2011) to identify ways in which the proportion of his samples (estimated as 20%) experience ST and how this might be extended into other groups, for example, via 'EPP interventions' (see Chapter 9).

Further resources

We recommend you explore Wong and Reilly (2017) as a model of meaning seeking and ST:

Wong, P.T.P. & Reilly (2017). *Frankl's Self-Transcendence Model and Virtue Ethics.* Web site post 2nd May.)

Reading

Consider which of the theories of growth you are drawn to in this chapter – or a theory you know of and not included here. Consider spending more time deepening your understanding of how you may grow in this way.

The following is a classic and rich text in this subject area:

Waterman, A.S. (Ed). (2014). *The Best Within Us: Positive Psychology Perspectives on Eudaimonia*. Washington. American Psychological Association.

References

Allport, G.W. (1961). *Pattern and Growth in Personality*. New York, Holt, Rinehart & Winston.

Buhler, C. (1935). The Curve of Life as Studied in Biographies. *Journal of Applied Psychology*, 19, 405–409.

Buhler, C. (1965). Some Observations on the Psychology of the Third Force. *Journal of Humanistic Psychology*, 5, 54. doi.org/10.1177/002216786500500105

Chinen, A.B. (1985). Fairy Tales and Transpersonal Development in Later Life. *The Journal of Transpersonal Psychology*, 17, 99–122.

Chinen, A.B. (1986). Elder Tales Revisited: Forms of Transcendence in Later Life. *The Journal of Transpersonal Psychology*, 26, 171–192.

Csikszentmihalyi, M. (1975). *Beyond Boredom and Anxiety: Experiencing Flow in Work and Play*. San Francisco, Jossey Bass Publishers.

Csikszentmihalyi, M. (1993). *The Evolving Self*. New York, Harper Collins.

Erikson, E.H. (1959). Identity and the Life Cycle. *Psychological Issues*, 1, 18–164.

Erikson, E.H. & Erikson, J.M. (1997). *The Life Cycle Completed: Extended Version*. New York, W.W. Norton.

Erikson, E.H., Erikson, J.M. & Kivnick, H.Q. (1986). *Vital Involvement in Old Age*. New York, W.W. Norton.

Fowler, J.W. (1981). *Stages of Faith*. New York, Harper and Row.

Frankl, V. (1946 / 2020). *Yes to Life, Inspite of Everything*. London, Random House.

Frankl, V. (1959 / 1992). *Man's Search for Meaning*. London, Random House.

Frankl, V. (1966). Self-Transcendence as a Human Phenomenon. *Journal of Existential Psychiatry*, 97–106. doi.org/10.1177/002216786600600201

Frankl, V. (1969 / 2004). *The Doctor and the Soul: From Psychotherapy to Logotherapy*. Revised from the original edition and published in London by Souvenir Press.

Hartman, D. & Zimberoff, D. (2015.) *Self-Transcendence and Ego Surrender*. Issaquah, WA, The Wellness Press.

Hoffman, E. (1999). *The Right to Be Human: A Biography of Abraham Maslow*. New York, McGraw Hill.

Jahoda, M. (1958). *Current Concepts of Positive Mental Health*. New York, Basic Books.

Jung, C.G. (1930). Die Lebenswende. *Gesammelte Werke 8*. Olten, Germany, Walter-Verlag, 1982.

Jung, C.G. (1933). *Modern Man in Search of a Soul* (W.S. Dell & C.F. Baynes, Trans.). New York, Harcourt, Brace & World.

Kaufman, S.B. (2020). *Transcend: The New Science of Self-Actualisation*. New York, Tarcher Perigee.

Kivnick, H.Q. & Wells, K.W. (2013). Untapped Richness in Erik H. Erikson's Rootstock. *The Gerontologist*, 54(1), 40–50. DOI: 10.1093/geront/gnt123

Levinson, D.J., Darrow, C.N., Klein, E.B., Levinson, M.H. & McKee, B. (1978). *The Seasons of a Man's Life*. New York, Ballantine Books.

Levinson, D.J. & Levinson, J. (1996). *The Seasons of a Woman's Life*. New York, Alfred Knopf.

Loevinger, J. (1976). *Ego Development.* San Francisco, Jossey-Bass.

Maslow, A.H. (1964). *Religions, Values and Peak-Experiences.* New York, Viking Compass.

Maslow, A.H. (1968). *Toward a Psychology of Being* (2nd Edition). New York, Van Nostrand Reinhold.

Maslow, A.H. (1970). *Motivation and Personality* (3rd Edition). New York, Harper Collins.

Maslow, A.H. (1971). *The Farther Reaches of Human Nature.* London, Penguin Books.

May, R. (1953). *Man's Search for Himself.* New York, W.W. Norton.

May, R. (1983). *The Discovery of Being.* New York, W.W. Norton.

May, R. (1960). *The Emergence of Existential Psychology.* Chapter in: May, R., Allport, G., Feifel, H., Maslow, A. & Rogers, C. (Eds.). *Existential Psychology.* New York, Random House.

McAdams, D.P. (2013). The Psychological Self as Actor, Agent, and Author. *Perspectives on Psychological Science*, 8(3), 272–295. doi.org/10.1177/1745691612464657

McAdams, D.P. (2015). *The Art and Science of Personality Development.* London, Guildford Press.

McAdams, D.P. (2018). Narrative Identity: What Is It? What Does It Do? How Do You Measure It? *Imagination, Cognition and Personality: Consciousness in Theory, Research and Clinical Practice 2018*, 37(3), 359–372. doi.org/10.1177/0276236618756704

Norton, D.L. (1976). *Personal Destinies: A Philosophy of Ethical Individualism.* Princeton, Princeton University Press.

Quoidbach, J., Gilbert, D.T. & Wilson, T.D. (2013). End of History Illusion. *Science*, 339, 96–98. doi: 10.1126/science.1229294

Reed, P.G. (2008). Theory of Self-Transcendence. Chapter in: Smith, M.J. & Liehr, P.R. (Eds.). *Middle Range Theory for Nursing* (2nd Edition). Cham, Switzerland, Springer Publishing.

Rogers, C.R. (1957). The Necessary and Sufficient Conditions of Therapeutic Personality Change. *Journal of Consulting Psychology*, 21(2), 95–103. https://doi.org/10.1037/h0045357

Rogers, C.R. (1961). *On Becoming a Person.* Boston, Houghton Mifflin.

Ryan, R.M., & Deci, E.L. (2001). On Happiness and Human Potentials: A Review of Research on Hedonic and Eudaimonic Well-Being. *Annual Review of Psychology*, 52, 141–166. https://doi.org/10.1146/annurev.psych.52.1.141

Ryff, C.D. (1989). Happiness Is Everything or Is It? Explorations on the Meaning of Psychological Well-Being. *Journal of Personality and Social Psychology*, 57(6), 1069–1081. https://doi.org/10.1037/0022-3514.57.6.1069

Ryff, C.D. (2014). Eudaimonic Well-Being and Health: Mapping Consequences of Self-Realization. Chapter in: Waterman, A.S. (Ed.) *The Bests Within Us: Positive Psychology Perspectives on Eudaimonia.* Washington, American Psychological Association.

Ryff, C.D. (2018). Well-Being with Soul: Science in Pursuit of Human Potential. *Perspectives on Psychological Science*, 13(2), 242–248. https://doi.org/10.1177/1745691617699836

Ryff, C.D., & Singer, B.H. (2008). Know Thyself and Become What You Are: A Eudaimonic Approach to Psychological Well-Being. *Journal of Happiness Studies*, 9, 13–39. https://doi.org/10.1007/s10902-006-9019-0

Stein, M. (1998 / 2015). *Jung's Map of the Soul: An Introduction.* Chicago, IL, Open Court Publishing Company.

Stein, M. (2006 / 2018). *The Principle of Individuation: Toward the Development of Human Consciousness*. Ashville, NC, Chiron Publications.

Tornstam, L. (1997). Gerotranscendence: The Contemplative Dimension of Ageing. *Journal of Aging Studies. Summer 1997*, 11(2), 143–155.

Tornstam, L. (1999). Transcendence in Later Life. *Generations, Winter 1999–2000*, 10–14.

Tornstam, L. (2005). *Gerotranscendence: A Developmental Theory of Positive Aging*. New York, Springer Publishing Company.

Tornstam, L. (2011). Maturing into Gerotranscendence. *The Journal of Transpersonal Psychology*, 43(2), 169–180.

Vaillant, G.E. (1977.) *Adaptation to Life*. Boston, Little, Brown.

Vaillant, G.E. (2002). *Aging Well*. Boston, Little Brown.

Vaillant, G.E. (2012). *Triumphs of Experience: The Men of the Harvard Grant Study*. Cambridge, The Belknap Press of Harvard University Press.

Waterman, A.S. (2014). Considering the Nature of a Life Well Lived – Intersections of Positive Psychology and Eudaimonist Philosophy. Chapter in: Waterman, A.S. (Ed.). *The Bests Within Us: Positive Psychology Perspectives on Eudaimonia*. Washington, American Psychological Association.

Waterman, A.S. & Schwatz, S.J. (2014). Eudaimonic Identity Theory. Chapter in: Waterman, A.S. (Ed.). *The Bests Within Us: Positive Psychology Perspectives on Eudaimonia*. Washington, American Psychological Association.

Wong, P.T.P. (2010). What is Existential Positive Psychology? *International Journal of Existential Psychology and Psychotherapy*, 3(1), July.

Wong, P.T.P. (2016a). Existential Positive Psychology. *International Journal of Existential Psychology and Psychotherapy*, 6(1), February.

Wong, P.T.P. (2016b). Meaning-Seeking, Self-Transcendence, and Well-Being. Chapter in: Betthyany, A. (Ed.). *Logotherapy and Existential Analysis. Proceedings of the Viktor Frankl Institute* (Vol. 1, pp. 311–322). Cham, CH, Springer.

Wong, P.T.P. (2017). *From Viktor Frankl's Logotherapy to the Four Defining Characteristics of Self-Transcendence*. Web site post 2nd January.

Wong, P.T.P. & Reilly (2017). *Frankl's Self-Transcendence Model and Virtue Ethics*. Web site post 2nd May.

Wong, P.T.P. (2021). Existential Positive Psychology (PP 2.0) ad Global Wellbeing: Why It Is Necessary During the Age of Covid-19. Posted by Paul Wong | Jan 5, 2021 | Existential Psychology, Positive Psychology, Writing. Available online at: http://www.drpaulwong.com

Worth, P. (2000). Localised Creativity: A Life Span Perspective. Unpublished PhD thesis, Open University, Milton Keynes, U.K.

Worth, P. (2016). The Hero's Journey. Chapter in: Ivtzan, I., Lomas, T., Hefferon, K. & Worth, P. *Second Wave Positive Psychology: Embracing the Dark Side of Life*. London, Routledge.

Worth, P. & Smith, M.D. (2021). Clearing the Pathways to Self-Transcendence. *Frontiers in Psychology*, April. doi: 10.3389/fpsyg.2021.648381

Yaden, D.B., Haidt, J., Hood, R.W. Jr., Vago, D.R. & Newberg, A.B. (2017). The Varieties of Self-Transcendent Experience. *The Review of General Psychology*, May 1–18. doi.org/10.1037/gpr0000102

Chapter 4

The journey's hero
Birth of an existential self

Lee Newitt

> *Transformative process is a journey in which there is not simply movement*
> *from one place to another or stage to another, but in which the landscape, the*
> *destination and the journeyer shift and change as part of that movement.*
> (Hartelius, Rothe, & Roy, 2015, p. 10)

Learning objectives

- To extend our understanding of the Hero's Journey by investigating the transformation of the Hero
- To identify the qualities of the Hero that are being transformed
- To explain the transformation of these qualities through a developmental process towards an existential self

Part I. The Hero's Journey

The landscape of life

Life may be a struggle for us all, for some of the time and to some degree: physically, socially, psychologically or developmentally. The modern world still faces the age-old challenges of hate, inequality, prejudice, war, famine and disease and now with the looming ecological crisis life for some may seem, and for others maybe, a literal fight for survival (Fellows, 2019; Thorne, 2002). This worldview suggests that an existential crisis is taking place, a self-created crisis of personal and collective meaning, purpose and values, that may require self-created solutions (Helminiak, 2008; Wong et al., 2012). The challenges faced in the world today invite each of us to become more, to commit and strive to reach our fullest, personal and collective potential.

Becoming more inevitably requires 'soul work', liberating the potentiality of the psycho-spiritual 'self-seed' within us by surrendering to the will of its inherent natural force for growth (Hillman, 1996; Jung, 1956; Maslow, 1964; Rogers, 1951). This may be a 'heroic' journey, demanding the transcendence

DOI: 10.4324/9781003132530-4

of our 'smaller nature' to become the truest, most actualised self needed to live existentially fully and contribute to an overcoming of this crisis (Wigglesworth, 2012). This, for the purposes of this chapter, is the 'existential self', the aspects of our being that will take on and live out, with commitment, the deepest expressions of our being; the context of this book makes clear that our being is fluid and will change and unfold with time.

The metaphor of myth

This chapter aims to explore and extend Joseph Campbell's (1949) 'Hero's Journey' beyond Worth's (2016) contemporary interpretation, by identifying universal patterns of transformation that may occur through and within the Hero. In doing so, the intention is to bring to the fore the relevance of key EPP and Transpersonal Psychology (TP) theories. By casting EPP and TP theory against the backdrop of a heroic transformation of character, it may further illuminate and contextualise the transforming qualities of the hero.

The chapter will be a pathway through the 'archetypal' metaphors of the Hero's Journey, which is as much about everyday effort, courage and perseverance as it is popular ideas of heroism. Within the Hero's Journey, there is a connection to everyday heroism wrapped up in mythic imagery. Every life journey may be thought of as being both heroic and mythic in nature. 'Mythic' because every person faces in life the same universal challenges of finding their own path, coming into a relationship with others, finding and experiencing their own meaning and coming to terms with their own potential, limitations and finitude (Yalom, 1980). Facing these existential challenges may be considered 'heroic' when 'heroism' is understood as the active participation in the transformation of life that occurs through everyday struggles. In essence, heroism may be a person's stand towards and engagement with the challenges of living, growing and becoming that are so often the focus of mythology (Allison, Goethals, & Kramer, 2017; Franco, Efthimiou, & Zimbardo, 2016; May, 1993).

Mythic imagery such as the Hero may be understood as a metaphoric projection of inner psychological content and process, and as such, the myth acts as a vessel for deeper truths and expressions of deeper meanings, pertaining to the universal nature of existence and character (Le Grice, 2013). The everyday heroic struggle may be grounded in experience that becomes encapsulated in the metaphorical. Lakoff and Johnson (2008) suggest that metaphor may be the basis for the inference by which we live our lives. Similarly, Campbell suggested that myths provide a sense of participation in the universal, infinite and abundant nature of existence and character. Myth brings the sociological and cosmological within as the psychological and metaphysical, thus guiding and instructing, individuals and societies (Campbell, 1993, 2002, 2004). In essence, myth offers an opportunity to unify our inner and outer worlds. As readers, we are invited to sense through the images of transformation, to be influenced by the deeper universal patterns and psychological qualities behind a myth and metaphor and, in doing so, reveal more of our own deeper nature.

Wheels within wheels

The Hero's Journey is described as an ongoing transformative process or cycle of self-actualisation and ST (Allison, Goethals, & Kramer, 2017; Campbell, 1949, 2004). The Hero cycle may be considered transformative by the nature of it converting unknown inner potentiality into known actuality; thus, it may also be considered self-expansive (Ivtzan, 2015; Le Grice, 2013). The resources for this self-expansion may be deep psychological structures contained within a 'self-seed', qualities of an original and authentic, core image of self (Hillman, 1996; Steele, 2014; Wilber, 1996). These unconscious and potentially repressed qualities of character have yet to be fully known by ourselves, owned and lived, hence their potentiality. Yet, these potentialities may still strive to become storied and lived (Bauer, McAdams & Pals, 2008; Bauer, Schwab, & McAdams, 2011). From this perspective, it is possible to see the Hero cycle as 'self-actualising'. As Maslow (1964) later suggests, there may be a need for this actualised potentiality to transcend the Hero through a further process of ST that may also be at work (Kaufman, 2020; Le Grice, 2013; Reischer et al., 2020). What is transformed by the 'Journey' within the person may also be transmitted, communicated to and shared with the World. These newly acquired insights and profound learning experiences may be shared or communicated, shaping and influencing our external world (Allison, Goethals, & Kramer, 2017; Capra & Luisi, 2014).

The Hero's Journey is a monomyth depicting a universal pattern of human transformation. It is a synthesis of the psychological projections found within numerous cultural myths and as such may comprise symbolic meanings within meanings. To 'decode' the symbolic meaning, it is necessary to see through the imagery and metaphor to a deeper, latent level of meaning that may be experienced beyond the conceptual. To do this within the context of this chapter, it is suggested that your reading might be unrushed, with frequent pauses to contemplate and reflect on the imagery to experience its meaning (Campbell, 1949, 1993, 2002, 2004). Let us now consider the metaphors of the Hero, World and Journey and in Figure 4.1.

The Hero as Content: The Hero metaphor may be thought of as representing that which is known to a person of themselves, their personal reality of what and who they think they are. This may be the actuality of their perception that includes all of who they currently know themselves to be of their character, story and personal identity (Allison, Goethals, & Kramer, 2017). From this perspective, the Hero may be seen as equating with a person's self-image. A 'Figure of Being' consciously differentiated from and drawn out of their inherited cultural landscape and evolutionary history by their own adaptations and traits (McAdams & Pals, 2006). This 'Figure of Being' may be encoded within the autobiographical story of a person's journey, their life story (McAdams, 1993). The Hero metaphor

World	Hero
Mythos	Logos
Unknown	Known
Transpersonal	Personal
Ground of being	Figure of being
Inherent	Acquired
Complexity	Continuity
Potentiality	Actuality
Relatedness	Separateness
Universal	Individual
Whole	Part

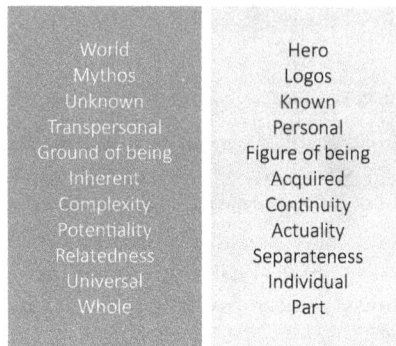

Figure 4.1 The Hero and world metaphors.

as a conscious 'Personal' identity, the self-constructed image, at the centre of a person's reality with the power to choose and act to survive, aligns with the psychological concept of the conscious personal 'I' (Assagioli, 2007), the 'Ego' (Jung, 1969), the 'Egoic Self' (Vaughan, 2000; Wilber, 1996) and the 'Ideal Self' (Rogers, 1951).

The World as Context: The 'World' metaphor reaches far beyond the physical realm of events and actions alone. The 'World' is a rich and complex image representing that which is known and unknown to a person of themselves and their life (Allison, Goethals, & Kramer, 2017). Therefore, the world metaphor may be thought of as the innate qualities of who a person can become contained within a self-seed, a psyche or soul. The transpersonal self holds the potentiality of the yet to be perceived that includes all of who they believe themselves not to be as well as all that is unknown or hidden to themselves, their story yet to be lived and their unconscious pattern of being, (Vaughan, 2000). The World metaphor is a potent image of unlived potential and transformation as well as a wasteland of the rejected debris and the unresolved conflict; it is a source of a personal identity, an organising principle (Somers & Gordon-Brown, 2002; Vaughan, 2000). The World as a source of personal identity is dualistic; it is both the evolutionary and cultural womb of the Hero, a story wanting to be lived from within and without, a 'Great Mother' and a 'Ground of Being' (Somers & Gordon-Brown, 2002; Le Grice, 2013; Neumann, 1954).

The Hero's Journey may be thought of as a pilgrimage or mindful journey through the inner and outer landscape of the World. The Hero is caught between the non-material 'World within' of complex, chaotic inner desires and emotional forces, and the material 'World without', what we perceive as cause and effect. If the Hero is to gain a mastery of their life, they need to learn to bridge and balance these dual Worlds 'within and without'. The Hero's Journey is then a journey inwards, through and outwards, and a journey of participation, interaction and connection (Newitt, Worth, & Smith, 2019). From this perspective, the Hero and the World are in a dynamic and evolving relationship, consciously or unconsciously creating and shaping each other. This developing Hero–World relationship is an 'alchemical marriage' that may give rise to the birth of a fuller, truer, more authentic and self-actualised 'existential self' (Edinger, 2004; Somers & Gordon-Brown, 2002; Vaughan, 2000). This existential self is a deeper truth of being found when a person's conscious identity, 'I', is more aligned with their unconscious transpersonal source 'Self', a profound 'I–Self' relationship. The existential 'I–Self' may be differentiated from the egoic 'I' by the fact it is freeing itself from inherited cultural conditioning and norms, an important aspect of EPP perspective. The World metaphor aligns with the psychological concept of the unconscious transpersonal 'Self' (Assagioli, 2007; Jung, 1969; Vaughan, 2000; Wilber, 1996), the 'Real Self' (Rogers, 1951), the 'More' (James, 1929) and the 'World Unconscious' (Aizenstat, 1995).

The Journey as Process: The Journey can be thought of as representing a person's changing understanding of reality that is the result of the Hero–World relationship or the relational process by which the unknown in the World becomes known to the Hero. The journey may be seen as a dynamic process of both creating and being created. Our experience of life creates who we are and who we are creates our experience of life (Bruner, 1997). The Journey is then the transforming process of the Hero; it is the ongoing transformation of consciousness, the actualisation of inner potentiality. The process of the journey transcends the person as it is fully integrated and lived (Allison, Goethals, & Kramer, 2017).

Perhaps then, life's purpose may be found in discovering our gifts, wherein life's meaning may be found in giving these gifts away (Viscott, 1993). In fully accepting the invitation and opportunity that life's journey affords, there is the potential to bring the relationship between the Hero and the World into an 'I–Self' at-one-ment of wholeness, and balance and harmony. Therefore, the Journey metaphor does not represent a sequence of events alone. It may also represent the ongoing process of transforming consciousness that marries and unifies the Hero with the World through direct experience.

From this perspective, successful completion of the 'Hero's Journey' may be seen as arriving at a perception of a higher order of physical, social, cosmological or metaphysical reality that transforms the dialectical tension between inner and outer experience. (Campbell, 2002; Fowler, 1995; Le Grice, 2013). Facing life's trials and overcoming worldly challenges may be both the spark and the crucible for the Hero's transformation (Allison, Goethals, & Kramer, 2017). The Journey may be the transformative response to the question of life, a synthesis of an 'answer' that becomes lived. As a metaphor, the journey reflects the inward and outward arc of life, the descent and ascent into higher consciousness and the separation and unification of selfhood. This aligns with developmental models such as Individuation (Jung, 1956), Acorn Theory (Hillman, 1996), the Development of Faith (Fowler, 1995), the Organismic Valuing Process (Rogers, 1951), the Exceptional Human Experience Process (Brown, 2000) and the Atman Project Life Cycle (Wilber, 1996).

Part II. The Journey's Hero

Building-Up

The process of 'building-up' is the preparation for the Hero's Journey that, in turn, creates the journey's hero. As Ram Dass (Catto, 2019) suggests you have to develop an 'ego', a sense of self, as part of the process of 'building-up' prior to the 'Hero's Journey'; and the ego may then paradoxically be 'given away' in support of others. This is a process of becoming someone, the someone who we *believe* ourselves to be, our personal identity or 'I' consciousness. There are no shortcuts to 'becoming', life is a journey that is lived through and like the caterpillar destined to become the butterfly, so we are all to some degree, destined to become 'More' of who we can be, our innate potentiality (Elkins, 2013; Stein, 1998; White, 1994).

To what extent we become 'More' is a choice. The ongoing process of accepting and becoming more of ourselves is our psycho-spiritual development, the ongoing process of self-expansion and the creation and unfolding of a life story from both the inside out and outside in (Newitt, Worth, & Smith, 2019). As such, self-expansion may be both the continuous growth and stepwise transformation of our personal consciousness.

Literature suggests that self-expansion may primarily occur through identifying with and integrating unlived potentiality so that it differentiates identity and worldview from what is and transcends what was (Ivtzan, 2015; Vaughan, 2000; Wilber, 1996). As this fuller, truer and more whole self emerges, it also entails letting go or loosening our psychological grip on old ways of seeing ourselves and the world, so new understanding may be accommodated, a psychological flexibility (Ciarrochi & Kashdan, 2013). The identification and integration of something 'More' of ourselves may, in some cases, be easy and seamless, especially in childhood, whereas in other instances and times, the trans-forming of consciousness may be a life's work and seemingly endless struggle for it to become fully accepted in ourselves and lived. As such, 'building-up' may be a continuous process of psychologically transitioning by breaking-out, breaking-through and breaking-in.

Ken Wilber (1996) proposes a Human Life Cycle encompassing three broad developmental phases: pre-personal (subconscious), personal (conscious) and transpersonal (superconscious). 'Building-up' may be seen as the developmental period leading up to a transition and transformation. Vaughan (2000) describes the formation of identity as moving through stages of identification with aspects of self, a Body Self (I am my sensations), to an Emotional Self (I am my emotions) and to an Egoic Self ('I am my thoughts' leading to 'I am my identity'). Each subsequent stage encompasses and transcends the previous level of consciousness. Transposing Fowler's (1995) Development of Faith over these may afford a tantalising glimpse of why transformation might take place and why it may be a painful crisis or an ecstatic revelation. Fowler's qualitative research suggests that 'development is the transformation of consciousness' and Faith may be, in part, a way of being, seeing and knowing ourselves and the world. In essence, a person might live the stories about themselves that are inherited from their families, community and culture. As such, this may create a misalignment or separation of the personal identity from its unconscious source unless they 'radically or heroically' break-out of this inherited identity (Fowler, 1995). This 'breaking out' is from the conditioning and subsequent beliefs or ideals that have been internally and externally built up, for a person to 'break-in' to their own true identity, or at least a first self-response to the existential questions 'Who am I?' and 'What is my purpose?'

Reflection 'symbolic life'

Create three symbolic representations of the past (where you came from), the present (where you are now) and the future (where you are going). You might create 'pictures' or collages, collect objects, photos or whatever feels right for you. Importantly be led by your intuitive heart do not spend time in your head thinking. Get into a flow, let go and go with what is coming through even if it is abstract. Do not interpret. STOP READING NOW.

When finished, place the pictures in sequence and create a symbolic story about a hero or heroine living this life. Reflect on the story. What would you change? What would you grow? What would you keep? What would you let go?

Adapted from Vaughan (2000).

Before travelling further, let us remember this chapter is an attempt to identify universal characteristics of the transforming of Hero as a result of their journey.

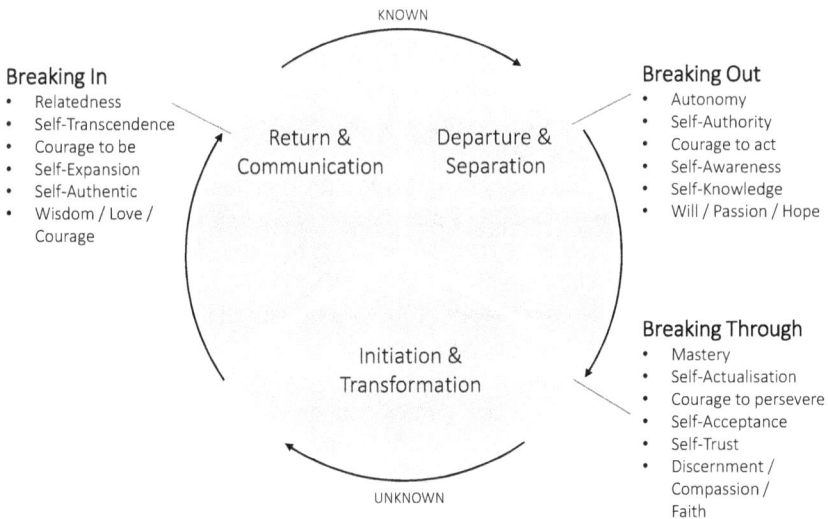

Figure 4.2 Transformation of the Journey's Hero.

To this end, the next three sections have been influenced and inspired by an analy-sis of Dante's 'Divine Comedy', an exemplar symbolic 'Hero's Journey'. Dante's journey through the 'Inferno', 'Purgatory' and 'Paradiso' will provide the general symbolic backdrop and emotional undertone required to explain the transforma-tion of the 'Hero' (Alighieri, 2019).

Breaking-Out

Breaking-out is a departure from what is known, from the 'who I am and have become'. It is a departure from the life that has been culturally given, the life that has been personally lived and the life that may have been mindlessly building-up. Breaking-out might then be a psycho-spiritual descent or opening up and, for some, an existential fall or 'cracking up' (Grof & Grof, 1986; Wong, 2019, 2020). It might also be the start of a journey inwards to an 'under-World' that is soften-ing and humbling. In venturing into the unknown, the security of the known is left behind, and it takes courage and humility to choose a way that may involve making mistakes in steps towards growth (Hollis, 2001). The way is symbolically 'downwards', towards a centre that will take the Hero towards their inner 'heat', to encounter the 'inferno' of the very life force that is the passion of an authentic self within us all (Hillman, 1996; Steele, 2014). The Hero is invited to experience the force and heat of this passion for it to be transformative that it might soften and re-shape the Hero with all its potential growing pains. In this way, the Hero will metaphorically have to 'die' to an existing perception to be reborn for the World within to live through the Hero of tomorrow (Jung, 1956; Neumann, 1954; Stein, 1998). Why should such a dramatic and drastic image be created by Alighieri and others of the 'Hero's Journey'? Perhaps because there is a recognition within EPP of a vital and core trans-forming role of challenge and suffering in both develop-ing an authentic way of being and sustaining well-being (mature happiness). The Hero will be tested by the World within and without to choose between sacrificing their 'soul' to conformity or facing the risks and challenges that may come with 'standing out' (Wong, 2019, 2020).

Breaking-out may be an awakening that has the potential to be both existen-tial crisis and personal revelation, it may be an awakening to the realisation of having wandered off life's path, revealed at a time of crisis, through feeling lost, wounded or blocked. Alternatively, the awakening may be a calling from deep within, the desire for an innate way of being or living that is meaningful and purposeful and that has been an ever-present passion waiting in the wings of life. Nietzsche outlines a similar awakening in the story of the 'Metamorphosis of Spirit' when the 'Camel', which carries the burden of cultural expectations, transforms to the 'Lion' the innate force of individuality within (Nietzsche, 1997). Either way, the World is letting the Hero know all is not as it might be on life's journey. The innate natural forces are calling the Hero back to its 'source'. Accepting the World's call is a departure that inevitably means break-ing-through the 'womb of culture'; the awakened transpersonal destiny asks a person to follow their own path to fulfil more of their potentiality (Hollis, 2001; Le Grice, 2013).

Within the awakening that a crisis or revelation may bring, there is usually an early encounter with an unknown World that 'holds up a mirror' to the Hero. Such encounters may be seen as synchronous nudges or 'ghosts' from the past with unfinished business, which calls for choice and commitment (Hillman & Shamdasani, 2013; Hollis, 2013). This World's mirror may reveal glimpses of the Hero's personal and universal depth that had been previously obscured, thus raising awareness of deficiencies and excesses that may cause doubt, denial and overwhelm (Hollis, 1996). How the Hero responds to this preparatory test, with either hubris or humility, may determine how the threshold to the next stage is crossed. It takes humility and courage to unlearn beliefs, whereas hubris denies this learning and distorts the awareness of what support may be needed (Le Grice, 2013). Breaking-out may be both an awakening and a departure as a test of will is passed. In encountering a force larger than its own and in realising the limits of its own control and centrality, the Hero's grip is loosened on life's direction allowing new questions to exist. To what extent do I dare commit to this journey? For what do I hope? For what will I suffer? Who am I really?

Reflection 'who am I really'

Ask yourself, who am I?

Then, write your response as a short list of qualities 'I am. . .'. Try to write this with little thought, even if you repeat yourself or make errors. When finished, repeat this process and make a list of who 'I am not. . .'. Do not analyse as you write.

When finished, look at the lists; can you recall an everyday example of each? Can you recall an example of the opposite? In what ways are you More than you think you are? Might the 'story' that these statements imply be rewritten?

Adapted from Millichamp (2018).

Summary: Breaking-out may be the stage of the Hero's *awakening* to the possibility of the 'World' within that they might be living is shaped or influenced by someone else. From this potential crisis or revelation, there is the inevitable invitation for *departure* from the life currently lived that is a test of will.

What is motivating? An innate truth or an inherent passion is fuelling willpower, the choice and commitment to act in the direction of hope.

What is confronted? In being 'called', a person is faced with confronting an existing limited vision of their personal identity. Simultaneously, there may be an encounter with a greater awareness and knowledge, 'the More', a force greater than their own, their 'Transpersonal Self'.

Paradoxically, doubt may be a gift that develops a greater courage to act.

What is developing? Through the autonomous courage to act, a greater self-authority is being brought to bear on life's journey.

Breaking-Through

If breaking-out is awakening to the possible discord, incongruence or dissonance in the relationship between the Hero and the World, then breaking-through is the self-fulfilling prophesy of the Hero's becoming that restores and transforms this relationship. As such, 'breaking-through' is the transformation that comes with letting go of 'who I have become' as the person 'who I am becoming' simultaneously emerges. It is the metamorphosis within, an incubation where the organism is neither 'caterpillar nor butterfly' (Stein, 1998).

Breaking-through might be an evolving personal response to the existential questions of crisis and revelation. It is a reforging of personal identity between the seemingly immovable 'anvil' of inner forces, the passion and will of individual growth and the unstoppable 'hammering' of cultural norms, societies expectations and allotted duties (Luke, 1993; Le Grice, 2013). With the initial heat and intensity of the 'inferno' behind, this next stage by comparison is a long and winding 'road of trials' that may be a slow and precarious uphill climb. The 'road of trials' are the repeated 'tests' encountered on life's individual path that require the Hero to gain the mastery and maturity synonymous with a seasoned traveller, a pilgrim.

The Hero often *needs to* surrender to the will of the unconscious World within, to the shifts in understanding we may be more than we believe, to gain mastery. It requires the Hero to 'sacrifice' former beliefs and conditioning, and this inevitably means confronting the 'thou shalt's of the cultural 'Dragon' (Nietzsche, 1997). This 'sacrificial surrender' is the Hero's psycho-spiritual death and rebirth, a letting go of what was and the control this story has to be reborn into an 'I–Self' alignment. The transformative rebirth into the totality of a person, a greater authentic and existential truth of being, is the slow birth of the 'existential self' (Vaughan, 2000).

This transformation is ultimately about self-mastery and the discernment of the forces within. The Hero *needs to* repeatedly overcome the resistance of these forces to the uncertainty and risk that transformation brings instead of favouring the safety and continuity of the story lived with its 'weight of history' (Hillman & Shamdasani, 2013). Simultaneously, the Hero *needs to* learn how and when to stand firm, to not be overwhelmed or inflated by the force of energy and power that may be experienced when encountering the transpersonal 'Self'. In the terms of the Nietzschean story mentioned earlier, this means answering, 'Who will tame the Lion, now the Lion has tamed the Dragon?' (Le Grice, 2013). To stand firm and endure the will of the World within, the Hero *needs to* learn discernment, that is, to be able to judge when and how to follow their passions (Luke, 1993; Vaughan, 2000). Will without discernment is potentially chaotic and destructive. Discernment involves a perseverance, patience and compassion that come from walking a 'road of trials'. With each step and each learning comes a renewed faith in the Hero's developing relational way of being, seeing and knowing that might renew hope (Fowler, 1995; Scioli & Biller, 2010).

Breaking-through is, therefore, an ongoing process, a learning journey of trial and error that requires a different sort of courage, a vital courage, the courage to persevere, to keep going despite suffering. It is a test of endurance (Pury & Lopez, 2010).

As such, breaking-through may be thought of as the purification that comes through enduring the repeated and often bruising encounters between the outer World and the Hero. 'Purification' is a stripping away of what does not serve the 'soul' anymore, a disidentifying or cleansing of that which is inauthentic to reveal a deeper truth (Edinger, 2004; Luke, 1993).

In submitting to the 'fires and waters' of purification, the Hero is destined to confront the repeated tests of the World within and without to learn the required lessons (Hollis, 2001; Stein, 1998). Facing 'failure and weakness' may strip away and cleanse a person of the falsehoods that limit growth. This is a process of learning to disidentify with imagined self-concepts and emotional self-pity, shame or guilt. If successful, a person may fully accept themselves and grow, forgive their own mistakes and learn to trust their true being (Edinger, 2004; Hollis, 1996; Luke, 1993). Moving to self-acceptance and self-trust may be gradual, seemingly imperceivable and yet the thirsts and aches from the strivings to become, suggest otherwise (Thorne, 2002). The necessary forging and purifying in breaking-through is a 'purgatory', a reckoning of that which is unresolved from the past, a debt to be repaid. The Hero's repressed past, suppressed emotion, distorted reality and denied truth may come back like apparitions or memories to be repeatedly endured until their energies are eliminated (Hollis, 2013). What is my life in service of? What greater purpose lives through me? What is my meaningful life?

Reflection 'my meaningful life'

Go to a place that is sacred, meaningful or important to you. It might be home, a workplace or a leisure place.

Go there, get comfortable and look around, daydream about what makes this important to you for a while. Notice any item of meaning and importance that really draws your interest, pick this object and study it carefully. STOP READING NOW.

Write a description of the chosen object, but instead of naming it, write 'I am . . .' in place of the name. What do you learn?

Adapted from Joseph (2016).

Summary: 'Breaking-through' may be the stage of the Hero's *transformation*, the 'road of trials', that is, *learning* to live an individual life despite the suffering this may bring. Breaking-through is a test of endurance that purifies and removes that which was acquired but not required. The *integration* of this learning is the birth of a deeper, truer and more authentic self, an existential self.

What is motivating? It may be with compassion that discernment and faith grow. Action and choices taken with discernment may build this faith in our own way of being, seeing and knowing ourselves and the world.

What is confronted? In being 'initiated', a person is faced with bringing the Hero and the World into alignment. There may be a 'see-sawing' of trial and error of lived experiences to overcome to develop the self-acceptance and self-trust required for a natural flow of life that is an 'I–Self' alignment. An experience of suffering may be the gift that develops a courage of perseverance.

What is developing? Through the courage to persevere, a greater mastery of life may be developed that is maturing and self-actualising.

Breaking-In

Breaking-in may be a reunion and a transcendence: a reunion because it reconnects a person with what was, an 'involution', a turning inwards that is a return to the source, and a transcendence because it goes beyond what is, to what is becoming, an 'evolution' that is a raising of consciousness (Wilber, 1996). As a reunion, breaking-in may be the 'alchemical marriage' of the personal identity 'I' with the transpersonal source 'Self', giving rise to a more aligned 'I–Self' consciousness, the existential self (Edinger, 2004; Vaughan, 2000). This 'marriage' is a re-union of identity with a natural and innate flow of life, an authentic way of being and living that honours the potentiality of the self-seed (Hillman, 1996). When a person surrenders to the possible fate of the potentiality seeded within their 'soul' at birth, they unlock the destiny of the Hero's Journey to become more of their true nature. Mythologically speaking, it is this initial 'twist of fate' of an individuality that makes each destiny unique and simultaneously 'turns the world' that is to say contributes to an evolving culture (Meade, 2012). To explain this re-union, Nietzsche uses the image of the 'child' to suggest a 'potentiality' that was innate and an 'ease' that comes from being oneself freely. The 'child' is an image of wholeness that paradoxically only comes with the maturity of the journey (Nietzsche, 1997). The wholeness of the child image may be an intuitive and self-determined way of being that unifies the conceptual with the experiential (Wilber, 1996). When life is lived in service to wholeness, it may flow with a natural grace and spontaneity that is harmonious and balanced, and expressed in a profound sense of gratefulness (Campbell, 1993, 2004; Steindl-Rast, 1999). Perhaps this is a 'gratefulness of being' that comes from the 'suffering of becoming', a suffering that is a profound teacher. As such, breaking-in may be a return to a love of life that unites passion with compassion (Campbell, 1993). With an acceptance of our uniqueness expressed through passion maybe a 'gratefulness of being' will be found? With an acceptance of universal humanity expressed through compassion may a 'gratefulness in serving' be found?

The self-transcendence of the breaking-in may be the impact on the world that this individual's authentic way of being has (Kaufman, 2020; Maslow, 1964;

Rogers, 1951). A way of being that may radiate an 'existential' or 'spiritual' intelligence capable of transforming others (Kaufman, 2020; Wigglesworth, 2012). This is not to suggest there is a perpetual state of bliss, awe, inspiration or elevation. Suffering, challenge and adversity are destined to return. However, as the Hero evolves, so might their stand towards suffering (Yalom, 1980). In facing the suffering that may accompany the Hero's Journey, is hope transcended by faith to become courage? Is our will transcended by discernment to become wisdom? And is passion transcended by compassion to become love? If so, the emerging pattern is one of actions leading to insight to become value-led behaviour (Van Deurzen, 1997). Between the fate held within the self-seed and the destiny of life's inevitabilities, there lies a heroic journey that calls a person to live a self-determined life (May, 1999). Furthermore, self-determination may be key to psychological development, and as this chapter suggests, this may sequentially unfold through periods of transition. Life invites every person to make this heroic journey. The extent to which a person accepts life's invitation is a choice that rests on finding self-authority in cultures of 'shoulds and musts'. It is a freely given response to the question of 'Who am I?'. Life's journey is heroic because whatever the response, suffering is at times inevitable. Perhaps, the question then becomes 'For what will I suffer?'. When a person's answer aligns with the meaning in their soul, then there might be a greater purpose to their suffering, and more vital personal lessons to be learned or messages to be received from life's trials. To 'know thyself' through suffering may be a stepping-stone to truly 'owning thyself' (Joseph, 2016). If a person is not tested, how might they gain the self-mastery needed to realise more fully the potentiality within their soul? Who I am really? From suffering, answers may emerge, and a person may find a deeper truth that is both unique and universal. Is it this deeper truth that transcends a person as a 'way of being'? Is it also this deeper truth that invites others to accept their call to the Hero's Journey? Perhaps, now more than ever, we are each required to find our deepest truth, if we are to overcome the potential challenges and crises of our times, this is the gift we have to give, this is the destiny we have to realise through the birth of the existential self.

Reflection 'radiating life'

Imagine your truest, most authentic, most wise, courageous and loving self. Be generous and take the time needed to really immerse in this self within. Make this a special experience. Know you are completely safe, thoroughly and unconditionally loved by this self. Remember this is your most courageous, wisest and most loving you. Fully experience this. Just be.

Where do you most experience this self? When do you most experience this self? What are you doing when you most experience this self? Ask what would this self do?

Adapted from Vaughan (2000).

Summary: 'Breaking-in' may be the Hero's *reunion* with the 'World' that brings about an authentic 'way of being' and living. This 'way of being' *transcends* the individual and in its authenticity has the potential to transform the 'World without' and become a stand towards suffering.

What is motivating? It may be from a love for life that a person finds courage and draws wisdom.

What is confronted? In 'returning', a person is faced with the challenge of living in the world from this 'I–Self' alignment despite learning that life involves suffering. The sacrifice of certainty may be the gift that invites each end to become a new beginning.

What is developing? Through the courage to be, a greater depth of connectedness and relatedness with all life may be realised that is transformative for others.

This chapter

- Describes heroism as everyday acts of authentic being despite the suffering this might cause
- Summarises the Hero's Journey through ongoing processes of self-actualisation and self-transcendence
- Explores the symbolism of the Hero's Journey in terms of a 'multiplicity of self'
- Proposes a model of transformation based on the changing interrelationship between these 'selves' that suggests certain qualities of character might develop as a result

Reflection?

Reflection is built into the chapter text.

An existential perspective?

Adversity, challenge and suffering may have an important role to play in psychological growth. The 'stand' a person takes towards suffering may also develop across the lifespan. Finally, the chapter also illustrates how we encounter our existence through story.

Research questions or possibilities?

The writer proposes we need to further understand the role played by a 'struggle of suffering' (as opposed to trauma) in healthy psychological growth. And what implications does this have towards how some mental health 'problems' are conceptualised (Hillman, 2013)? Could we also further understand how this 'struggle of suffering' may shape meaning in life stories?

Further resources?

Reading – alternatives to the *Hero's Journey*:

- Plotkin, B. (2021). *The Journey of Soul Initiation: A Field Guide for Visionaries, Revolutionaries, and Revolutionaries*. Novato, CA, New World Library.
- Somers, B. (2004). *The Fires of Alchemy: A Transpersonal Viewpoint*. Dorset, Archive Publishing.

Websites

- Joseph Campbell Foundation – www.jcf.org/
- Johnathan Young, Center for Story and Symbol – https://folkstory.com/resources.html
- Michael Meade, Mosaic Voice – www.mosaicvoices.org/podcast

Media

- YouTube: TED – MY STROKE OF INSIGHT – Dr Jill Bolte Taylor.

References

Alighieri, D. (2019). *The Divine Comedy*. London: Penguin Random House.
Allison, S. T., Goethals, G. R., & Kramer, R. M. (Eds.) (2017). *Handbook of Heroism and Heroic Leadership* (pp. 379–400). New York, London: Routledge.
Assagioli, R. (2007). *Transpersonal Development: The Dimension Beyond Psychosynthesis*. Findhorn, Forres, Scotland: Inner Way Productions.
Aizenstat, S. (1995). Jungian psychology and the world unconscious. In: Roszak, T., Gomes, M. E., & Kanner, A. D. (Eds.). *Ecopsychology: Restoring the Earth, Healing the Mind*. San Francisco, CA: Sierra Club Books.
Bauer, J. J., McAdams, D. P., & Pals, J. L. (2008). Narrative identity and eudaimonic well-being. *Journal of Happiness Studies*, 9(1), 81–104. https://doi.org/10.1007/s10902-006-9021-6
Bauer, J. J., Schwab, J. R., & McAdams, D. P. (2011). Self-actualizing: Where ego development finally feels good? *The Humanistic Psychologist*, 39(2), 121–136. https://doi.org/10.1080/08873267.2011.564978
Brown, S. V. (2000). The exceptional human experience process: A preliminary model with exploratory map. *International Journal of Parapsychology*, 11(1), 69–111.
Bruner, J. (1997). A narrative model of self-construction. In *Annals of the New York Academy of Sciences* (Vol. 818, pp. 145–161). Chichester: Blackwell Publishing Inc. https://doi.org/10.1111/j.1749-6632.1997.tb48253.x
Campbell, J. (1949). *The Hero with a Thousand Faces*. Princeton, NJ: Princeton University Press.

Campbell, J. (1993). *Myths to Live By*. London: Arkana Publishing, an imprint of Penguin Books.

Campbell, J. (2002). *The Inner Reaches of Outer Space: Metaphor as Myth and as Religion* (Vol. 2). Novato, CA: New World Library.

Campbell, J. (2004). *Pathways to Bliss: Mythology and Personal Transformation* (Vol. 16). Novato, CA: New World Library.

Capra, F., & Luisi, P. L. (2014). *The Systems View of Life: A Unifying Vision*. Cambridge: Cambridge University Press.

Catto, J. (2019). *Becoming Nobody*. [Video file]. USA; RocoFilmsVOD. www.youtube.com/watch?v=aLWJ5WjIc6k

Ciarrochi, J. V., & Kashdan, T. B. (2013). *Mindfulness, Acceptance, and Positive Psychology: The Seven Foundations of Well-Being*. Oakland, CA: New Harbinger Publications.

Edinger, E. F. (2004). *The Sacred Psyche: A Psychological Approach to the Psalms*. Canada: Inner City Books.

Elkins, D. N. (2013). *Beyond Religion: A Personal Program for Building a Spiritual Life Outside the Walls of Traditional Religion*. Wheaton, IL: Quest Books.

Fellows, A. (2019). *Gaia, Psyche and Deep Ecology: Navigating Climate Change in the Anthropocene*. Abingdon: Taylor & Francis Publishing.

Fowler, J. W. (1995). *Stages of Faith: The Psychology of Human Development*. London: Harper Collins Publishers.

Franco, Z. E., Efthimiou, O., & Zimbardo, P. G. (2016). Heroism and eudaimonia: Sublime actualization through the embodiment of virtue. In: Vittersø, J. (Ed.). *Handbook of Eudaimonic Well-Being*. Cham: Springer International Publishing.

Grof, C., & Grof, S. (1986). *Spiritual Emergency: The Understanding and Treatment of Transpersonal Crises*. New York: Tarcher/Perigee Books.

Hartelius, G., Rothe, G., & Roy, P. J. (2015). A brand from the burning: Defining transpersonal psychology. In: Friedman, H. L. & Hartelius, G. (Eds.). *The Wiley Blackwell Handbook of Transpersonal Psychology*. Chichester: John Wiley & Sons Ltd.

Helminiak, D. A. (2008). *Spirituality for Our Global Community: Beyond Traditional Religion to a World at Peace*. Washington, DC: Rowman & Littlefield Publishers.

Hillman, J. (1996). *The Soul's Code: In Search of Character and Calling*. Random House.

Hillman, J., & Shamdasani, S. (2013). *Lament of the Dead: Psychology After Jung's Red Book*. New York: W. W. Norton.

Hollis, J. (1996). *Swamplands of the Soul: New Life in Dismal Places*. Toronto: Inner City Books.

Hollis, J. (2001). *Creating a Life: Finding Your Individual Path*. Toronto: Inner City Book.

Hollis, J. (2013). *Hauntings: Dispelling the Ghosts Who Run Our Lives*. Asheville, NC: Chiron Publications.

Ivtzan, I. (2015). Spirituality – transcending the self. In: Ivtzan, I., Lomas, T., Hefferon, K., & Worth, P. (Eds.). *Second Wave Positive Psychology: Embracing the Dark Side of Life*. Abingdon: Routledge.

James, W. (1929). *The Varieties of Religious Experience: A Study in Human Nature*. The Gifford Lectures. New York: Penguin Group.

Joseph, S. (2016). *Authentic: How to Be Yourself and Why It Matters*. Boston: Little, Brown Book Group.

Jung, C. G. (1969). *The Collected Works: The Structure and Dynamics of the Psyche* (Vol. 8). New York: Routledge.

Jung, C. G. (1956). *The Collected Works: Symbols of Transformation* (Vol. 5). New York: Routledge.

Kaufman, S. B. (2020). *Transcend: The New Science of Self-Actualization*. New York: Tarcher Perigee and imprint of Penguin Random House Publishing Group.

Lakoff, G., & Johnson, M. (2008). *Metaphors We Live By*. Chicago, London: University of Chicago press.

Le Grice, K. (2013). *The Rebirth of the Hero: Mythology as a Guide to Spiritual Transformation*. London: Muswell Hill Press.

Luke, H. M. (1993). *Dark Wood to White Rose: Journey and Transformation in Dante's Divine Comedy*. New York: Parabola Books.

May, R. (1993). *The Cry for Myth*. New York: W.W. Norton.

May, R. (1999). *Freedom and Destiny*. New York: W. W. Norton.

Maslow, A. H. (1964). *Religions, Values, and Peak-Experiences* (Vol. 35). Columbus: Ohio State University Press.

McAdams, D. P. (1993). *The Stories We Live by: Personal Myths and the Making of the Self*. New York: Guilford Press.

McAdams, D. P., & Pals, J. L. (2006). A new big five: fundamental principles for an integrative science of personality. *American psychologist*, *61*(3), 204. https://doi.org/10.1037/0003-066X.61.3.204

Meade, M. (2012). *Fate and Destiny: The Two Agreements of the Soul*. Aurora, CO: Mosaic Multicultural Foundation.

Millichamp, S. (2018). *Transpersonal Dynamics: The Relational Field, Depth Work and the Unconscious*. Glasgow: Kaminn Media Limited.

Neumann, E. (1954). *The Origins and History of Consciousness*. London: Princeton University Press.

Newitt, L., Worth, P., & Smith, S. (2019). Narrative identity: From the inside out. *Counselling Psychology Quarterly*. https://doi.org/10.1080/09515070.2019.1624506

Nietzsche, F., & Common, T. (1997). *Thus Spoke Zarathustra*. Stanstead: Wordsworth Editions.

Pury, C. L., & Lopez, S. J. (2010). *The Psychology of Courage: Modern Research on an Ancient Virtue*. Washington, DC: American Psychological Association.

Reischer, H. N., Roth, L. J., Villarreal, J. A., & McAdams, D. P. (2020). Self-transcendence and life stories of humanistic growth among late-midlife adults. *Journal of Personality*, *89*(2), 305–324. e12583. https://doi.org/10.1111/jopy.12583

Rogers, C. R. (1951). *Client-Centered Therapy: Its Current Practice, Implications and Theory*. London: Constable.

Scioli, A., & Biller, H. (2010). *The Power of Hope: Overcoming Your Most Daunting Life Difficulties – No Matter What*. Oxford: Oxford University Press.

Somers, B., & Gordon-Brown, I. (2002). *Journey in Depth: A Transpersonal Perspective*. Dorset: Archive Publishing.

Steele, K. E. (2014). *Sacred Space: Embracing the Spiritual in Person-Centred Therapy*. Create Space Independent Publishing Company.

Stein, M. (1998). *Transformation: Emergence of the Self*. College Station, TX: Texas A & M University Press.

Steindl-Rast, D. (1999). *A Listening Heart: The Spirituality of Sacred Sensuousness*. Chesnut Ridge, NY: Crossroad Publishing Company.

Thorne, B. (2002). *The Mystical Power of Person-Centred Therapy: Hope Beyond Despair*. Chichester: Wiley.

Van Deurzen, E. (1997). *Everyday Mysteries: Existential Dimensions of Psychotherapy.* Abingdon: Routledge.

Vaughan, F. E. (2000). *The Inward Arc: Healing in Psychotherapy and Spirituality.* New York, NY: Authors Guild Backinprint.com.

Viscott, D. (1993). *Finding Your Strength in Difficult Times.* Chicago, IL: Contemporary Books of Chicago.

White, R. A. (1994). Exceptional human experience and the more we are: Exceptional human experience and identity. In *Academy of Religion and Psychical Research Proceedings Annual Conference, 75*(1), 1–13.

Wigglesworth, C. (2012). SQ21: *The Twenty-One Skills of Spiritual Intelligence.* New York, NY: SelectBooks.

Wilber, K. (1996). *The Atman Project: A Transpersonal View of Human Development.* Wheaton, IL: India: Quest Books, The Theosophical Publishing House.

Wong, P. T. (2019). Second wave positive psychology's (PP 2.0) contribution to counselling psychology. *Counselling Psychology Quarterly.* https://dio.org/10.1080/09515070.2019.1671320

Wong, P. T. (2020). Existential positive psychology and integrative meaning therapy. *International Review of Psychiatry,* 1–14. https://doi.org/10.1080/09540261.2020.1814703

Wong, P. T., Wong, L. C. J., McDonald, M. J., & Klaassen, D. W. (2012). *The Positive Psychology of Meaning and Spirituality: Selected Papers from Meaning Conferences.* Birmingham, AL: Purpose Research, LLC.

Worth, P. (2016). The hero's journey. In: Ivtzan, I., Lomas, T., Hefferon, K., & Worth, P. (Eds.). *Second Wave Positive Psychology: Embracing the Dark Side of Life.* Abingdon: Routledge.

Yalom, I. D. (1980). *Existential Psychotherapy.* New York: Basic Books.

Chapter 5

Our symbolic journey – heroes or heroines?

Diane Herbert

Introduction

The hero's journey is an allegory for how the process of development and change occurs, our 'quest' to find a meaningful life and make sense of our lives (Worth, 2016). Whilst Campbell (1949/2008) maintained that his metaphor applied equally to women and men, from my personal and professional experience, I question whether the hero's journey is as universally applicable as Campbell would have us believe. Campbell suggests that the myth of the hero's journey is a call to embark on an adventure to become more of who we truly are, yet there appears to be an assumption that the journey towards authenticity is the same for men and women. This chapter aims to explore the symbolic journey of development from a distinctly and unapologetically feminist perspective to consider to what extent the hero's journey may be relevant to women's experience and how the heroine's journey (Murdock, 2013) differs in its approach and assumptions. I will propose that whilst men and women may experience a call towards discovering their authentic self, the objectives and the nature of the journey may be experienced differently. I will explore how the hero's journey may not capture some women's experience as they seek to reach their full potential and suggest characteristics of what the heroine's journey may represent in this context. This chapter reflects some early attempts to make sense of how symbolic journeys of change, and developmental psychology, more broadly, capture and reflect my lived experiences and those I have worked with.

A brief word on sex and gender assumptions. Biological sex is not the same as gender. The terms *female* and *male* typically refer to biological sex. Gender is considered the socially constructed term used to encapsulate people's expectations, behaviours, and roles according to their gender identity (Mikkola, 2011). The terms *feminine* and *masculine* are typically used to denote gender. Greene (1997) described 'feminine' as a complex web of symbols and language embedded in culture that define what it means to be female.

Of course, some individuals do not identify with the constructed boundaries of biological sex or gender. I have used the words feminine when referring to the heroine's journey and masculine to refer to the hero's journey to represent the

DOI: 10.4324/9781003132530-5

journey rather than the sex or gender of the traveller. Reference to Jung's archetypes of Feminine and Masculine is capitalised to differentiate archetype from gender. The archetypal Feminine, present in women and men, represents strengths such as feeling, relatedness and creativity. The Masculine archetype is associated with logic and reason. Masculine archetypal qualities are valorised over Feminine attributes, which creates a division and differentiation that position Feminine qualities as somehow lacking or less critical. Jung proposed that as people move towards wholeness (individuation), the Masculine and Feminine side of their nature are integrated. However, Feminine archetypal qualities are often confused with femininity or characteristics of women.

In presenting a feminine perspective of the hero's and heroine's journey, I am mindful of not falling into the trap of assuming that my thoughts and experiences are universal. Women's experiences and development are shaped by their social, cultural and historical context. It would be inappropriate to criticise assumptions that masculine experience equals all experience if I assumed that all women's experience is similar (Jordan et al., 2004).

Learning objectives: at the end of this chapter, you will

Have been introduced to some female-centric perspectives on developmental psychology.

Recognise the importance of relationships to psychosocial development, especially for women.

Appreciate the heroine's and hero's journey as symbolic journeys of growth that may apply irrespective of gender.

The Heroine's Journey

The Heroine's Journey: Women's Quest for Wholeness (Murdock, 2013) was written in response to Campbell's psycho-spiritual development model. As a student of Campbell's, Murdock argued that there were different stages involved in contemporary women's journey towards fulfilment, its primary aim being to accept and integrate her feminine nature. Murdock states that in responding to her recognition of women's different developmental needs, Campbell remarked that women needed to recognise that they were the place people were aiming to get to and did not need to make the journey themselves (Murdock, 2016). In Campbell's model of the hero's journey, women are cast in the role of mothers, daughters, lovers or temptresses who seek to distract the masculine hero from their quest. As a feminist, Campbell's assertion that women do not need to make the journey sparks frustration and outrage. Indeed, Murdock expressed her incredulity at Campbell's statement, as through her clinical work as a family therapist, she had repeatedly noticed female clients being disconnected from their feminine nature (Davis, 2005). Murdock's motivation to write *The Heroine's Journey* was in recognition of the need she had recognised in her clients and to capture what she believed were the different stages of women's development (Murdock, 2016). Perhaps, we should not judge Campbell too harshly as he was writing in an era when women's role and expectations were substantially different from that of contemporary women. However, Campbell's stance brings into sharp relief the challenges that early female pioneers in psychology faced as they fought to have their voices heard. For example, Betty Friedan's (1963) *The Feminine Mystique* is credited with spearheading the 'second wave' of feminism. Her study of highly educated classmates revealed the extent to which they were dissatisfied and marginalised by society.

In exploring mythology, Campbell would likely come across a predominance of masculine heroes in fairy tales. As Gilligan (1982) notes, mythology portrays adventure as a masculine activity. If a woman were to embark on such an adventure, she would typically dress as a man, reflected in some contemporary film such as Disney's Mulan (Caro, 2020) and the character of Eowyn in Lord of the Rings (Jackson, 2002). Strayer (1996) observed that fairy tales are a narrative mechanism for understanding lifespan development. However, fairy tales often portray older women as witches and hags, who become invisible as their beauty and, therefore, power fades. It is less common to see men portrayed in fiction in similar negatively associated stereotypes (Bazzini et al., 1997; Stoddard, 1983).

Perlman (1992) suggests that the hero archetype emphasises rationality and places value on order over chaos, 'one' right way instead of a pluralistic perspective. Rationality is typically seen as positive (and Masculine), and Feminine qualities such as emotional expression generally are undervalued, being seen as negative and weak (Neumann, 1954; Whitmont, 1992). However, suppose one can look past the clumsy use of language to perceive the 'woman' in Campbell's words as the Feminine archetype rather than a person. In that case, Campbell may be saying that the objective is for the hero to integrate the Masculine and Feminine aspects of their character to achieve balance, rediscover their strengths of creativity, compassion and empathy, which are typically associated with the archetypal Feminine (Harris, 1996). The issue comes when archetypes are conflated with people and social expectations (Carriger, 2020). However, in stating that a woman does not need to make the journey, Campbell appears to be dismissive of women's developmental journey, which may be different to men's, but no less important, relevant or worthy of academic study.

In essence, the hero's journey is one of separation from the group. The hero finds their strength from within and must accomplish their mission alone before returning to the group as a changed person. By contrast, the heroine's journey is perceived as a journey into the self and the self in relation to the world. However, Murdock is quite clear that the journey to rediscover the feminine applies to men and women. The heroine's journey emphasises the inner journey to accept and integrate all aspects of one's Feminine nature. It starts with the **separation from the feminine,** which may be a rejection of a feminine role model, such as a mother figure or mentor, or a rejection of socially prescribed roles. The heroine rejects traditional expectations to find her path, which may involve adopting masculine roles or traits to succeed in a patriarchal world. Archetypal Feminine qualities, often considered deviant and undervalued, are rejected in favour of qualities that the heroine perceives may help her succeed. In **identifying with the masculine**, the heroine's journey seeks recognition and success by adopting masculine traits. She has learned throughout her life that to succeed, she must reject her feminine nature, and she seeks to break free from societal constraints and expectations of her life options.

Having left the safety of her known world, the heroine experiences **the road of trials**: the challenges she faces as she seeks to find her authentic self. Along the road are those who seek to dissuade her from her path or try to 'destroy' her. Furthermore, she may experience conflicting emotions as she questions her ability to overcome the hurdles she faces. The 'dragons' she encounters may represent her self-doubts or perceptions of her deficiencies. As the heroine continues to measure herself against standards and expectations that are inauthentic, she struggles with feelings of inadequacy.

The heroine works hard to overcome the obstacles she faced and has learned to succeed in her new world. However, she experiences **the illusory boon of success**. She has the symbols of success, the position, job title or degree, yet experiences a sense of something missing or not being 'enough'. She asks herself what the purpose of this success is (Murdock, 2013). The heroine experiences a sense of loss, a recognition that her new life is lacking something important. In her **descent to the goddess**, she recognises that she feels empty and deflated after striving so hard to succeed. She realises that she is not living an authentic life. Murdock encourages the traveller to permit themself to *be* in the descent and seek support from others, a critical but difficult task. EPP directly addresses the need to accept challenges of life rather than suppressing or rejecting them. However, our human tendency to suppress or deny difficult emotions to ease pain and anxiety means it is difficult to just 'be' in the descent. Furthermore, Murdock emphasises the need for the heroine to listen to her inner voice, to quieten the voices of others around her who seek to influence her choices and direction. The heroine is required to hold the tension of being in transition, with all of the uncertainty that brings, until the way forward becomes clear. The importance of having supportive others who can mentor and provide companionship through this challenging stage is a critical and important opportunity for EPP interventions to offer assistance.

In her **yearning to reconnect with the feminine**, the heroine recognises that she needs to reconnect with parts of herself that have been ignored for some time. In her quest for authenticity, the heroine begins to **heal the mother/daughter split**. She starts to rediscover her feminine strengths and values, seeing them from a new, more compassionate perspective. In the stage of **healing the wounded masculine**, Murdock (2013) describes 'masculine' as an archetype that, when out of balance, becomes critical, destructive and defensive. In learning to accept and use her strengths of creativity, intuition and emotion (archetypal qualities associated with the Feminine), the heroine can achieve a greater balance and integration of head and heart. Instead of seeing the world as a binary construction, the heroine can **integrate the masculine and feminine** and appreciate the complex blend of archetypal qualities that enable her to become her authentic self.

The psychological development of women

Whilst gender equality in 2021 is still not where it needs to be, much has changed for women since 1949 when Campbell wrote *Hero with a Thousand Faces*. Contemporary women have more choices and opportunities than their post-war predecessors. However, those choices and options present different challenges or 'trials' not least because the organisations in which women work and society more generally continue to be structured along patriarchal lines. Research (e.g. Del Boca et al., 2020; Sevilla & Smith, 2020) examined differences in housework and childcare commitments during the COVID-19 pandemic. Findings suggested that a higher proportion of domestic responsibility fell on women, regardless of their work status. Adams-Prassl et al. (2020) indicate the requirement to juggle additional responsibilities at home with work commitments may impact women's mental health and have implications for work progression and gender pay gaps.

Campbell was not alone in his assumptions that male experience equals all experience. Many psychosocial development theories have historically assumed masculine experience to be normative, with feminine experiences often considered a deviation from the norm (McClelland, 1975). Jordan et al. (1991) argue that developmental theories that emphasised the importance of separation, independence and self-sufficiency as indications of health and maturity consistently reinforced the stereotype of women as overly emotional and dependent. Gilligan's (1982) influential work *In a Different Voice* addressed problems perceived to be methodological (selecting male participants for studies) and theoretical (men's lives were of interest, and women were seen as derivative and uninteresting) (Gilligan, 2012). However, Gilligan emphasised that the different voice was thematic rather than gender-specific, presenting different modes of thought rather than generalising about men or women. Greene (2014) suggests a 'one size fits all' approach reflects the extent to which patriarchal assumptions have dominated developmental theory. The impact on women over time of difference being continually perceived as deficient should not be underestimated and is, indeed, a wound that needs to be healed. In 1989, Mednick argued that difference is frequently used as a basis for exclusion, and in 2021 (Robinson, 2021). Gergen (1990) argues that theories of women's development tend to focus predominantly on biological factors, an observation mirrored by Clark and Schwiebert (2011). They argued that developmental theories focus on feminine development milestones such as forming (romantic) heterosexual relationships and having children. Suppose women's growth is measured by biological function. What does that say about women's development in later years as they move beyond childbearing or, indeed, are not able to, or choose not to, reproduce?

The extent to which psychosocial development theories appear not to capture the fullness of women's lived experience has led some feminist scholars (e.g. Gilligan, 1982; Sorrell & Montgomery, 2001) to question how relevant or helpful major developmental theories are in explaining women's experiences. Feminist critiques of Erikson (1963) and Levinson et al. (1978) point to the emphasis on development as a process of separation and individuation, indicative of such theories' androcentric nature. Gilligan argued that Erikson's focus on separation–individuation rather than care and relationship rendered it a male-oriented theory. Building on Gilligan's assertion, Franz and White (1985) suggested an eight-stage process of relational development to sit alongside Erikson's model. However, Franz and White argued that the shortcomings of Erikson's model were not that it was a male theory, but that it failed to take sufficient account of the importance of interpersonal attachment to both men's and women's development. In contrast, Kroger (2002) argues that Erikson's stages encompass the importance of relationships in the stages, maintaining that the context in which trust, autonomy, identity or intimacy are developed are interpersonal in origin. It would appear that, in many cases, the term 'individuation' has been equated with 'individual'. The Jungian concept of individuation represents the journey to find self-realisation, discover meaning and purpose in life, and integrate polarities such as conscious and unconscious, personal and collective, life and death: to become all of who we are (Schlamm, 2014). In this sense, individuation is differentiated from individualism.

The heroine's journey centres on finding one's identity as both individual and part of a community. Gilligan (1982) maintained that the key to understanding women's development was by recognising the centrality of attachment across the lifespan. The importance of relationships was central to pioneers of women's development, such as Miller (1976/2012) and her colleagues at the Stone Centre. They developed relational-cultural theory (RCT: Jordan, Kaplan, Baker Miller et al., 1991). Rather than the goal of human development being separation or individuality, RCT scholars recognise the centrality of relationships to our development: that growth, for both men and women, occurs through and towards relationship which provides meaning and purpose to our lives (Jordan et al., 2004). Jordan (2017) argues that women's growth (and likely men's growth) is connected with others and that theories of development that posit that we move from dependency to autonomy are not an accurate reflection of human experience. Therefore, for women, the notion of individuation requires achieving a balance between identity as an individual and identity in relation to others (self-in-relation: Baker Miller, 2012). When viewed as a polarity, separation and integration appear problematic for explaining women's development and a source of dualistic tension. Just as relationships are central to women's development, so is individuality.

Erikson (1963) asserts that who we are and how we develop comprises biological, psychological and social aspects, each connected and influenced by the others. In so doing, Erikson was beginning to describe the systemic nature of development. However, perhaps a product of his environment or his background in Freudian psychoanalysis, Erikson appeared to overly emphasise the biological aspects of women's development, assuming that a woman's identity was linked to the formation of an intimate (heterosexual) relationship. Several feminist writers have proposed a dynamic systems perspective as a way of thinking about women's development (Fausto-Sterling, 2008; Martin & Ruble, 2010). As part of the system, an individual is at the centre. However, factors such as the individual's agency, self, experience, identity, age, social context and expectations are forces that impact how the individual's subjective experience unfolds. Taking a complex systems perspective, Csikszentmihalyi (1993) considered the developmental process to be a cyclical process of integration and differentiation. Csikszentmihalyi described differentiation as the extent to which a system is composed of parts that have a different structure or function from each other (such as the brain, an individual and a family), integration as the extent to which those parts communicate and enhance each other's goals. A developmental system's approach captures the ebb and flow of developmental stages and emphasises the interconnectivity and relationships between all aspects of the system. Periods of stability are punctuated with periods of change and instability, occurring due to environmental, societal, biological and/or psychological adaptations (Urban et al., 2011). Murdock (2013) maintained that symbolic journeys occurred at multiple points throughout the lifespan, pointing to the possibility that a symbolic journey occurs at life stage transition points as we seek to re-adjust between stages. Referring to the influence of environment on experience, Patricia Miller (2006) commented that male-dominated society impacts development at different points across the lifespan.

One such time is the mid-life transition, which is an important transition point for women. McQuaide (1997) proposed that developmental tasks for women at mid-life include reconstructing their identity and discovering purpose for the second half of their life, developing their self-expression and self-awareness and using their strengths of love and creativity to counterbalance the increasing awareness of the finite nature of life. Hyman (1988) commented that mid-life is when women seek to integrate their multiple roles in personally meaningful ways, reassess goals and become more self-directed. Rather than a narrative of decline for women, mid-life may offer a hopeful and creative opportunity for change (Ryan, 2020). McAdams (2008) describes narrative identity as the evolving internal stories people use to make sense of their lives. What happens when those stories are distorted by societal expectations and reinforced narratives that cast women in a particular and unhelpful light?

In her book *Paths to Fulfilment: Women's Search for Meaning and Identity*, Josselson (2017) followed the developmental journey of 26 women over 35 years, following them as they progressed through life from their college years to their mid-50s. Josselson documented how the women's identities developed and adapted over time and how they found meaning in life. Her findings supported the importance of relationships to women's development in their home and work life. However, whilst Josselson comments that the course each of the women's lives took differed, the group were united by their shared belief in the importance of choice: the ability to choose to live their lives on their own terms without undue imposition of societal values. They valued their freedom to make their own decisions about what it meant to be a woman.

How does it relate to EPP?

As discussed in Chapter 1, EPP reconnects with its existential and humanistic roots and considers how individuals survive and flourish in life, both as individuals and as part of a collective. It invites us to explore how we develop from the inside out to discover our true nature. As 'Second Wave Positive Psychology' (Ivtzan et al., 2016) and the emerging 'Third Wave' (Lomas et al., 2020) remind us, life comprises polarities in tension. Throughout this chapter, the polarities of heroine and hero, female and male and self and other are at the forefront of discussion and writing. I will now turn to another polarity that sits at the heart of the developmental journey for women: differentiation and integration.

The process of differentiation and integration has two qualities. It exists at the individual and collective levels. For an individual, the first step in their developmental journey is creating distinction as they begin to differentiate themselves from their caregiver. They begin to form a concept of themselves as a distinct person, define their life goals and values and free themselves from the control of other people's opinions and values (Csikszentmihalyi, 1993). At a collective level, differentiation represents women as a distinct field of study that authentically represents our voices, experience and growth. However, women have been historically, culturally and socially differentiated (marginalised) at a collective level for not being men. In discussing the individual process of differentiation, it is important to emphasise that the term as used in the context of this chapter refers to a developmental process of growth and change.

Csikszentmihalyi (1993) describes a dialectical process of differentiation and integration throughout life, a continual process of turning one's attention inwards and then outwards, from self to other in an ascending spiral towards integrating self-focused goals and other-focused goals in a way that is authentic and personally meaningful. The call to differentiation is a challenging stage of the journey for the heroine. Our self-concept may be based as much on our relational self as on our unique characteristics in continual navigation between 'self' and 'other' (Brewer & Gardner, 1996). Societal and familial expectations exert a strong influence over her and may try hard to maintain the status quo. Feelings of guilt and self-doubt may accompany the heroine's call to differentiation as she questions her motives. However, the heroine has the *right* to differentiate, to distinguish herself from other people that she relates to in a continual dance between herself as an individual and herself as part of a collective. As the heroine seeks to balance the paradox of her need for integration and differentiation, some reflective questions that may be considered are

- When I strip away others' expectations and the 'oughts' and 'shoulds' I put in my way, who am I at my core?'
- Whose life am I living? My authentic life or the one others want for me?

- What aspects of my true self am I hiding away?
- What possibilities may I uncover were I to bring my hidden strengths into the light?

If we are brave enough to ask ourselves the question 'who am I in essence' and seek a meaningful answer to that question, where does gender fit? It is part of our identity, part of our world view, but rather than being opposites, the qualities of Masculine and Feminine exist within us. We live in the presence of Feminine principles within a world that sees duality. The nature of reality is dialectic. I wonder what we are afraid of in accessing our Feminine qualities. It is worth considering that what people fear is what they deny, and it is that which is needed most.

Integration is concerned with becoming who one is on one's own terms, accepting the fullness of oneself as an individual and in relation to others. However, it is also concerned with integrating conscious and unconscious, the archetypal Male and Female aspects of our nature, strengths and shadow sides. We can choose to accept or reject those qualities. However, in so doing, we limit the possibility of becoming our authentic self. Integration is a potentially tricky stage because it may involve the disintegration of previous patterns, relationships and selves in search of synthesis towards new differentiation and integration. Firestone et al. (2013) describe the continual struggle to balance existential and environmental challenges of integration and differentiation. We are unique individuals who seek autonomy, yet we are social beings who need to belong and be cared for. And the social environment that is essential for our well-being imposes restrictions on how we express our feelings, discover meaning in life and live harmoniously together and apart. The Heroine's journey requires us to examine aspects of ourselves that we have suppressed, denied or rejected and potentially accept them as part of who we are in our fullness. Because if we are to integrate fully, we must integrate that which we have denied. And that is, indeed, an arduous and heroic journey.

Sartre's (2007) slogan of existence precedes essence is a central tenet of existentialism, and for me, a hopeful message that is reflected in EPP. Who we become is a matter of choice. Each individual is responsible for finding meaning in their life. Meaning is contextual and personal, and, as individuals, we are shaped by the choices we make (Webber, 2018). With the responsibility offered by the freedom to choose who we are and what we become also comes the anxiety of choice: anxiety provoked by polarities such as freedom and constraint, self and other and integration and differentiation. In seeking authenticity, one must balance one's identity as an individual and as part of a collective. We must balance our distinctive voice with the integration of who we are in relationship with others. Against a backdrop of societal pressures for conformity, the enormity of options available may, indeed, feel overwhelming. In addition to environmental constraints are those that an individual may put in their own way. Anxiety provoked by realising one's responsibility to create meaning may limit change possibilities. Choice can be overwhelming. Similarly, not knowing how to change or uncertainty regarding potential consequences of change may mean a choice is made that the certainty of the present situation, however unsatisfactory, is more tolerable than the uncertainty of embarking on a process of change. The heroic quest is to accept the inevitability and power of choice. Becoming one's authentic self is a critical but potentially difficult journey. EPP's significant contribution is to develop interventions that can support those wishing to undertake a heroic journey to reclaim their identity, authenticity and meaning in life.

Way forward?

At the beginning of this chapter, I commented that it reflected a personal journey to make sense of women's lived experience and seek out women's voices on developmental psychology. It is a journey that I have begun but certainly not ended. Reflecting the emergence of future 'waves' of positive psychology theorising, if the hero's journey represents the thesis of male experience as normative and the heroine's journey as the antithesis, differentiating women's experience, perhaps EPP can offer a synthesis and look beyond polarisation to accept the complexity of human development and the search for meaning for everyone? Carriger (2020) points out the human tendency to dichotomise and pigeonhole people into a binary conception of a hero or heroine's journey because it makes things simple. It fits our need for consistency and order. To achieve wholeness requires moving beyond polarities of masculine/feminine, rational/emotion, hero/heroine towards a balance and integration of polarities, accepting our individuality in relation to others. A central message of the hero's and heroine's journey is that our growth and development encompass dark and light experiences, whatever journey we undertake. To become our true self, we must face and overcome the challenges that life puts in our way (Worth, 2016).

Rather than making assumptions about either the Hero or Heroine's journey, perhaps we should refer to it as a 'symbolic journey of growth' which provides an opportunity to consider *both* the heroine *and* the hero's journey? Our symbolic journey of growth is about discovering our authentic self by whatever means feels most appropriate. In emphasising the nature of the quest rather than the gender of the traveller, we can recognise that both types of the symbolic journey may be experienced at different times and, as Murdock suggested, even simultaneously. The key is to understand each traveller's goals and support them in that journey with care and compassion.

If we accept that the Hero's and Heroine's journey are types of developmental journey rather than reflecting the gender of a 'traveller', does the gendered language matter? In my view, yes. Language has a powerful role in shaping one's experiences and creating reality. When men are cast in the role of hero and women as the 'prize', it is understandable that some may reject the stereotype and not see themselves reflected in the story. Reinharz (1986) reflected that frequently used and seemingly innocuous language (such as 'old wives' tales' or 'little old woman') perpetuates gendered stereotypes. It is also essential to remember that women may experience their developmental journey differently from men, and those differences are not adequately addressed or appreciated in much psychological theorising. As positive psychology continues to evolve, there is ample opportunity to continually celebrate difference, not as a deviation from the norm but as a reflection of the rich diversity that people bring and see feminine characteristics (whether exhibited by men or women) as strengths rather than deficiencies. As Gilligan (2012) argued, by dividing human qualities into masculine and feminine, we create divisions in the psyche, separating men and women from parts of themselves.

A challenge of the Heroine's journey is to find a synthesis between integration and differentiation, where we are both sufficiently integrated and differentiated. Where we can hold in balance ourselves as unique individuals and ourselves as part of a collective. It is just as necessary for men to integrate their Feminine side and reject the imposition of unhelpful constraints regarding what 'real men' should feel or do. Continually trying to squash pieces of ourselves into a shape that does not fit will be a source of tension, and while we may attempt to ignore the tension, it will find its way to the surface, whether we like it or not. Belonging in our own skin, irrespective of gender, is an aspiration towards healing, belonging and fulfilment, which may be viewed by many as the ultimate success. If we were able to talk about our differences without fear of reprisal or shame, it may become possible to reach the culminating stage of the heroine's journey and integrate the Masculine and Feminine.

Women need role models and mentors who have travelled a similar path and can share their challenges and experiences of achieving authenticity. Similarly, there is an opportunity for EPP to develop interventions focusing on how to help people along their journey to discover their authenticity. I hope that, by surfacing these debates, we may continue a meaningful conversation regarding the psychological development of women across the lifespan and rediscover the many inspirational women who write about psychological development.

Summary of this chapter

This chapter

- Introduces a woman-centred perspective on psychological development
- Emphasises the importance of relationship to women's development
- Proposes the possibility of an integrated 'symbolic journey of growth' that encompasses discovering our authentic self on our own terms rather than binary and gendered concept of heroes and heroines.

Reflective questions

Are you drawn to aspects of either or both symbolic journeys?
These questions are in text (p. 86)

- When I strip away others' expectations and the 'oughts' and 'shoulds' I put in my way, who am I at my core?'
- Whose life am I living? My authentic life or the one others want for me?

- What aspects of my true self am I hiding away?
- What possibilities may I uncover were I to bring my hidden strengths into the light?

Ideas for future research

- Research into developmental psychology from diverse perspectives such as ethnicity, disability, LGBTQ+ and neurodiversity
- How women of different age groups experience their psychosocial development

Resources

Gunderson, C., Graff, D., & Craddock, K. (2018). *Transforming community: Stories of connection through the lens of relational-cultural theory.* Whole Person.
This book presents the application of relational–cultural theory to topics such as education, race, white privilege, LGBTQ+ and girl-centred practice.
Miller, J. B. (2012). *Toward a new psychology of women.* Beacon Press.
An updated version of the classic text that spearheaded the development of relational–cultural theory. The book discusses the strengths and diversity of women and demonstrates how stereotyping restricts women's psychological development.
Frankel, V. E. (2010). *From girl to goddess: The heroine's journey through myth and legend.* McFarland & Company Inc.
An alternative to Murdock's Heroine's Journey.
Murdock, M. (2020) *The heroine's journey workbook: A map for every woman's quest.* Shambhala Publications Inc.
An updated compilation of practical exercises and reflexive questions to guide people through the heroine's journey.

Website

Wellesley Centres for Women – information, publications and resources from the Jean Baker Miller Training Institute
www.wcwonline.org/JBMTI-Site/relational-cultural-theory

References

Adams-Prassl, A., Boneva, T., Golin, M., & Rauh, C. (2020). Inequality in the impact of the coronavirus shock: Evidence from real time surveys. *Journal of Public Economics, 189.* https://doi.org/10.1016/j.jpubeco.2020.104245
Baker Miller, J. (2012). *Toward a new psychology of women.* Beacon Press.
Bazzini, D. G., McIntosh, W. D., Smith, S. M., Cook, S., & Harris, C. (1997). The ageing woman in popular film: Underrepresented, unattractive, unfriendly, and unintelligent. *Sex Roles, 36*(7–8), 531–543. https://doi.org/10.1007/BF02766689
Brewer, M. B., & Gardner, W. (1996). Who Is This "We"? Levels of collective identity and self representations. *Journal of Personality and Social Psychology, 71*(1), 83–93. https://doi.org/10.1037/0022-3514.71.1.83

Campbell, J. (2008). *The hero with a thousand faces*. New World Library.

Caro, N. (2020). *Mulan*. Walt Disney Studios Motion Pictures.

Carriger, G. (2020). *Heroine's journey: For writers, readers, and fans of pop culture*. Gail Carriger LLC.

Clark, S. H., & Schwiebert, V. L. (2011). Penelope's loom: A metaphor of women's development at midlife. *The Journal of Humanistic Counseling, Education and Development, 40*(2), 161–170. https://doi.org/10.1002/j.2164-490x.2001.tb00114.x

Csikszentmihalyi, M. (1993). *The evolving self: A psychology for the third millennium*. HarperCollins.

Davis, M. (2005, Summer, 3). Maureen Murdock. *C. G. Jung Society of Atlanta Quarterly News*. www.jungatlanta.com/articles/summer05-maureen-murdock.pdf

Del Boca, D., Oggero, N., Profeta, P., & Rossi, M. (2020). Women's and men's work, housework and childcare, before and during COVID-19. *Review of Economics of the Household, 18*(4), 1001–1017. https://doi.org/10.1007/s11150-020-09502-1

Erikson, E. (1963). *Childhood and society* (2nd ed.). WW Norton & Company.

Fausto-Sterling, A. (2008). *Myths of gender: Biological theories about women and men*. Basic Books.

Firestone, R., Firestone, L. A., & Catlett, J. (2013). *The self under siege: A therapeutic model for differentiation*. Routledge.

Franz, C. E., & White, K. M. (1985). Individuation and attachment in personality development: Extending Erikson's theory. *Journal of Personality, 53*(2), 224–256. https://doi.org/10.1111/j.1467-6494.1985.tb00365.x

Friedan, B. (1963). *The feminine mystique*. WW Norton & Company.

Gergen, M. M. (1990). Finished At 40. *Psychology of Women Quarterly, 14*(4), 471. https://doi.org/https://doi.org/10.1111/j.1471-6402.1990.tb00225.x

Gilligan, C. (1982). *In a different voice: Psychological theory and women's development*. Harvard University Press.

Gilligan, C. (2012). Looking back to look forward: Revisiting in a different voice. *Classics@, 9*. http://chs.harvard.edu/wa/pageR?tn=ArticleWrapper&bdc=12&mn=4025

Greene, S. (1997). The 1997 PSI lecture: Psychology and the re-evaluation of the feminine. *Irish Journal of Psychology, 18*(4), 367–385. https://doi.org/10.1080/03033910.1997.1010558157

Greene, S. (2014). *The psychological development of girls and women: Rethinking change in time*. Routledge.

Harris, A. S. (1996). *Living with paradox: An introduction to Jungian psychology*. Wadsworth Publishing Company.

Hyman, R. B. (1988). Four stages of adulthood: An exploratory study of growth patterns of inner-direction and time-competence in women. *Journal of Research in Personality, 22*(1), 117–127. https://doi.org/10.1016/0092-6566(88)90028-1

Ivtzan, I., Lomas, T., Hefferon, K., & Worth, P. (2016). *Second wave positive psychology: Embracing the dark side of life*. Routledge.

Jackson, P. (2002). *Lord of the rings: The two towers*. New Line Cinema.

Jordan, J. V. (2017). Relational-cultural therapy. In M. Kopala & M. Keitel (Eds.), *Handbook of counseling women* (pp. 63–73). SAGE Publications.

Jordan, J. V., Hartling, L. M., & Walker, M. (2004). *The complexity of connection: Writings from the stone center's Jean Baker Miller training institute*. Guilford Press.

Jordan, J. V., Kaplan, A. G., Baker Miller, J., Stiver, I. P., & Surrey, J. L. (1991). *A review of Women in connection : Writings from the stone center*. Guilford Press.

Jordan, J. V., Kaplan, A. G., Stiver, I. P., Surrey, J. L., & Miller, J. B. (1991). *Women's growth in connection: Writings from the Stone Center*. Guilford Press.

Josselson, R. (2017). *Paths to fulfilment: Women's search for meaning and identity*. Oxford University Press.

Kroger, J. (2002). Commentary on "feminist perspectives on Erikson's theory: Their relevance for contemporary identity development research. *Identity: An International Journal of Theory and Research, 2*(3), 257–266. https://doi.org/10.1207/S1532706XID0203

Levinson, D. J., Darrow, C. N., Klein, E. B., Levinson, M. H., & McKee, B. (1978). *The seasons of a man's life*. Ballantine Books.

Lomas, T., Waters, L., Williams, P., Oades, L. G., & Kern, M. L. (2020, August). Third wave positive psychology: broadening towards complexity. *Journal of Positive Psychology*. https://doi.org/10.1080/17439760.2020.1805501

Martin, C. L., & Ruble, D. N. (2010). Patterns of gender development. *Annual Review of Psychology, 61*, 353–381. https://doi.org/10.1146/annurev.psych.093008.100511

McAdams, D. P. (2008). Personal narratives and the life story. *Handbook of Personality: Theory and Research*, 242–262. https://doi.org/10.1136/ewjm.173.1.32

McClelland, D. C. (1975). *Power: The inner experience*. Irvington.

McQuaide, S. (1997). Keeping the wise blood: The construction of images in a mid-life women's group. *Social Work with Groups, 19*(3–4), 131–144. https://doi.org/10.1300/J009v19n03_11

Mednick, M. T. (1989). On the politics of psychological constructs: Stop the bandwagon, I want to get off. *American Psychologist, 44*(8), 1118–1123. https://doi.org/10.1037/0003-066X.44.8.1118

Mikkola, M. (2011). Ontological commitments, sex and gender. In C. Witt (Ed.), *Feminist metaphysics* (pp. 67–83). Springer. https://doi.org/https:/doi.org/10.1007/978-90-481-3783-1_5

Miller, P. H. (2006). Contemporary perspectives from human development: Implications for feminist scholarship. *Signs, 31*(2), 445–469. https://doi.org/10.1086/491680

Murdock, M. (2013). *The heroine's journey: Woman's quest for wholeness*. Shambhala Publications.

Murdock, M. (2016). The heroine's journey. In D. A. Leeming (Ed.), *Encyclopedia of psychology and religion*. Springer.

Neumann, E. (1954). *The origins and history of consciousness*. Harper & Brothers.

Perlman, M. S. (1992). Toward a theory of the self in the group. In M. Stein & J. Hollwitz (Eds.), *Psyche at work: Workplace applications of Jungian analytical psychology* (pp. 174–193). Chiron.

Reinharz, S. (1986). Friends or foes: Gerontological and feminist theory. *Women's Studies International Forum, 9*(5–6), 503–514. https://doi.org/10.1016/0277-5395(86)90042-7

Robinson, B. (2021). Gender discrimination is still alive and well in the workplace in 2021. *Forbes.Com*. www.forbes.com/sites/bryanrobinson/2021/02/15/gender-discrimination-is-still-alive-and-well-in-the-workplace-in-2021/?sh=1e210b337f1c

Ryan, L. (2020). *"Embracing the middle years" How do female executives aged 45 and over describe their experience of midlife and how does this experience influence their career decisions?* [Unpublished doctoral thesis]. Liverpool.

Sartre, J. P. (2007). *Existentialism is a humanism* (C. Macomber, Trans. and J. Kulka, Ed.). Yale University Press.

Schlamm, L. (2014). Individuation. In *Encyclopedia of psychology and religion* (2nd ed., pp. 866–867). Springer Reference.

Sevilla, A., & Smith, S. (2020). Baby steps: The gender division of childcare during the COVID-19 pandemic. *Oxford Review of Economic Policy, 36*, S169–S186. https://doi.org/10.1093/oxrep/graa027

Sorrell, G. T., & Montgomery, M. J. (2001). Feminist perspectives on Erikson's theory: Their relevance for contemporary identity development research. *Education, 3488*(919435511), 37–41. https://doi.org/10.1207/S1532706XID0102

Stoddard, K. M. (1983). *Saints and shrews: Women and aging in American popular film* (Vol. 39). Praeger.

Strayer, J. (1996). Trapped in the mirror: Psychosocial reflections on mid-life and the queen in snow white. *Human Development, 39*(3), 155–172. https://doi.org/10.1159/000278434

Urban, J. B., Osgood, N. D., & Mabry, P. L. (2011). Developmental systems science: Exploring the application of systems science methods to developmental science questions. *Research in Human Development, 8*(1), 1–25. https://doi.org/10.1080/15427609.2011.549686

Webber, J. (2018). *Rethinking existentialism.* Oxford University Press.

Whitmont, E. C. (1992). *Return of the goddess.* Continuum.

Worth, P. (2016). The hero's journey. In *Second wave positive psychology: Embracing the dark side of life* (pp. 175–196). Routledge.

Chapter 6

The relational context of change

Andrew Machon

> Do we recall the whole in which our part finds meaning?
>
> Machon (2018, p. 114)

Learning objectives – at the end of the chapter, the following will inform your practice:

- You will gain insight into the essential relational nature of developmental change, from source through to practice.
- You will develop a growing awareness of the psychological identity and presence of the practitioner in you.
- You will gain insight into how to activate and prime your 'self as an instrument'.
- You will become more aware of how you can develop your 'instrumentality', through a study and appreciation of key 'markers' vital to our practice and how we relate, namely:
  - Three key attributes – being alert, authentic and able
  - Three key qualities – detached involvement, empathy and compassion
  - Three key innate instruments that collectively comprise our innate 'instrumentality' in practice – an inner 'spirit-level', compass and mirror
- A 'fruit' of a dedication to practice, which may mark the furthest extent to which we are able to truly relate and develop, namely, love, will more fully be explored in Chapter 8, examining 'Developing Insight'.

Introduction

The chapter is written in a way that is conceptual, practical and personal. I am writing as a practitioner–researcher, who learns auto-ethnographically, from my own experience and from those I work with as a Master Coach. The contents of this chapter have been presented and feedback gained in practitioner development contexts over many years. Working in the field of positive psychology, we are invited to live and model the principles that we discover and research. How do we bring our learning to life, through developing ourselves, others and the systems in

DOI: 10.4324/9781003132530-6

which we work? Irrespective of your level of experience as a positive psychology practitioner, the insights offered to you in this chapter will inform and guide you in how to facilitate change and develop your capability as a practitioner.

The single intent of this chapter is to 'crystallise' and share essential learning. Do not see 'my way' as 'the right way', more a chance and opportunity for us to share in our experiences and to learn together to inspire and inform our practice. As a Visiting Teaching Fellow in Positive Psychology, whenever asked a question, my first response would always be: 'What do you think?'. There is something more important than my own answers that behind every good question is an equally good answer just waiting to be made conscious and voiced. The more we permit others to speak that which remains unspoken, the more we enable others to discover their resourcefulness and self-confidence (Kimsey-House et al., 2011). Throughout this chapter, there will be natural breaks 'reflective moments' marked by key questions for you to respond and include your own experience, before moving forward. Take what time you need to sit and be with these questions and permit your own response.

This may be the ideal time to write this chapter with the emergence and scope of EPP as described by Wong (2010, 2016, 2021) together with a claim for a further third wave of evolution developing more complexity and scope for potential growth (Lomas et al., 2020). A doorway is opened inward that places value on our shared experiences and includes qualitative as well as quantitative study. This invites the rare chance to turn our attention 'inside out'. To profoundly deepen the connection with ourselves and come to know who we really are beyond the person we think we are. The opportunity is presented to look more deeply into the psychology of change, the evolution of consciousness and the identity of the practitioner. And, central to this chapter, how we develop ourselves as an 'instrument' (Cheung-Judge, 2001) that can, in turn, develop others.

The nature of self as an instrument

When working with groups of developing practitioners, I will often ask the question: 'What is the essential instrument of change?' Responses commonly include 'listening, questioning and mirroring', and then after a period of silence, one of the group members will say: 'Hold-on, it's me, I am the instrument'. It is well to pause at this point . . . and allow such a realisation to settle fully into awareness . . . for self is, indeed, your vital instrument.

Worth (2017) importantly reminds every positive psychology practitioner that whenever you meet and or connect with another person, your first intervention is always through yourself. Every time you intervene, influence or relate, yourself is a potential instrument, the only question is whether you are conscious of this or not? You will also realise from your own life experiences that 'self' is not fixed or absolute. Throughout our lives and illustrated in Chapters 2 and 3, self-development may occur across our lifespan (Vaillant, 1977, 2002). Self is not fixed. Identity evolves and changes. It is valuable to reflect, therefore, on who you are when you operate as a practitioner.

Reflection

What characterises when you are operating at your 'best' and 'worst', as a practitioner?

Take a little time to reflect and note your responses before reading on.

Two versions of ourselves

Commonly when we think about who we are as a practitioner, we become aware of different versions of ourselves. We may describe them as a pseudo and an original self (Fromm, 1942) or a false and true self (Winnicott, 1960; Whitfield, 1991; Miller, 2004). In the coaching field, the seminal work of Timothy Gallwey (2000) explored the nature of self in practice of what he named as self 1 and 2. Self 1 was distracted and defensive, largely unable to focus attention on others due to an overriding inner critic that is profoundly distracting and creates self-doubt. He noted how we revert to self 1 when under pressure and feeling anxious or fearful. Self 2 in marked contrast emerges only when we can free ourselves from the fear, doubt and over-controlling inner judgements of self 1. Gallwey describes how self 2 is resourceful and may operate effortlessly, expressing desire and joy and demonstrating great agility. Throughout my work with groups of practitioners including coaches (Machon, 2010) and healthcare practitioners wishing to develop a best practice in the compassionate care (Roberts & Machon, 2015), it has been vital to develop awareness and a list of key characteristics that comprehensively describes these two selves.

Self 1 – 'smaller version'	Self 2 – 'larger version'
Self-protective – self-preserving	Able to be in-service of self and others
Outwardly orientated	Able to face inward and outward
'My way is the right way' – political	Open to exploration – apolitical
Cynical and negative – problem focused	Appreciative and creative
Partial	Wholistic
Differentiating	Able to integrate and synthesise
Un-reflective, compelled to answer	Reflective, free to question
Content focused	Context and content aware
Non-relational – objectifying, un-empathic	Relational and empathic
Reacts to conditioning from the past	Responsive – able to be unconditional
Compulsive doing	Responsive being
Missing present reality	Present in and to the moment
Strongly rational – overthinking	Able to also feel, sense and intuit
Perfectionist – invulnerable	Able to accept vulnerability
Lacks purpose	Aware of values and reason for being
Lacks meaning	'Makes meaning'

Reflection

> Do you recognise these contrasting versions of yourself and these characteristics?
>
> What would you add, change or remove from your own experience?

Permit yourself what time you need to respond, before reading on. . .

Note how these two versions of ourselves are markedly contrasting and apparent opposites. One is non-relational and the other is deeply relational. And, literature suggests that the non-relational version of our-self is where we spend most of our time. Baumeister et al. (1998) and Muraven et al. (1998) supported that we may focus and concentrate our attention for as little as 5% of the time. Despite the temptation to automatically identify with self 1, might this be a dormant form of 'self as an instrument' that first requires priming and activation? And, if so how? If you try to control and directly stop the inner critical voices, we only create more worry and rumination (Gallwey, 2000). There may not be a direct off-switch, but could there be an *on-switch* to enabling 'self as an instrument'?

> the exit we seek, might be an entrance.
>
> Machon (2018, p. 98)

Priming self as an instrument

For all those of you who play musical instruments, you will realise the necessity of first tuning before you play.

Reflection

But, 'how do you 'at-tune' to yourself?'

Are you able to prime yourself to be an instrument in service of others?

Take what time you need to respond before reading on. . .

Such a 'tuning' necessitates that we as practitioners are able to 'make' a psychological somersault, learning how to turn yourself 'inside out' (Machon, 2010, p. 132). This involves two related steps – firstly, a refocusing of attention inward, and then, becoming self-aware.

Mindful priming

Before reading on, if you wish to explore your own experience of this mindful self-priming in practice, an example of a guided exercise will be made available on a website supporting this book content. Over time, such a practice may become second nature and self-priming more immediate.

By focusing and redirecting your attention inward and increasingly becoming aware of yourself from the 'inside out' – you build self-consciousness, becoming aware of a new centre of gravity, a place within from which you can operate, that is uniquely characterised as consciousness free from content (Firman & Gila, 2002). Mindfulness practice develops your ability to focus and pay attention to the present moment, being able to bear witness to any experiences as they come and go, with acceptance and without judgement (Bishop et al., 2004; Ludwig, 2008). In practising mindfulness in this way, we reduce attention hopping, rumination and emotional avoidance (Gilbert & Choden, 2014) negative thinking and emotional reactivity (Harenski & Hamann, 2006; Hölzel et al., 2007). And show a heightened capacity to inwardly attune, an ability to control attention and an increased awareness of new sources of inner information plus enhanced self-efficacy and self-regulation (Cavanagh & Spence, 2013). Remarkably, this describes how we can shift from reactivity to responsiveness and the ability to 'at-tune' to 'self as an instrument'. Siegel (2007) describes the nature of this mindful shift as waking up from life being spent on autopilot. Rarely, the central importance of this shift is highlighted and reported; this may be because self 1 – who we are on autopilot – is largely unconscious. Yet, for the practitioner, this is the key to activating 'self as an instrument', becoming receptive to what you may be thinking, feeling, sensing and intuiting as well as being aware of what you see and hear.

Developing instrumentality

We will now explore how we develop 'self as an instrument' and discover our innate 'instrumentality' – by exploring three key attributes, three key qualities and three innate instruments to illuminate the relational context of change.

Three key relational attributes – being alert, authentic and able

I will often in a jovial spirit remind practitioners that before practising, to check that they have their 'triple A rating' – that they are Alert, Authentic and Able. Let's examine how this 'triple A rating' of the practitioner operates in practice.

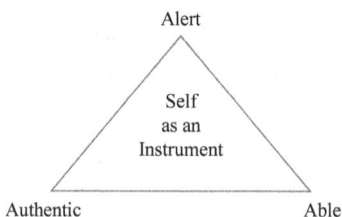

Alert

Finding the answer, by relinquishing the search.

Machon (2018, p. 49)

We have explored how in priming the 'self as an instrument' we are able to transition from compulsive doing to responsive being (Machon, 2010). May (1983) points to *being* as a distinctive aspect of our existence and that which remains and withstands. If you reflect on your own being, what often emerges is awareness of presence. Cuddy (2016) describes presence as the degree to which we can authentically attune to and relate with ourselves as well as with another. The seminal relational work of Rogers (1980) highlights the importance of unconditional presence and how being non-judgemental deepens the relationship, allowing the practitioner to step into the experience of others and observe how experiences change over time. When you experience the presence of an attentive other, you experience being seen and heard as you are and without condition and you feel cared for, even loved (Worth, 2017). Rogers further describes the experience of being prized, of feeling loved, appreciated unconditionally and not possessively and expresses that a person will likely blossom. So, the extent we are alert is a measure of our being, the measure of our being is the extent of our presence and the extent of our presence is the degree to which we are aware of the present moment. Worth (2017) reminds the practitioner that when the compulsion to extrapolate and the process ends, then and only then can we begin to see and hear what is actually in front of us.

Note also that when you reflect upon your own being, how you may quickly become aware of an innate dynamism therein, because 'being' has a 'twin', 'becoming' (Machon, 2005). Jung (1954) states from his early relational work that if you stay true to your being your developmental journey will inevitably unfold. We are, therefore, beings who are ever in the process of becoming more whole and complete (May, 1983).

Authentic

Stillness,
how the superficial recall their depth.

Machon (2018, p. 16)

A mindful practice, as we have examined is one in which we increasingly become aware of ourselves from the 'inside out' and our receptivity and sensitivity to what we experience, sense and intuit. It's remarkable to realise that who you really are is not what you think. Rogers (1967, 1980) once again in his seminal work on the nature of relationships expresses the importance of being genuine and congruent, whereby the practitioner can align their awareness, experience and communication. He further highlights the importance of meeting realness in oneself and the other as vital opportunities for growth. Such authenticity we may consider to be a measure of the extent to which we are able to be faithful to ourselves (Harter, 2002). How well we are able to come to know ourselves our deeper values and beliefs. Cuddy (2016) reminds how the presence and being in tune with oneself, permits the practitioner to more comfortably and fully express their thoughts, feelings, values and how this is central to fostering relationships and the potential for growth. With authenticity, the practitioner operates openly and genuinely, free from the confines of any 'should, must and or ought'. As authenticity grows, we appear to become 'transparent', more real to ourselves and so more relational. Rogers (1980) shares the view that the more we discover of ourselves inwardly, the more we are able to outwardly relate. And, Bruce et al. (2010) agree that being mindfully in-tune with oneself develops our capacity to relate.

What we accept in ourselves, we can accommodate in others.

Machon (2018, p. 94)

It appears there is a self-fulfilling prophecy that the more we continually open to our own personal growth, the more we can enable growth in others by offering a 'mirror' or becoming a role model for another person. The innate power of the inner mirror we will explore later in the chapter.

Able

May (1983) notes that there is a natural dynamism to human growth that involves our becoming someone more. Let's explore how this innate motivation appears to be the core and source, offering a purposeful directionality to development. Jung (1969, 1971) describes how we are motivated to unfold our authentic personality through the process of individuation. Kohut (1984) equally supports the concept that we may be programmed from within by a 'nuclear self'. Winnicott (1987) supports how we are inwardly motivated towards the actualisation of a true self. Rogers (1967) affirms the existence of an 'actualising tendency', with which we may align to potentially fulfil our possibilities. Finally, Firman and Gila (2002) go further not only in acknowledging the developmental process of self-realisation but also how the unfolding of authentic personality is dependent on the presence of this vital axis – the 'I–Self' – throughout our lives. This aligns with Buber's (1970) work on the existence of 'I–thou' and how human beings are deeply relational and aware of an ultimate unity of being that Self is the source to which we can meaningfully relate. Assagioli (1965, p. 37) refers to the innate interrelationship between the 'I' and 'Self' and specifically states how the ' "I" is a reflection of Spiritual Self' and, therefore, ever in a meaningful dialogue. In this psychological presence, the 'I' – your sense of 'I am-ness', appears never to exist in isolation, but as we have affirmed is ever in an intimate relationship and communion with the transpersonal Self. Assagioli goes further in affirming this

relational existence by expressing that there are not really two independent enti-
ties, but one. Firman and Gila (2002) express how the unfolding of our authentic
personality is ever-present in relation to the existence of 'I–Self' throughout our
lifespan. This offers profound insight to the title of this chapter – the relational
context of change – and how we are inextricably psychologically in relation to the
source of our development.

Returning to the work of the practitioner, the continual opportunity to re-align
and orientate with source permits the setting of our vital co-ordinates, those that
inform our chosen directionality and the next step that we intend to make. Staying
true to our aligning with this source offers an innate purposeful directionality to
our life and work. Rogers (1980) recognises that as we align, we unblock a flow
of experiencing that we then permit to run its uninhibited course. Csikszentmihalyi (1997) equally supports that becoming aligned and absorbed with that which
motivates results is effortless action and being in flow. Yaden et al. (2017) point
out how in being absorbed we forget ourselves and paradoxically can in such a
transcendent experience increase our connectedness and a felt connection with
others. Note how in being able to respond – we become 'response-able' – you not
only can intentionally set 'your own course' but equally enable this prospect for
others. This is highlighted later in the chapter with the value of the inner compass.

Three key relational qualities – detached-involvement, empathy and compassion

We explored in the last section how the 'I' exists in a union with 'Self'. Wilber
(2004) compares the 'I and 'Self' in relation to a mirror and its reflection and
implies how this may support the practitioner in being able to witness and notice
all objects that enter the field of experience. Notice how the 'I' in one way stands
apart from 'Self' and yet is also intimately and inextricably related. It may not,
therefore, be surprising that one of the key qualities of the practitioner when operating from this emergent centre of awareness is one of detached involvement.

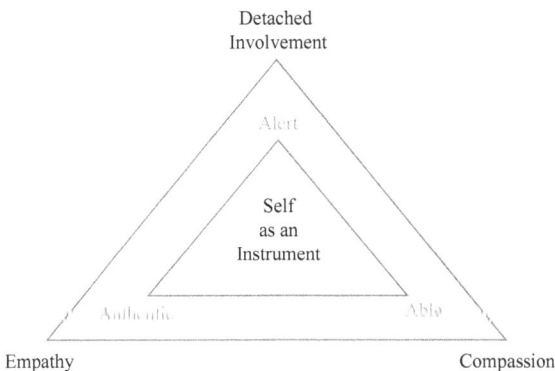

Detached involvement

As practitioners, we can be both stand 'apart from' and 'step into' the experience of others, cultivating the paradoxical quality of 'detached involvement' in practice. Such a relational quality may, on the one hand, create the reflective space in which the client can feel fully heard and seen whilst also offering the practitioner the choice to intervene at any time through questioning, sensing and intuiting. Such a paradoxical quality in practice permits both holding and agility (Tobin, 2005) and frees the practitioner to potentially respond irrespective of what the other person may present. This enables the practitioner to be present and to choose to act and enable, even when strong feelings and/or conflictual polarities are presented.

Empathy

Firman and Gila (1997) describe the capacity of the 'I' to be in a continual relationship with 'Self', as one that brings empathy to the relationship. This quality by definition provides the practitioner with the capacity 'to feel into' the experience of others. This offers the practitioner the chance to understand the client from the other's point of view.

Rogers (1980) expresses how with empathy, the practitioner can enter in the private world of another and follow in their experiences, moment by moment. And how empathy cultivates sensitivity, the ability to accurately sense, acknowledge and mirror emotions that enables the other person to make meaning of their experiences. Listening with empathy, Rogers acknowledges to be a way of prizing and valuing the other person.

Gilbert (2013) reminds us how in the absence of judgement and the demonstration of empathy in a relationship, the prospect arises for the practitioner to engage with and tolerate whatever feelings the other may present. Gilbert goes further to express how deep relating involves the practitioner being able to accommodate and accept, complexity, tolerating distress, without a need to solve. In demonstrating empathy, the practitioner is essentially able to enter into the life of the other, building an intimate togetherness that creates the opportunity to come to know the client more fully and deeply fostering trust and safety (Rogers, 1967). Empathy early in a developmental relationship predicts later success by fostering learning and change (Rogers, 1980). When practitioners listen with empathy, they may sense what is not yet spoken, a hidden emerging consciousness behind what is communicated. The practitioner may with sensitivity mirror with the other what they are experiencing in service of fostering the self-awareness. I often consider this experience as one where the other person is essentially borrowing *my eyes* to know themselves more deeply and fully. We as practitioners in service of our clients lay down what we think so that the other can come to know themselves more fully. We may tolerate 'not knowing' and focus on experiencing so that the other can come to know themselves better.

Compassion

Whereas empathy demonstrates a willingness to share in the inner world and experiences of another, compassion goes further, with the intent to enable purposeful action. Fredrickson (2003) notes that when we feel compassion, we don't just sit and suffer with another but are motivated to make bearable, reduce and/or enable an end to their suffering. As a practitioner, there are three useful stages in working with and appreciating the nature of compassion: firstly, an attention to and a noticing of the suffering of another; secondly, a showing of empathic concern and thirdly, an acting to enable the other to relieve their suffering (Kanov et al., 2004). Gilbert (2013) affirms that there is value in acknowledging and learning how to 'bear suffering', for when we are able to face our fears, there we may discover courage. The compassionate desire to support and enable recognises a common humanity and the value in sharing the experiences of being human. Compassion offers caring and kindness in the face of distress and potential feelings of failure. This quality permits a 'facing into' experiences that we may be tempted to 'turn away' from. In facing in and accepting, we may learn the nature of self-transcendence, the ability to include and go beyond the presenting struggles and suffering (Frankl, 2004). Compassion enables the practitioner to 'face' and 'embrace' suffering in a relationship and not to disconnect (Gilbert, 2013).

Three key innate instruments of practice – spirit level, compass and mirror

If we consider the 'instrumentality' of the self, we may commonly observe three vital instruments in practice: the spirit level, compass and mirror (Machon, 2010).

Reflection

Do you recognise your inner spirit level, compass and mirror?
  If so, consider how you may operate them in your practice?
  What value do they offer to you and your client?
  Take what time you need to respond before reading on. . .

Your inner spirit level

If you have not seen a 'spirit level' before, it is a simple device often used in manual work to show that something is balanced and level. All practitioners aspire to be able to offer a 'balanced viewpoint', to be able to stand firm and strong in support of the other person. Also, to be as free from bias and conditioning as possible, offering an unconditional presence and so able to mediate and facilitate

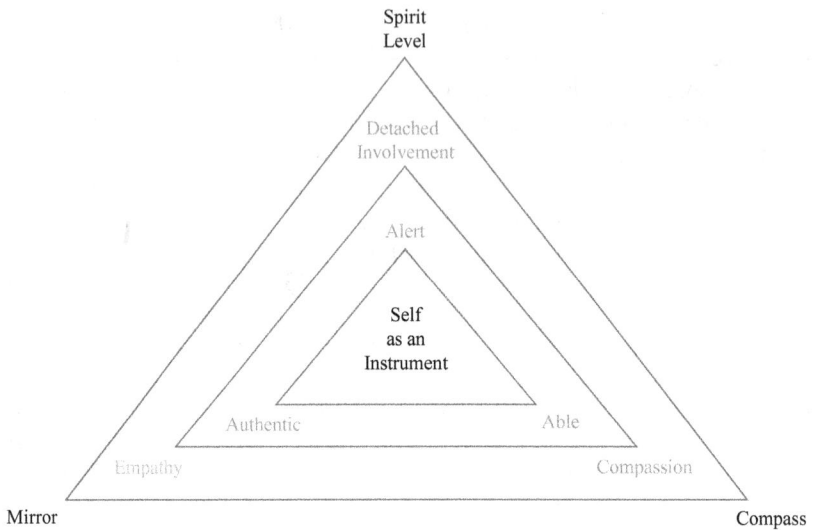

the growth of another (Rogers, 1980). This invites the discovery of a symbolic 'spirit level' within ourselves. Firman and Gila (2002) note how the emergent 'I' is a place from which we may pivot and balance, building awareness, making choices and taking action. Operating from this emergent centre of awareness, the practitioner remains still and paced, balanced and reflective, alert and observing, noticing and listening and sensing and intuiting (Machon, 2010).

Becoming an expert in 'not knowing'

> learning how not to know,
> may be our greatest act of intelligence.
>
> Machon (2018, p. 66)

I will often ask groups of practitioners – 'when you operate as a practitioner what are you an expert in?' Responses may commonly include questioning, listening, paraphrasing, mirroring . . . all of which are true. I would then add 'are you not experts in not knowing?'

When we resist the temptation to know (and not give our own answers), we permit the other person the chance to come to know themselves better. Only when we have learned how 'not to know' do we gift the other person the creative space and chance to discover the answer for themselves – unimpeded. This is when the spirit level is present and operational, helping the practitioner to remain open, listening and balanced, in essence, comfortable in 'not knowing' in service of another (Machon, 2010). Notice how when you find your own answers, this may foster your own personal accountability and willingness to act and follow through, building your autonomy, engagement and resourcefulness. Also, detached involvement – a quality we have previously explored, closely associated with the spirit level – allows the other person the chance to become more fully aware of and learn through what they are experiencing. Rogers (1980) recalls the vital role of the practitioner is to enable the other to learn through whatever experiences that they may present.

As one example, here is a recent coaching interaction with a senior business executive, which highlights the importance of operating the inner spirit level in service of the client. I have been working with this person for two coaching sessions and are in the middle of the third.

	"What do you think is the way forward?"
Client:	"I don't know?"
	"Look again?" *I smile and sit back – I notice the temptation to give my answer and to be over-helpful, but my spirit-level is in action, so I remain intent on letting the client discover her own answer*
Client:	"but Andrew, I don't know?"
	"Look again? *I smile and nod – I feel the pull once more to answer but recognise that this would not be in service of the client's learning and the opportunity for self-discovery*
Client:	"Mm (long pause) . . . Okay, I think I should do what I have longed to do for a long time".
	"Oh, what is that?"
Client:	"To take some time out and to take the trip I have dreamt of taking . . .".
	"What opportunity does that offer you?"
Client:	"It would be 'a dream come true"
	"And if you permitted your dream come true?"
Client:	"Then the world would be my oyster"
	"Can we reflect for a moment on what just happened?"
Client:	"Sure"
	"You seemed determined not to answer" *I smile at her*
Client:	"Yes, I know"
	"Look at how valuable your answer is!"
Client:	"I know" *we both laugh*
	"So, do we need to play this game anymore?"
Client:	"No"
	"What have you learned?"
Client:	"I am more resourceful than I give myself credit, I just need to be patient and to reflect deeply to find my way – I do need to speak my truth, that feels new"
	"What valuable learning! That you are more resourceful than you had thought, and you will and are able to speak your truth"

Notice what would have been taken away from the client if the inner 'spirit level' were not operational – the chance to realise her own resourcefulness and experience speaking her truth. The spirit level is an invaluable inner instrument that allows the practitioner to be useful but not over-helpful.

Compass

We have explored earlier in the chapter, how being and becoming are intimately related. And how a vital innate directionality exists to development. The inner compass is the vital instrument that enables the practitioner to be a useful reference and opportunity to orientate and set direction. The compass allows the client to be continually clear about where they are. With an inner compass, the practitioner is always reminded to check intention – where the person is right now? And where they ideally would like to get? The inner compass allows you to share in the 'vital coordinates' of the person you are with and the key goals or outcomes that they wish to achieve. The compass enables a setting of intent, aligning with one's will or choice to act and make purposeful and potentially meaningful progress. If the intention is set, then the goal is likely to be reached. If it's not, then you are likely to lose your way. Henry Ford reminds us that our beliefs of whether we can or can't perform in a certain way will be correct. A note, therefore, to all practitioners – don't set off without a compass.

Let me offer a very recent use of the inner compass in a coaching session with an executive. This session typically shows how the compass is valuable in setting the clients 'vital co-ordinates' for the coaching conversation:

"What would you like to work on today?"
Client: "I'm not sure?"
"Take a moment to decide" *we pause . . .*
Client: "I want to understand why I am getting so angry in key meetings?"
"Why are you getting so angry?"
Client: "Yes, I am so frustrated at the moment"
"You are feeling frustrated and angry yes *pause . . .*".
Client: "Yes, it's happening a lot *pause . . .*".
"So, what would you ideally like to walk away with when we end today?"
Client: "Let me think *pause . . . .* More insight. . . . And maybe an action plan"
"How will we know when you have found your insight and action plan?" – *we go one step further to allow the client to become aware of their measure of success*
Client: "I will feel such relief, I know it will take courage – but it will be worth it"
"So, you will feel 'such relief'"
Client: "Yes, I will be able to relax so much more"
"Have you your courage?"

Client: "I am feeling courageous"
           "So, shall we begin?"
Client: "Yes, I'm ready to go now!"

Notice the energy when a person aligns with what is most important to them when they set clear intent. Also notice how exploring measures of success 'fuels' their intention.

Mirror

> Knowing less, seeing more.
>
> Machon (2018, p. 34)

The third vital inner instrument of the practitioner is the 'mirror', offering the capacity for reflection and mirroring back what you see and experience. Empathic mirroring is vital to our development in early life and across the lifespan (Gruhn et al., 2008). However, the full scope and impact of the inner mirror are often overlooked and underplayed in practice. One important aspect of mirroring is to reflect back to the client, key words or phrases (paraphrasing) to demonstrate listening, show understanding and build trust. However, mirroring back what we hear and see represents only one aspect of the scope of this vital inner instrument. Operating as an *authentic mirror* – we have a measure of the full scope of this instrument in practice. Stein (2006) notes how a clean and clear mirror is one free from identifications to any internal content. The authentic mirror is one that sensitively reflects back what you notice, sense and intuit about the other, without judgement or condition. And essentially includes what we may feel, sense and intuit as well as what we can see and hear (Machon, 2010).

Let me offer a recent example of the value of the authentic mirror from a coaching conversation with another senior client. This is our first coaching session, and I notice that I am experiencing my client to be energetic, charismatic and charming. However, as I deeply reflect, I experience strongly a feeling of 'not being good enough'. Now, at times I can and do experience the feeling of 'not being good enough', but this experience with the person feels particularly 'strong' (somehow greater than my own self-reservations) and upon reflection, not all mine. So, this is how I responded by deploying the inner 'authentic mirror', in service of my client.

> "Can I share something with you that I am experiencing, which seems strangely paradoxical"
> *Client:*   "Please do"
> "I experience you are charismatic and charming and yet, also, more deeply, I sense a feeling of 'not good enough' – is this a useful reflection to you?
> *Client:*   *Long pause* "Andrew, you have outed me" *we both smile*
> "In what way?"

Client: "Folk generally focus on how good they think I am, but I actually feel a bit of an imposter . . . deep down . . .".
"An imposter?"
"Yes, *long pause* I often feel not good enough and it undermines me a lot"
"Is this an important area for us to work?"
"Most, certainly".
We continue with the exploration . . .

Recognise the value of the authentic mirror of how you might develop and deploy this valuable inner instrument in your own work?

An essential 'fruit' of dedication to practice

Chapter 8 explores the nature of 'Developing Insight', and we will examine more a key 'fruit' that may emerge from a dedication to personal development and practice – namely, Love. What does this offer the practitioner? Love – may be a remarkable relational quality, 'when two are at one' (Machon, 2018). Might this be a measure of our coming to fruition, making conscious a source and original way of being?

As we conclude, we may recall some of the key questions of EPP that Wong (2004, p. 1) poses including how will we survive and, indeed, thrive within a world of conflicts including hope and despair, love and hate, courage and safety and so on? We need to look no further than the work of the practitioner to answer this question. For if we prime and fashion 'self as an instrument', then we can enable others not only to survive but also, indeed, to thrive within a conflictual world. The practitioner learns the secrets of how to manage their psychological state and presence in service of developing others:

* How to be comfortable with discomfort
* How to see the strength that resides in accepting vulnerability
* How to enable others to see their blindness and awaken
* How not to know, to surrender to 'not knowing', so that others may come to know themselves better
* How to be useful and not over helpful
* How the extent to which we accept ourselves is the same degree to which we are able to relate to others

Our capacity to relate – to connect and our sense of connectedness – is something that we may learn from the 'inside out'. Research often places an emphasis on the 'What', from this work the present and future primary focus may necessarily be the 'How'. Tolle (2005) affirms that it is in the *How* of *What* we do that is a measure of our fulfilment.

Such a research focus will reveal more insights into 'self as an instrument' and its remarkable attributes and qualities, in practice, and the developmental medium we call relationship.

Summary – this chapter has. . .

- Shown originality in providing insight into the relational nature and context of change from source through to practice
- Explored the evolution and psychological identity of the practitioner. When we practice, we operate from an emergent centre of awareness – a new centre of gravity – where consciousness is free of content – namely, the 'I–Self'
- Shown a vital priming is necessary to the activation of 'self as an instrument' through mindful practice.
- Illustrated how the activation of 'self as an instrument' creates reflexivity and receptivity that permit the practitioner to relate more deeply through sensing, listening and intuiting
- Explored how the work of the practitioner is a consequence of

  - Three relational attributes – being alert, authentic and able – that mark the transition from a compulsion to do to a being and becoming responsive. These attributes have been shown in this chapter to align and marry with being unconditional, presence, prizing, congruence, integrity and response-ability.
  - Three relational qualities – detached involvement, empathy and compassion – that mark a vital shift from non-relational and rational objectivity to the ability to be able to deeply relate and respond.
  - Three innate instruments vital to practice – the spirit level, compass and mirror – that demonstrate the innate 'instrumentality' of self, in practice.

- Ultimately, there may be key fruits of dedication to development and practice including love, more fully explored in Chapter 8.

Reflective questions

(Are contained within the text).

Existential perspective

This approach to articulating the relational context of change highlights how the inner awareness of a practitioner can both focus their own work and elicit and support the 'being' of a client.

Research questions or opportunities

Notice how, in what way, the ideas and experiences described in this chapter appear in your own work, either on yourself, or when working with others, or both.

What questions do these experiences raise for you?

In what way, or place, can you explore those experiences further?

References as resources

If you wish to follow up ideas and further reading from this chapter.

Assagioli, R. (1965). *Psychosynthesis: A Manual of Principle and Techniques*. New York, Hobbs Dorman.

Baumeister, R. F., Bratslavsky, E., Muraven, M. and Tice, D. (1998). Ego Depletion – Is the Active Self a Limited Resource? *Journal of Personality and Social Psychology*, 75(5), 1252–1265. DOI: 10.1037//0022–3514.74.5.1252

Bishop, S. R., Lau, M., Shapiro, S., Carlson, L., Anderson, N. D., Carmody, J., Segal, Z. V., Abbey, S. and Speca, M. (2004). Mindfulness: A Proposed Operational Definition. *Clinical Psychology: Science and Practice*, 11(3), 230–241. doi.org/10.1093/clipsy. bph077

Bruce, N. G., Manber, R., Shapiro, S. L. and Constantino, M. J. (2010). Psychotherapist Mindfulness and Psychotherapy Process. *Psychotherapy: Theory, Research, Practice, Training*, 47(1), 83. DOI: 10.1037/a0022062

Buber, M. (1970). *I and Thou*. Translated by Walter Kaufmann. New York, Charles Scribner's Sons.

Cavanagh, M.J. and Spence, G.B. (2013). Mindfulness in Coaching. In J. Passmore, D.B. Peterson, and T. Freire (Eds.), *The Wiley Blackwell Handbook of the Psychology of Coaching and Mentoring*. Chichester, Wiley Blackwell, pp. 112–134.

Cheung-Judge, M. (2001). The Self as an Instrument – A Cornerstone for the Future of OD. *OD Practitioner*, 33(3).

Csikszentmihalyi, M. (1997). *Finding Flow – The Psychology of Engagement in Everyday Life*. New York, Basic Books, Perseus Books Group.

Cuddy, A. (2016). *Presence – Bringing your Boldest Self to Your Biggest Challenges*. London, Orion Publishing Group Ltd, pp. 18–34.

Frankl, V.E. (2004). *Man's Search for Meaning – The Classic Tribute to Hope from the Holocaust*. London, Rider Classics, an imprint of Penguin Books.

Firman, J. and Gila, A. (1997). *The Primal Wound – A Transpersonal View of Trauma, Addiction and Growth*. New York, State University of New York Press, p. 72.

Firman, J. and Gila, A. (2002). Psychosynthesis – *A Psychology of the Spirit*. New York, State University of New York Press.

Fromm, E. (1942). *The Fear of Freedom*. London, Routledge and Kegan Paul 2001, p. 175.

Fredrickson, B.L. (2003). Positive Emotions and Upward Spiral in Organisations. In K.S. Cameron, J.E. Dutton and R.E. Quinn (Eds.). *Positive Organisational Scholarship – Foundations of a New Discipline*. San Francisco, Berrett-Kochler Publishers Inc.

Gallwey, T.W. (2000). *The Inner Game of Work*. New York, Random House Trade Paperbacks. pp. 43–56.

Gilbert, P. (2013). *The Compassionate Mind*. London, Constable and Robinson.

Gilbert, P. and Choden, P. (2014). *Mindful Compassion*. Oakland, CA, New Harbinger Publications Ltd. p. 135.

Gruhn, D., Rebucal, K., Diehl, M., Lumley, L. and G. Labouvie-Vief. (2008). Empathy Across the Adult Lifespan – Longitudinal and Experience – Sampling Findings. *Emotion*, 8(6), 753–765.

Harenski, C.L. and Hamann S. (2006). Neural Correlates of Regulating Negative Emotions Related to Moral Violations. *NeuroImage*, 30(1), 313–324. DOI: 10.1016/j. neuroimage.2005.09.034

Harter, S. (2002). Authenticity. In C.R. Snyder and S.J. Lopez (Eds.), *Handbook of Positive Psychology*. Oxford, Oxford University Press, pp. 382–394.

Hölzel, B.K., Ott, U., Hempel, H., Hackl, A., Wolf, K., Stark, R. and Vaitl, D. (2007). Differential Engagement of Anterior Cingulate Cortex and Adjacent Medial Frontal Cortex in Adept Meditators and Nonmeditators. *Neuroscience Letters*, 421(1), 16–21.

Jung, C.G. (1954). *The Development of Personality*. Princeton, Princeton University Press Bollingen Series XX.

Jung, C.G. (1969). *The Archetypes and the Collective Unconscious*. Princeton, Princeton University Press.

Jung, C.G. (1971). *Psychological Types*. 20 vols. Vol. 6, Bollingen Series XX. Edited by J. Read, M. Fordham, G. Adler, and W. McGuire. Princeton, Princeton University Press.

Kanov, J., Maitlis, S., Worline, M.C., Dutton, J.E., Frost, P.J. and Lilius, J. (2004). Compassion in Organisational Life. *American Behavioural Scientist*, 47, 808–827. doi.org/10.1177/0002764203260211

Kimsey-House, H., Kimsey-House, K. Sandhal, P. and L. Whitworth (2011). *Co-Active Coaching – Changing Business Transforming Lives*. Boston, MA, Nicholas Brearley Publishing.

Kohut, H. (1984). *How Does Analysis Cure?* Edited by A. Goldberg. Chicago, IL, University of Chicago Press.

Ludwig D.S. (2008). Mindfulness in Medicine. *JAMA*, 300(11), 1350–1352.

Lomas, T., Waters, L., Williams, P., Oades, L.G. and Kern, M. (2020). Third Wave Positive Psychology: Broadening Towards Complexity. *The Journal of Positive Psychology*. DOI: 10.1080/17439760.2020.1805501

Machon, A. (2005). *Just Beyond the Visible – the Art of Being and Becoming*. Croyden, Arem Publishing Ltd.

Machon, A. (2010). *The Coaching Secret – How to Be an Exceptional Coach*. London, Pearson Business.

Machon, A. (2018). *Guiding Lights: Images and Words Inspired by the Aurora Borealis*. Penarth, Wales, Oliver's Books.

May, R. (1983). *The Discovery of Being – Writings in Existential Psychology*. New York, W.W. Norton and Company.

Miller, A. (2004). *The Drama of Being a Child- The Search for the True Self*. London, Virago Press, p. 45.

Muraven, M., Tice, D. and Baumeister, R.F. (1998). Self Control as a Limited Resource: Regulatory Depletion patterns. *Journal of Personality and Social Psychology*, 74(3), 774–789. DOI: 10.1037//0022-3514.74.3.774

Roberts, G.W. and Machon, A. (2015). *Appreciative Healthcare Practice – A Guide to Compassionate Person-Centred Care*. Keswick, Cumbria, M&K Publishing, an imprint of M&K Update Ltd, Keswick.

Rogers, C.R. (1967). *On Becoming a Person: A Therapist's View of Psychotherapy*. London, Constable, p. 414.

Rogers, C.R. (1980). *A Way of Being*. New York, Houghton Miffin Company.

Siegel. D.J. (2007). *The Mindful Brain*. New York, W.W. Norton.

Stein, M. (2006). *The Principle of Individuation – Toward the Development of Human Consciousness*. Ashville, NC, Chiron Publications.

Tobin, J. (2005). Chapter 4 – *The Role of the Leader and the Paradox of Detached Involvement in Complexity and the Experience of Leading Organisations* – Edited by D. Griffin and R. Stacey. Abingdon, Oxon, Routledge.

Tolle, E. (2005). *A New Earth*. London, Penguin Books.

Vaillant, G.E. (1977). *Adaptation to Life*. Cambridge, MA, Harvard University Press.

Vaillant, G.E. (2002). *Ageing Well*. Boston, Little Brown.

Whitfield, C.L. (1991). *Co-dependence: Healing in the Human Condition*. Deerfield Beach, FL, Health Communications.

Wilber, K. (2004). *The Simple Feeling of Being – Embracing Your True Nature*. Boston, MA, Shambhala Publications.

Winnicott, D.W. (1960). Ego Distortion in Terms of True and False Self. In *The Maturational Process and the Facilitating Environment: Studies in the Theory of Emotional Development*. New York, International Universities Press, Inc., pp. 140–157.

Winnicott, D.W. (1987). *The Maturational Processes and the Facilitating Environment*. London, The Hogarth Press and the Institute of Psycho-Analysis.

Wong, P.T.P. (2004). Existential Psychology for the 21st Century. *International Journal of Positive Psychology*, 1(1), 1.

Wong, P.T.P. (2010). What Is Existential Positive Psychology? *International Journal of Existential Psychology and Psychotherapy*, 3(1), July.

Wong, P.T.P. (2016). Existential Positive Psychology. *International Journal of Existential Psychology and Psychotherapy*, 6(1), February.

Wong, P.T.P. (2021). Existential Positive Psychology (PP 2.0) and Global well-being -Why Is It Necessary During the Age of Covid-19. *International Journal of Existential Psychology and Psychotherapy*, 10(1), 1–16.

Worth, P. (2017). Positive Psychology Interventions in Practice: The First Intervention is Our Self. In C. Proctor (Ed.), *Positive Psychology Interventions in Practice*. Cham, Switzerland, Springer International Publishing, AG.

Yaden, D.B., Haidt, J., Hood, R.W. Jr., Vago, D.R. and Newberg, A.B. (2017). The Varieties of Self-Transcendent Experience. *The Review of General Psychology*, May 1–18. doi.org/10.1037/gpr0000102

Chapter 7

An introduction to the trans-theoretical model of change

Piers Worth

Introduction

I have been a 'student' of human change, personal change, for over 40 years, exploring different theories and models as I encountered them. I first learned of the trans-theoretical model (TTM) in 2005, in Carr (2004), a textbook on positive psychology, where he presented it as a model for 'positive change', weaving the TTM theory and positive psychology together. I was enthralled in that this seemed a clearer and more structured framework and understanding of change than I felt I had seen before. This prompted me to explore the chapter of James Prochaska and his colleagues – something that I would encourage all readers of this chapter to do, with references cited at the rear of the chapter. This chapter is a summary of their work. It will not replace the need for a more detailed follow-up of their work in the original publications if you wish to use make use of this model.

In the design of the Buckinghamshire New University MAPP programme and the 'Journey of Change' module,[1] our intention became to give the post-graduate students an awareness of the 'context' and possible structure of change, not just the 'content' in positive psychology interventions (PPIs). There are many possible models of the process of change which could have been used. The TTM was chosen because of its research base, and the 'face validity' of its structure to individuals unused to the process of change. Additionally, one of the gifts of the TTM is it invites us to explore whether we as individuals, or our clients, are actually ready for a process of intentional change and what might be the states that precede a readiness to change; I felt this perspective was not visible in positive psychology as a discipline. Prochaska et al. (1994) proposed that 80% of individuals they encountered in research or clinical work were *not* ready to initiate change without further preparation. Prochaska and Prochaska (2016) refer to the human experiences and emotions that may characterise an individual not yet considering a change or being only tentative about the choice; they make clear that these states deserve and need compassion. There is a role of acceptance and if needed education of the feelings and perceptions of those currently unready to change. Perhaps, positive psychology as a discipline assumes we all would wish to move towards a 'positive' future in some aspect of our lives. The TTM illustrates that is not necessarily the case. If we open to that possibility,

DOI: 10.4324/9781003132530-7

then 'positive psychology practitioners' have an educative and preparatory stage for change in their work that is not yet given a full presence in the teaching of the discipline.[2] There are new aspects to positive psychology practice yet to be developed, and they will be tentatively explored later in this chapter.

In that context, the learning objectives of the chapter are

At the end of the chapter, you will

- **Comprehend** in outline the structure of the TTM of Change – the stages, processes and levels.
- **Recognise** indicators of your or other individuals' readiness for change.
- **Appreciate** that any process of change takes readiness and preparation in appropriate detail, prior to taking action.
- **Identify** potential ways in which positive psychology may contribute to the TTM of change.
- **Consider** and understand potential criticisms of the TTM.

Background to the TTM of change

The TTM of change has been researched and used for over 40 years with an estimated 4,000 research papers produced in that time (Prochaska & Norcross, 2018). The background to the model, read 'through time, is a fascinating pathway of research questions and unfolding development of this way of working.

In communicating the TTM, Prochaska et al. (1994) acknowledge there are decades of research and clinical experience in the work of personal and client change. A gift they bring to any reader and practitioner is their acknowledgement of learning not only from research and clinical practice but also from the experiences of clients, and particularly the stories of 'self-changers', who don't necessarily appear in therapeutic or research work. In developing their model, the work was foundational in that it explored established and successful patterns and processes of change *as well as* reports from individuals who were successful self-changers. Their work reflects and synthesises profound learning from both of these directions. I would acknowledge as they do that unconditional caring is foundational and environmental to successful self-change. This quality is further explored for readers and practitioners in Chapter 6 of this text, the relational nature of change.

The meaning and contribution of the 'trans-theoretical' perspective

Prochaska (1979, Prochaska & Norcross 2018), Prochaska and DiClemente (1984) and Prochaska et al. (1994) acknowledge that there currently exist approximately 400 different methods of psychotherapeutic support and change. For someone seeking or needing change, this is a potentially bewildering number and level of divergence and differentiation within the work of therapeutic support from which to choose. They reflect (e.g. Prochaska & Norcross 2018) that any creative process, such as psychotherapy, diverges as part of an evolution to explore the nature of human needs and ways of achieving change, yet differentiation and divergence eventually have to involve some kind of integration and synthesis to focus on the gains of their field. This focus on integration in and of this knowledge is a driving energy behind their perspective.

Prochaska (initially in 1979 and revised with fellow authors in eight subsequent editions till 2018) undertook an astonishing review of the commonalities across psychotherapeutic and psychological processes of treatment as a way of asking whether it was possible to combine the profound insights of multiple disciplines and theories to establish their common components and a synthesis – the structure of intentional change. He described this as the 'grand tie' across treatments (Prochaska, 1999), one which gives insight to the activities within a facilitated session, and the daily life of those seeking change. Prochaska asserts that the hundreds of therapies, which may have very differing views on the causes of problems, share a substantial commonality in processes of change which are summarised later in the chapter. In the awareness of this commonality, someone seeking change or those facilitating change in others can work in a systematic manner. In the act of working from research on the synthesis of therapeutic change processes and the successes of self-changers, their proposals build the competencies of those facilitating change or seeking to achieve it.

Prochaska et al. (1994) propose that an 'action paradigm' or orientation has dominated thinking on personal change for decades – that as individuals, when changes are needed, the assumption is we are ready to act. Their work argues for the contrary, in a manner which I interpret is profoundly human and compassionate. They propose that (Prochaska & Prochaska, 2016) most people do not know how to change nor are they ready to. Therefore, adopting an assumption of a readiness to change risks excluding from support or frustrating those who are not ready. Change portrayed by this model occurs in a sequence of controllable, predictable stages. This being the case, then a personal awareness, on the part of an individual facing or seeking change, or a practitioner facilitating change, is to understand what 'stage' of change an individual is in at that point in time (Prochaska et al., 1994).

In their research and clinical work, Prochaska et al. (1994) and Prochaska and Norcross (2018) assert that this model has been found applicable in multiple contexts of necessary change, for example, in the treatment and support of delinquents, drug addiction, alcoholism, depression, anxiety and panic disorders and health-related change. The reason this is the case, established in their research, is that the principles of change can be transferred from one context to another.

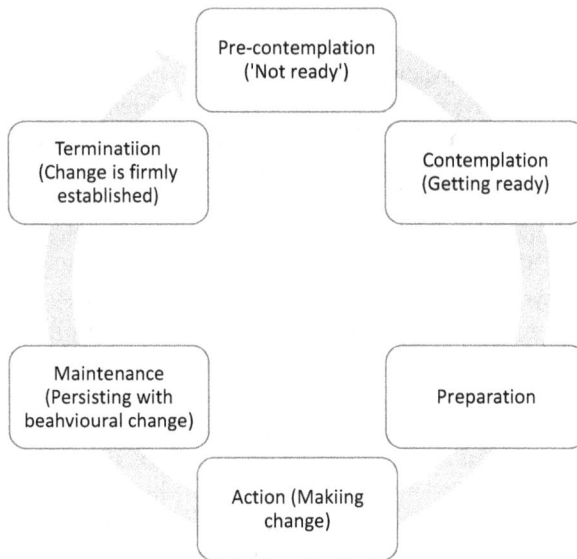

Figure 7.1 The six stages of change.

The stages of change

Prochaska and Norcross (2018) describe the stages of change as constellations of intention, attitudes and behaviours that reflect the individual's readiness for change. Prochaska et al. (1994) portray the stages as likely to involve periods of time and tasks to be accomplished before proceeding to the next stage. They emphasise from their research and clinical experience that many programmes of change work on an assumption of readiness and the task being one of moving to 'action'. A remarkably human quality of their work is the recognition embedded in the stages that we may not be contemplating or seeking change – or we may only be contemplating it – let alone preparing for and moving into change.

The six stages of change are illustrated in figure 7.1:

In highlighting the reality and humanity of change, they describe how, in some instances of change, we might get stuck at a stage and not progress. Yet realising that some circumstances in our lives might be long-standing to move from not contemplating change to contemplating action may be an achievement in its own right and create a possibility for eventual action on change.

Prochaska et al. emphasise that a key use of these concepts is to know what stage of change we are in, as this is, in turn, an indication of readiness and the type of processes of change that may be needed within them. Further, they pro-pose research-based timescales indicative of those needed or applying to progress within a stage. Prochaska and Prochaska (2016) offer a range of questionnaires to support an exploration of the stages later. A summary of the stages of change is as follows:

Pre-contemplation

This stage may have different qualities or characteristics which illustrate the humanity of change and the need for compassion and awareness as we approach it either as facilitators or those seeking change. If you are, for example, a positive psychology practitioner proposing a form of change reflected in a PPI, then an individual or group may have no awareness, consciousness or motivation for change to perceive the relevance of this suggestion. There is an educative task in establishing whether and why change should be undertaken at all, prior to action.

If the change relates to moving from some form of 'problem state', an individual may not be aware or resisting awareness of the difficulty needing change. The behavioural choice to be where they are would have made sense to an individual at some point in time and they may not perceive this rationale has changed. An individual may be aware of difficulty yet lack information or understanding about how to change; they may overestimate costs of change and underestimate benefits or gains (Prochaska, 1999). Through this, they may feel unready, disempowered or resistant to change. Alternatively, they may be demoralised because in the absence of awareness of the problem or how to change, there could be a sense of hopelessness. This may bring about behaviour that is defensive and distant about the prospect of change. Therefore, there may be a sense that the 'cons' for change are overwhelming; the 'pros', the reasons for change, must develop and increase. In this situation, 'action' may be distant, and the immediate need being one of education. Prochaska proposes that the step from 'precontemplation' to 'contemplation' may be the biggest in the model overall (Prochaska et al., 1994; Prochaska, 1999; Prochaska & Prochaska, 2016; Prochaska & Norcross, 2018).

Contemplation

This stage involves an awareness and even an acknowledgement of a problem or need to change, but not yet a decision to do so. Yet, there may also potentially be a lack of understanding of the problem state or the nature of the change – of causes, implications and possible solutions. Both pros and cons for change are evident. An individual may have uncertainty over the balance of them. The skill is to decrease the cons. Doubt exists which may, in turn, impact the motivation for change. Contemplating change can become habitual, even chronic – if no action is taken, there is no risk of failure. Alternatively, a risk is this stage may be rushed. Prochaska et al. (1994) propose that the indicator of readiness to move from contemplation to preparation is a shift of time focus, to the future rather than the past, and the solution possibilities, rather than the problem past (Prochaska et al., 1994; Prochaska, 1999; Prochaska & Prochaska, 2016; Prochaska & Norcross, 2018).

Preparation

For individuals in the preparation stage, a decision has been made to undertake intentional change. Planning for change is practical and likely to be well advanced and based on a move to action within a small number of weeks. This will be focused on the effort and demands needed for change. In this, and any of the stages, it involves putting *processes of change* in place relevant to the needs of a *stage* and ensuring that we have learned them sufficiently to support the action and maintenance stages that follow. Prochaska and his colleagues are specific that preparation rushed or not prioritised will tend to lead to a subsequent failure to achieve change. Planning and preparation involve a rational and emotional consideration of the 'before' and 'after' of change, what could be termed the 'ecology' or circumstance of the change and its implications (Prochaska et al., 1994; Prochaska, 1999; Prochaska & Prochaska, 2016; Prochaska & Norcross, 2018).

Action

In this stage, the focus is on changed behaviour, and if needed, the environment necessary to support this. Action is a combination of cognitive and behavioural methods focused and channelled into the processes of change. Action needs time, focus, skills and energy and is likely to be visible to others. We need to learn from and adjust to experience. We need to distinguish between action towards change and achieved change. This stage may involve the earliest experiences of change and the need to learn and adjust as we go. Prochaska and colleagues propose that where 'at risk' behaviours are involved, this stage will need at least six months of effort.

The processes involved in 'action' involve a belief in our ability to change and an intention to act on that belief. Commitment to making a change may need subsequent adjusting based on the experience of change and making improvements in choices based on experience gained (Prochaska et al., 1994; Prochaska, 1999; Prochaska & Prochaska, 2016; Prochaska & Norcross, 2018).

Maintenance

Prochaska and colleagues invite any reader to consider the meaning of the word 'maintenance': to maintain a chosen change and to keep this effort and experience in a good condition. When experience has been gained from action, and change is being achieved, then this phase involves supporting and consolidating what has been learned and changed. Additionally, it involves having coping methods to adjust to stress or distress that may emerge in change. Maintenance is a continuing of change and a consolidation of gains already achieved. They advocate developing a resource of positive substitutes or choices to be used in place of earlier coping methods which might have been unhealthy. Prochaska et al. highlight that comparable energy is needed to maintain change as it is to initiate it in the action stage. Further, that without concerted focus and time invested in maintenance some form or 'relapse' to earlier stages is possible and likely. The skills associated with responding to a relapse include recognising it as part of the overall process rather than 'failure' and learning to perceive and deal with the stresses or pressures that change may involve. The authors are striking in their humanity recognising in the face of difficulties that may occur in this stage, action towards change will be done at the individual's own pace (Prochaska et al., 1994; Prochaska, 1999; Prochaska & Prochaska, 2016; Prochaska & Norcross, 2018).

Termination

This phase represents change as being established and that an earlier problem or at-risk state is no longer a 'threat'. This implies an individual will have confidence in their own capability and self-efficacy in avoiding a return to earlier states.

Summary of processes of change

In his analysis of many different forms of psychotherapy, Prochaska (1979) and Prochaska and DiClemente (1984) assert that there are a small number of processes within their work that are common to all. Prochaska and Norcross (2018) assert that 35 years of research has demonstrated the presence of these processes and that they link to specific stages of change. They argue that to make sense of and find some common ground between many theories of psychotherapy, there has to be an identification of the common processes through which clients, and we as human beings, change. This argument and the research that underpins it is one of the primary creative contributions of the model of change led by Prochaska over time. An example of the research-driven nature of their work is that the proposed processes have been amended over time (e.g. Prochaska & DiClemente, 1982, 1983; Prochaska et al., 1994).

Table 7.1 is an adaptation and development of ideas contained in Prochaska et al. (1994), pages 26 and 33. These processes are described in detail in Prochaska et al. (1994) and Prochaska and Prochaska (2016), the latter involving and offering detailed questionnaires and descriptions of a process supportive of individuals seeking change or practitioners supporting change. Readers are encouraged to look at the work of James Prochaska and colleagues to obtain detailed descriptions. See the reference list at the end of the chapter.

With processes of change established, Prochaska describes turning to research based on successful self-changer feedback to determine the stages of change itself. He, and we, would find it striking how specific processes of change related to specific stages and situations of change – using a process at the right and relevant time and action (e.g. Prochaska & DiClemente, 1984). Additionally, Prochaska (1999) highlights that the use of the 'wrong' process at a point in time may stimulate resistance in the change-seeker.

Table 7.1 Summary of the processes of change

Primary Process of Change	Example of possible content
Consciousness raising	Information about self, context or change desired. Increasing consciousness through this. Asking questions to gain insight. Clarifying goals associated with change A release of difficult emotions associated with current circumstances
Social liberation	Creating an awareness and imagination of alternatives in a changed social context. Giving oneself 'permission' to change. Finding others who will support your change
Emotional arousal	A focus on emotions in the current context, positive and negative, and the balance of anticipated emotions in the changed context. Finding and creating emotional energy that can be harnessed to support change
Self-re-evaluation	Identifying needed feedback, and unhelpful thoughts or behaviours associated with the desired change. Considering the values that will support change. Goals that we move towards and away from. Re-evaluating yourself and the 'problem'
Supportive and helping relationships	Sources of information and support on the possible desired change. Professional and/or personal social support for the change process. A context in which you can discuss possible change
Commitment	A belief in our ability to change. A felt commitment and willingness to act. Commitment to a date and a process of change. Creating a plan of action
Rewards	Recognition of ourselves for the effort and change made. Recognition from others for the change
'Countering'	Identifying potential positive or healthy alternatives to existing negative behaviours. This can include ways of thinking and acting
Environmental control	Creating an environment that positively supports the direction of change and avoids the prompts for negative behaviour

Stages and processes of change

Table 7.2 links the stages and processes of change, and proposes possible PPIs. All of these proposals for the use of positive psychology in this context are speculative and would need research-based exploration in use. The majority of these ideas were created by a MAPP student group in 2019 – Clare Martin, Theresa Jaurequi, Margaret Rioga, Claire Farrell and Amelia Beddoe – and used with their permission.

Table 7.2 The stages and processes of change (with possible Positive Psychology Interventions)

Precontemplation	Contemplation	Preparation	Action	Maintenance
Consciousness raising	⇑			
Social liberation	⇑			
	Emotional arousal ⇑			
	Self-re-evaluation ⇑	Commitment		
			Rewards and recognition ⇑	⇑
			Countering	⇑
			Environment control ⇑	
			Helping relationships ⇑	

Potential contributions from positive psychology interventions

'Best possible self'
Strengths development
Growth mindset
Self-compassion
Gratitude
Snyder's model of hope
Change facilitated/created through personal strengths
'Grit'
CBT 'reframing', that is, 'ABCDE' process
'Broaden and build' positive emotions

Levels of change

A development from earlier writings on the model and evident in more recent descriptions is the acknowledgement of the TTM in discrete levels of change circumstances. They all reflect a 'problem' focus and imply 'at risk' behaviours; all are interconnected. The levels are

1   Symptom or situational problems
2   Maladaptive cognitions
3   Current interpersonal conflicts
4   Family or systems conflicts
5   Intrapersonal conflicts

(The level titles are from Prochaska & Norcross, 2018, p. 427.)

This chapter, and, indeed, this book, implies that the insights from this model may be a structure to support positive change, an idea originally reflected in Carr (2004). Carr makes a direct connection to the changes that occur and are needed in the context of our overall development and possible applications of this model, for example, breaking long-standing habits and dealing with pressures and conflicts that occur over time. Carr connects the TTM to our historical, contextual and personal strengths and proposes that they can all be linked to and drawn upon in our application and experience of the model of change – that our being and our responses are systemic and that these strengths will all reflect in how we change. Prochaska and Norcross (2018) recognise that the primary application focus of the TTM will start at the symptom or situational level. They acknowledge that the other levels are likely to imply older influences that may be outside personal awareness and are correspondingly more difficult to address given their potential impact on individual self-esteem as this proceeds. Perhaps that challenge or difficulty could be said of PPIs. The model of 'person activity fit' (described further in Chapter 9) used for the choices of potentially applicable PPIs for an individual increases the likelihood of a type of positive change being appropriate. My experience as a practitioner is that if some form of difficulty occurs in attempting the use of a PPI, then it will point towards a new and relevant question in the experience of the person exploring change, which can be an influence for further consideration.

The dynamics of the stages of change model

Descriptions of this nature run the risk of portraying change as linear and sequential. Prochaska et al. (1994) are touching in their humility and honesty in saying that they initially thought the process was linear in nature and then found the stages of change as a 'spiral' where our experiences may bring us back to memories or feelings related to earlier stages which, in turn, may need rechecking or attention. Prochaska and colleagues consider this to be 'normal', not a failure. The humanity of change is we may slip up or slip back at different points in our experiences before the capacity to move forward again. They propose that the only 'mistake' at this point is to be demoralised and to lose hope.

My experience as a practitioner is that individuals will often say or feel 'I am back to where I started' after some form of 'relapse'. My perception is that is never the case because all of us learn or change with a new experience. We might return to what feels like an earlier state, but it is always with the benefit of experience gained from which we can learn and then choose to progress change again. Prochaska et al. (1994) describe this dynamic as 'recycling' the stages rather than relapsing, a regression likely to involve revisiting the needs of an earlier stage.

Critical observations and evaluations

Prochaska and DiClemente (1984) acknowledge that their descriptions are based on the work and experience of *intentional* change that may be self-directed or occurring in a therapeutic coaching context. Yet they, and we in the context of writing this book, acknowledge that personal change may occur in lifespan developmental experiences. There is the scope, outlined in Chapters 2 and 9 for specific times in our lives, to create a context where the scope for change becomes explored and taken. Prochaska and DiClemente (1982) acknowledge that this combination of circumstances sometimes brings a conscious choice for change, or one that may be motivated outside our awareness.

Reviewing the literature for the purposes of writing this chapter, it is evident that the TTM is or has been used in a wide range of circumstances as illustrated in Table 7.3

(These example headings have been drawn from mention made in TTM literature and 'ebsco host' data base searches.)

Table 7.3 Examples of research-based application of the TTM.

Subject area example	Example Reference(s)
Addictions	Davidson (1998)
	DiClemente and Prochaska (1998)
Bullying and violence	Evers et al. (2007)
Exercise adherence	Husebo et al. (2013)
Financial difficulties	Xiao et al. (2004)
Increasing physical activity in young people	Callaghan et al. (2010)
Motivation to change in child molesters	Tierney and McCabe (2001)
Motivation to change in sex offenders	Tierney and McCabe (2005)
Multiple behaviours simultaneously	Prochaska et al. (2005)
Multiple domains of well-being	Prochaska et al. (2012)
Offender rehabilitation	Casey et al. (2005)
Smoking cessation	Prochaska et al. (1993)

Prochaska and Norcross (2018) acknowledge that approximately 4,000 research studies have been conducted on the TTM over the 40 years of its existence. In this, we see studies

- Initiated by Prochaska and colleagues to explore and establish the structure and dynamics of the model and to extend its use into new therapeutic areas.
- Reported by individuals and teams who have drawn upon the TTM in specific contexts.
- That have explored an extension of the model into new areas, and report on their measured success, or otherwise.

Criticisms or critiques I have been able to identify

- Challenge the stages of change as being discrete steps rather than a continuum.
- Question the time periods that Prochaska and colleagues allocate to each stage.
- Question the processes of change located in specific stages, proposing that some client groups appear to utilise them in a sequence different to the one proposed by Prochaska and colleagues.
- Question the effect size achieved by the model in specific groups.

What I would add or propose in response to these criticisms is

- The structure and time periods described within the model are communicated as emerging from research in therapeutic groups and particularly self-changers in research conducted by Prochaska and colleagues.
- A working ethos commented on repeatedly by Prochaska et al. (1994) and Prochaska and Prochaska (2016) is that as supporters of change *they take the client and their experience wherever it is*. Stated in a different way, they appear to communicate an approach, humanity and compassion in a way of working that is grounded in a client-centred perspective. This would argue that their model is not bound by a proscriptive way of working alone but can be adjusted to the status of the client. Therefore, while their research argues for a structure underpinned by periods of research-based time and processes, they adjust as clinicians in practice with their client.
- It is evident from literature that comes through data base searches that extensions to the use of the model continue to occur.

As mentioned in the introduction of this chapter, its intention is to offer a summary and introduction. A reader can gain further detail by searches of data bases such as ebsco host or Google Scholar. In my own searches, I used the name of the model as the primary words and, in addition, 'criticism' or 'critiques'.

If a reader wishes to look at examples of research and criticisms of the model, the following references are illustrative (identified and chosen by a MAPP student, Sarah Monk):

Adams, J., & White, M. (2005). Why don't stage-based activity promotion interventions work? *Health Education Research, 20*(2), 237–243.
Bowles, T.V. (2006). The adaptive change model: An advance on the transtheoretical model of change. *The Journal of Psychology, 140*(5), 439–457.
Brug, J., Conner, M., Harre, N., Kremers, S., McKellar, S., & Whitelaw, S. (2005). The Transtheoretical Model and stages of change: a critique: Observations by five commentators on the paper by Adams, J., & White, M. (2004). Why don't stage-based activity promotion interventions work? *Health Education Research, 20*(1), 244–258.
Littell, J.H., & Girvin, H. (2002). Stages of change: A critique. *Behavior Modification, 26*(2), 223–73.
Littell, J.H., & Girvin, H. (2004). Ready or not: Uses of the stages of change model in child welfare. *Child Welfare, LXXXIII*(4), 341–366.
Orford, J. (1992). Davidson's Dilemma: Comments on Davidson's 'Prochaska and diclemente's model of change: A case study? *British Journal of Addiction, 87*, 832–833.

This chapter

- Introduces and offers an overview of the TTM of change, including the stages and processes of change, and its origin in psychotherapeutic research and how successful 'self-changers' achieve their goals.
- Proposes how PPIs might be used and integrated within the model of the stages of change.
- Summarises uses and sources of recent research on the TTM.
- Explores and responds to possible criticisms of the model.

Reflective questions

How does the TTM reflect your own experience of change, personally, or in working with others?

Do you see this model as applicable to supporting group or organisational change?

Would you use this model in the 'foreground' as an overt structure through which to navigate change, or 'background' to support your own planning as well as use of other resources?

If you are working as a positive psychology practitioner, how would you assess an individual's readiness to take on a specific 'positive psychology intervention' – to enter the 'preparation' and 'action' stages?

Is there a part or perspective of this model you are resistant to using, consider why that is the case? What does the resistance tell you?

An existential perspective?

From the perspective of existential psychology, I would propose that the TTM prompts a focus on distinct aspects of our experience and seeks to draw us more consciously into their nature. It supports us in seeking an inner and outer orientation to what we wish to change in a period of time.

EPP has been defined and positioned specifically (Wong, 2004, 2010, 2016, 2021) as connected to our living the polarities and challenges of life along with its positives, becoming authentically ourselves and finding meaning and purpose in life. The TTM appears to have a structure for the support of change that is clear and usable and one which would support the acknowledgment and exploration of the polarity-type experiences. It is grounded in research focusing on stages and processes of change, is structured, while also having an advocacy of a client-centred approach.

Research questions or possibilities?

Might we explore, from existing research data, age ranges of TTM 'clients' to determine whether there is an association with the periods of transition and change predicted in lifespan developmental psychology?

How can the TTM be linked with a PPI to determine how it might support the achievement of positive change?

Resources

Prochaska, J.O. & Prochaska, J.M. (2016). *Changing to Thrive*. Minnesota, Hazelden Publishing.

This text offers a range of practical ways, often questionnaire based, to explore the circumstances and readiness for change.

Notes

1 Mentioned in Chapter 1 of this book.
2 The relational implications of being with someone considering change, or indeed ourselves, are explored in Chapters 6 and 8.

References

Adams, J., & White, M. (2005). Why don't stage-based activity promotion interventions work? *Health Education Research*, *20*(2), 237–243. doi.org/10.1093/her/cyg105

Bowles, T.V. (2006). The adaptive change model: An advance on the transtheoretical model of change. *The Journal of Psychology*, *140*(5), 439–457. doi.org/10.3200/JRLP.140.5.439-457

Brug, J., Conner, M., Harre, N., Kremers, S., McKellar, S., & Whitelaw, S. (2005). The transtheoretical model and stages of change: A critique: Observations by five commentators on the paper by Adams, J., & White, M. (2004). Why don't stage-based activity promotion interventions work? *Health Education Research*, *20*(1), 244–258. doi.org/10.1093/her/cyh005

Callaghan, P., Khalil, E., & Morres, I. (2010). A prospective evaluation of the transtheoretical model of change applied to exercise in young people. *International Journal of Nursing Studies, 47*, 3–12. DOI: 10.1016/j.ijnurstu.2009.06.013

Carr, A. (2004). Positive *Psychology: The Science of Happiness and Human Strengths.* London, Routledge Publishing.

Casey, S., Day, A., & Howells, K. (2005). The application of the transtheoretical model to offender populations: Some critical issues. *Legal and Criminological Psychology, 10*, 157–171. doi.org/10.1348/135532505X36714

Davidson, R. (1998). The transtheoretical model: A critical overview. In: Miller, W.R., & Heather, N. (Eds.), *Applied Clinical Psychology. Treating Addictive Behaviours* (pp. 25–38). New York, Plenum Press.

DiClemente, C.C., & Prochaska, J.O. (1998). Towards a comprehensive transtheoretical model of change: Stages of change and addictive behaviours. In: Miller, W.R., & Heather, N. (Eds.), *Applied Clinical Psychology. Treating Addictive Behaviours* (pp. 3–24). New York, Plenum Press.

Evers, K.E., Prochaska, J.O., & VanMarter, D.E. (2007). Transtheoretical-based bullying prevention effectiveness in middle schools and high schools. *Educational Research, 49*, 397–414. DOI: 10.1080/00131880701717271

Husebo, A.L., Dyrstad, S.M., Soreide, J.A., & Bru, E. (2013). Predicting exercise adherence in cancer patients and survivors: A systematic review and meta-analysis of motivational and behavioural factors. *Journal oof Clinical Nursing, 22*, 4–21. DOI: 10.1111/j.1365-2702.2012.04322.x

Littell, J.H., & Girvin, H. (2002). Stages of change: A critique. *Behavior Modification, 26*(2), 223–273. DOI: 10.1177/0145445502026002006

Littell, J.H., & Girvin, H. (2004). Ready or not: Uses of the stages of change model in child welfare. *Child Welfare, LXXXIII*(4), 341–366.

Orford, J. (1992). Davidson's Dilemma: Comments on Davidson's 'Prochaska and diclemente's model of change: A case study? *British Journal of Addiction, 87*, 832–833. doi.org/10.1111/j.1360–0443.1992.tb01976.x

Prochaska, J.O. (1979). *Systems of Psychotherapy.* Homewood, IL, Dorsey Press.

Prochaska, J.O. (1999). How do people change, and how can we change to help many more people? In: Hubble, M.A., Duncan, B.L., & Miller, S.D. (Eds.), *The Heart and Soul of Change: What Works in Therapy?* Washington, DC, The American Psychological Association.

Prochaska, J.O., & DiClemente, C.C. (1982). Transtheoretical therapy: Toward a more integrative model of change. *Psychotherapy: Theory, Research and Practice, 19*, 276–288.

Prochaska, J.O., & DiClemente, C.C. (1983). Stages and processes of self-change of smoking: Toward an integrative model of change. *Journal of Consulting and Clinical Psychology, 51*, 390–395. DOI: 10.1037//0022-006x.51.3.390

Prochaska, J.O., & DiClemente, C.C. (1984). *The Transtheoretical Approach: Crossing Traditional Boundaries of Psychotherapy.* Homewood, IL, Dorsey Professional Books.

Prochaska, J.O., DiClemente, C.C., Velicer, W.F., Ginpil, S., & Norcross, J.C. (1985). Predicting change in smoking status for self-changers. *Addictive Behaviors, 10*(4), 395–406. DOI: 10.1016/0306–4603(85)90036-x

Prochaska, J.O., Evers, K.E., Castle, P.H., Johnson, J.L., Prochaska, J.M., Rula, E.Y., Coberley, C., & Pope, J.E. (2012). Enhancing multiple domains of well-being by decreasing multiple health risk behaviors: A randomised clinical trial. *Population Health Management, 15*, 1–11. DOI: 10.1089/pop.2011.0060

Prochaska, J.O., & Norcross, J.C. (2018). *Systems of Psychotherapy* (9th Edition). Oxford, Oxford University Press.

Prochaska, J.O., Norcross, J.C., & DiClemente, C.C. (1994). *Changing For Good*. New York, Harper Collins.

Prochaska, J.O., & Prochaska, J.M. (2016). *Changing to Thrive*. Minnesota, Hazelden Publishing.

Prochaska, J.O., Velicer, W.F., Redding, C.A., Rossi, J.S., Goldstein, M., DePue, J., Greene, G.W., Rossi, S.R., & Sun, X. (2005). Stage-based expert systems to guide a population of primary care patients to quit smoking, eat healthier, prevent skin cancer, and receive regular mammograms. *Preventive Medicine, 41*, 406–416. DOI: 10.1016/j.ypmed.2004.09.050

Tierney, D.W., & McCabe, M.P. (2001). The validity of the trans-theoretical model of behaviour change to investigate motivation to change among child molesters. *Clinical Psychology and Psychotherapy, 8*(3), 176–190. doi.org/10.1002/cpp.285

Tierney, D.W., & McCabe, M.P. (2005). The utility of the trans-theoretical model of behaviour change in the treatment of sex offenders. *Sexual Abuse: A Journal of Research and Treatment, 17*(2).

Xiao, J.J., Newman, B.M., Prochaska, J.M., Leon, B., Bassett, R., & Johnson, J.L. (2004). Applying the transtheoretical model of change to debt reducing behaviour. *Financial Counselling and Planning, 15*(2), 89–100.

Xiao, J.J., O'Neill, B., Prochhaska, J.M., Kerbel, C.M., Brennan, P., & Bristow B.J. (2003). A consumer education programme based on the transtheoretical model of change. *International Journal of Consumer Studies, 28*(1), 55–65.

Wong, P.T.P. (2004). Existential psychology for the 21st century. *International Journal of Existential Psychology and Psychotherapy, 1*(1), 1–2.

Wong, P.T.P. (2010, July). What is existential positive psychology? *International Journal of Existential Psychology and Psychotherapy, 3*(1).

Wong, P.T.P. (2016, February). Existential positive psychology. *International Journal of Existential Psychology and Psychotherapy, 6*(1).

Wong, P.T.P. (2021). Existential positive psychology (PP 2.0) ad global wellbeing: why it is necessary during the age of covid-19. Posted by Paul Wong | Jan 5, 2021 | Existential Psychology, Positive Psychology, Writing. Available online at: http://www.drpaulwong.com

Chapter 8

Developing insight

Andrew Machon

Insight is born of perceiving blindness.

Machon (2018, p. 63)

Learning objectives: at the end of this chapter, you will

- **Realise** how the extent of your vision and perception of reality are determined from the 'inside out' and can profoundly change in parallel with your evolving self-consciousness.
- **Recognise** how you automatically revert to seeing reality as duality and appreciate how this can create developmental dormancy.
- **Discover** how studying the myths of the gods Janus and Hermes can provide vital clues to how we can activate and enable development.
- **Appreciate** seeing the paradoxical nature of reality can illuminate how the acceptance of vulnerability can gift vital strength and resourcefulness.
- **Understand** how paradox can elucidate the mechanism and motivation of ST.
- **Realise** the vital role of love in the work of the practitioner and how this can permit unconditional self-acceptance and facilitate the developmental through the experience of 'being at one' with oneself, others and, indeed, the world around us.
- **Clearly recognise** throughout the chapter, how changing perceptions of reality from seeing duality, to paradox and ultimately, 'at-one-ness', can profoundly impact how we see beginnings and endings and if and how we develop.

Introduction

The content of this chapter has been developed from its conception as a workshop taught on the final weekend of a module titled *The Journey of Change* for post-graduate students studying for an MSc in Applied Positive Psychology. A central theme is how our perceptions of reality can profoundly change from within, in parallel to the evolution of self consciousness, illuminating how we can develop insight. We will also explore how our changing perceptions of reality can

DOI: 10.4324/9781003132530-8

markedly influence if and how we develop. We refer to how we view endings and beginnings throughout as an illustration.

This chapter is written with positive psychology practitioners in mind. This includes everyone interested in self-development and facilitating the development of others, irrespective of your level of expertise and experience. Worth (2017) correctly reminds that whenever we meet with someone, a developmental opportunity is presented. The question is, are we conscious and able to choose to practise or not? This chapter is positioned as 'a natural build' from the content of Chapter 6, which explores the nature of 'self as an instrument', the essential attributes, qualities and roles important to being and becoming a practitioner in Positive Psychology.

The discipline of positive psychology has continued to evolve and encompasses an existential perspective (Wong, 2004, 2016, 2017, 2021a). This invites a more complete examination of the nature of our existence and how we develop across the lifespan, as experienced from the inside out. We can marry qualitative and quantitative approaches to more fully understand and inform the nature and complexity of our existence (Lomas et al., 2020). This chapter is a conscious response to these invitations.

Let's begin by considering how we commonly view endings and beginnings. The sight of any gravestone highlights when the journey of the person begins and ends. But can this stark reality be a measure of a life well-lived?

Reality as duality

Reflection

> From your personal perspective, how do you commonly experience 'endings and beginnings'?

Take your time to respond before reading on. . .

Tolle (2005) acknowledges an affliction of the human condition that we are commonly identified with our minds, become caught in our heads and compulsively overthink. As a result, we may not see reality as it is, but more as we think. The Bible similarly supports that 'there is nothing either good or bad but thinking makes it so' (Matthew 5:3). We as humans appear to be unique in seeing our existence to be a problem (Yalom, 2008). The self to which we automatically revert, therefore, appears to be a compulsive problem-solver seeing reality through an analytical lens (Machon, 2010). Endings and beginnings, when perceived through this lens, equally appear problematic, final and absolute. Death is conceived to be our ultimate end and, therefore, something to be feared (Iverach, Menzies, and Menzies, 2014). As Williamson (1992) reports, we equally fear our potential greatness and power and doing so 'step back' from living life to the full. Either way, when we perceive reality as binary and conflictual, we foster an inability to either fully face death or live life (Yalom,

2008). As a result, we may enter a state of developmental dormancy, as we will now explore.

Developmental dormancy

'Turning away from' what we fear has a major developmental consequence. We become caught in a 'nether land', an 'in-between' state, whereby life can be lived but only in part. May (1983) describes how we can become estranged from ourselves. Whilst Campbell (1949/1988) explains how in resisting our inner calling, we experience a 'wasteland'. It is as if we sleepwalk through our days (Machon, 2008) not unlike *Sleeping Beauty* of the famous fairy tale (Machon, 2010) who was said to have slept for a hundred years. Alternatively, we may consider ourselves to be like a dormant seed – a *seed-self* (Machon, 2008) awaiting the right conditions for germination and growth. Notice these descriptors all point towards how we may unwittingly become displaced or distracted from what we may most want (Stein, 2006). Einstein aptly described the human condition as one of suffering an *optical delusion*. As a result, we can commonly be 'blind to our blindness' and may need to 'borrow the eyes' of someone in whom we trust to see our blind spots (Machon, 2005). Our compulsion to process may result in our perception of reality as duality selecting what we think is right and rejecting and pushing away what we judge to be unwanted, bad, wrong and/or weak. What we may overlook, in our need to be right and safe, is how, in judging and rejecting aspects of ourselves, we divide our sense of wholeness, and experience separation (Wilber, 2004). In perceiving reality as binary, we appear to become caught within the very conflict we unconsciously create.

We are castaways on islands of our own making.

(Machon, 2018, p. 23)

How can we resolve this developmental conundrum? And to whom do we turn for guidance?

Mythological guidance

In a study of the myths and stories that have endured the test of time, we may discover vital symbolism and guidance to inform our own lives (Campbell, 1949/1988). Let's turn to the mythological gods Janus and Hermes to see how they may guide?

Janus

The visionary

The Roman god Janus was said to offer guidance into the nature of beginnings and endings. His presence was noted at important 'rites of passage' and ceremonial births. An expert in transitioning, he was agile and able to move with ease between passages and through doorways (Grimal, 1945) and equally 'bridge' different dimensions of existence (Holland, 1961). What particularly characterises the god Janus, and especially worthy of note to our inquiry, was his ability to see in two or more directions at the same time (Renard, 1953). Images of Janus characteristically show his head in three positions at once. This may offer clues to how we might learn to perceive reality differently. We have established how in perceiving reality as duality, we create judgement, bias and conflict, placing value on one side whilst rejecting another. The result of such critical analysis is a favouring of either 'this or that', 'right or wrong' and 'good or bad'. What if we could learn not unlike Janus to see in several ways at once, giving attention to both? This would add an **'and'** in place of an **'or'**. In the absence of any compulsion to judge, might we perceive reality to be more paradoxical than we may think?

Nature of paradox

Reflection

What is your understanding and experience of paradox?

How might a recognition of the paradoxical nature of reality inform your life and work?

Takes some moments to respond before moving on. . .

Paradox by definition describes how apparent contradictory features may actually interrelate and combine. Here is an imaginative description of paradox:

'If paradox were a person, then I would imagine a benevolent sage-like and peaceful character, in whose arms, opposites and difference would be embraced. Paradox would then hold together with empathy and love those aspects that appear to strongly oppose, be they right or wrong, while offering equal and considered space to both, without judgement and a need to solve. Through this quality of holding, paradox invites each of us to enter a third creative space, into which 'the something more' can emerge, from the rare encounter of truly meeting with, and facing, one's apparent opposition' (Machon, 2005, Section entitled Emerging).

Hermes

The inner mediator

Paris (1990) acknowledges Hermes to be an archetype of change. And, Hermes not unlike Janus was recognised to be an agile messenger and 'go between', who could navigate 'between-ness', transitioning with ease, the different realms of existence (Miller, 2004). Through Hermes, we may realise the essential role of the inner mediator in bringing about change. Mediation expands awareness, giving clues to how we may live more fully in the moment, creating the opportunity to respond by turning towards, rather than hurrying past our fears (Downing, 1993). This perception may offer hope for those recognising developmental dormancy as we will explore shortly.

The bridge

Agnel (1992) recognises that Hermes was able to 'bridge' two worlds. Mindful of the dream of Piers Worth during the composing this book and described in Chapter 1, might Hermes guide us to the developmental importance of inner 'bridging'? Hermes was mythically born, conceived of both man and god. Miller (2004) noted how his special winged sandals permitted swift and fluid movements, allowing him to mediate between the gods, human beings and the underworld. Also, a clue to the nature of transformation may come from his capacity to visit two disparate places at once (Williams, 1983). Hermes through 'bridging' different dimensions of existence was said to perceive the sacred in the ordinary, creating new possibilities for evolving consciousness (Stein, 2006). Miller (2004) notes that how Hermes has the remarkable ability to cross what we might think to be uncrossable, drawing our attention to previously unseen connections which we in our over-rational binary thinking, may have blindly overlooked. Through Hermes, we are drawn towards an appreciation of the interior and liminal spaces where transformation may occur (Stein, 2006). Further, Stein compares the nature of Hermes to the actions of spirit, who like the wind was powerful and impressive and yet equally subtle and invisible. Another ability of Hermes was said to be in writing, translation and the discovery of a new language. It was said he had the rare creative gift of being able to bring into a form what often resides outside of our human rational understanding, extending the limits of consciousness and creating distinctiveness (Palmer, 1969).

Key learning

What clues and learning might we distil from the myths of these gods that may guide and potentially liberate us from developmental dormancy?

1   The capacity to see differently is a central opportunity – to be able 'face into' what we would have judged and 'turned away from' may offer a vital developmental re-orientation.
2   The capacity to perceive paradox, to embrace and 'bridge' different dimensions of our existence and what we have judged to be contrastingly different and conflictual, may be vital to the development and how we change.
3   Becoming an agile and responsive mediator may be the key to unlocking how we can initiate and enable development.

Perceiving the paradoxical nature of reality

Chapter 6 highlighted how the capacity of the practitioner to enable development parallels changes in awareness and self-consciousness. And, how a mindful 'priming' is necessary for the activation of 'self as an instrument'. Further, how through this practice we can facilitate an inner role shift from a compulsive analyst and conditional doing to a responsive mediator and unconditional being. This transition, activated through the practice of refocusing and redirecting your attention inward, builds awareness of a new and emergent 'centre of gravity' within a place from where we can experience – consciousness-free from identification with any content (Tolle, 2005). This emergent centre of awareness is named the 'I–Self' (Firman & Gila, 1997, 2002). Assagioli (1965) describes the nature of the relationship between the 'I' (personal Self) and 'Self' (transpersonal Self) to be like a subject and its reflection in a mirror, wherein the two are more as one and intimately related, than separate. It may, therefore, not surprise that when we are consciously operating from this emergent centre of awareness, we can perceive the paradoxical nature of reality. The recognising of paradox and the emergence of the inner mediator may be vital to the initiation and fostering of development. What we may have once judged to be opposing, distinct and poles apart, can now in perceiving paradox be embraced. The work of Second-Wave Positive Psychology especially supports how apparent conflictual opposites may, in fact, be dynamically interrelated (Ivtzan et al., 2016). Might the discovery of this interrelatedness foster our own capacity to relate and develop? Let's examine this prospect.

'Facing into' what we have 'turned away from'

To name how seeing the paradoxical nature of reality may inform the work of the practitioner is to consider what developmental value there may be in being able to 'face into' what we have previously judged, feared and 'turned away from'. To examine what this may look like in practice, here is a case study that occurred during the writing of this chapter. My coaching client was progressing a major coaching and consulting opportunity with an international organisation and was comfortable that the content of our conversation be shared with you.

	"What would you like to work on today?"
Client:	"I have some strange feelings in relation to my work. I'm feeling overwhelmed and off balance. I have not felt like this before".
	"You are feeling overwhelmed and off balance, and this feels new?"
Client:	"Yes, it's a very strange feeling, as if my organs are all muddled up and going around and around here" – *he moves his hand in a circular motion around his chest and stomach.*
	"do you feel dis-orientated?"
Client:	"Yes *(pause)*".
	What ideally would you like out of our conversation?" – *I am inviting my client to set his own 'compass bearings' and goals, to be clear of his intention.*
Client:	*(long pause).* "I want to know what's going on with these emotions and I really want to find a good way forward".
	"How will you know when you discover your 'good way forward'?" – *inviting my client to go one step further to discover how he may experience success.*

Client: "I will feel better. I will be less anxious and more relaxed. And understand more of what's actually going on for me".

"You are clear with what you need – to discover what is going on for you with your emotions – and a way forward – so, where would you like to begin?".

Client: "I feel very off balance, very strange and a little frightened by these feelings".

"What are you fearing?" – *wondering if my client is willing and able to turn more towards his fear?*

Client: "I am fearing that I am losing control. I'm anxious and I am very rarely anxious. I'm not sure I have clear picture of what's actually going on, in my work?".

"You are experiencing losing control, feeling anxious and unclear" – *offering a clear non-judgemental mirror for him to see himself reflected*

Client: "Yes, it's true".

"What's it like to face into your fear?" – *I am wondering if and how 'facing into' his fear may potentially serve him?*

Client: "I feel some relief (*long pause*) strangely. It feels good to own that I have been feeling out of control and overwhelmed. And my emotional churning feels less now".

"Is owning your fear serving you?" – *I am curious again what opportunities there may be in 'facing into' his fear?*

Client: "Yes (*long pause*) I am feeling better and seeing things differently already".

"What more are you now seeing?"

Client: (*long pause*) "This may seem strange, but I am aware of new character inside me, who has just appeared – he's a Jester".

"A Jester (*we both share surprise and smile together*) can you describe him?" – *wondering if my client can come to know his Jester better?*

Client: "He's quite scary – he has a big smile – a big wide smile – you know like those clowns that can frighten you?".

"Yes (*pause*) so what will you call him?" – *I am aware the Jester can scare and create fear in my client and so I am curious if he can name and own him?*

Client: "He's 'The Jester', yes that's who he is – I will call him 'The Jester'".

"The Jester can be a bit frightening. Yes? Is there anything else you notice about him?" – *I am curious for what reason has he emerged?*

Client: "He makes me think of the Shakespearean Kings, he would be sitting at the foot of a Shakespearean King".

"What would his role be?" – *I am intrigued where my client is going and curious how this character may truly serve him?*

Client: "I sense he is the King's wise guide. He would be the one that the King would turn to for wise counsel".

"Indeed, every King should have a wise Jester" (*we laugh together*). "I wonder how your Jester will serve you as you move forward together?".

Client: "It's strange, I was wondering about that also (*long pause*)?".

"Might you ask him? *(we smile)*" – *I'm wondering if my client is able to practise having inner conversations with his Jester?*

Client: (*Long pause*) "He wants to help me, and can help me, if I let him (*pause*), he will calm me down, we can face things together, he will be a valuable guide".

"How do you feel about him now?"

Client: "I realise that I want and actually need him with me, though I have been pushing him away before, that's when I am feeling overwhelmed, I will now go to him for help" – *notice the 'turn around' – in facing into his fear, a vital inner character has emerged who he wishes now to remain close, rather than push away.*

"I am wondering if the Jester can help you right here and now?" – *can the client practise working with the Jester here – in this moment – now he is present?*

"*long pause* . . . I truly value his calming effect (*long pause*). He is consoling me with the overwhelming nature of the task in hand in the organisation. He is inviting me to come to him, to talk and to play/joke more often. To stand outside the madness and to talk with him more. Wow!"

"What's the Wow!?"

Client: "One of the issues I am facing is that when I am overwhelmed, I keep turning to my wife who is a very good coach. And I realise now, that I am over-burdening her with everything. I have been turning to the wrong person! I may be stronger than I think. I need to turn to my Jester for help, not my wife" – *notice how the client is discovering his own inner resourcefulness.*

"So, you may be stronger than you think – what are you learning?" – *I sense this may be a good time in the coaching conversation for client to crystallise out key learning.*

Client: "I am learning that what I need is what I was pushing away – the Jester. He's a god-send really. I was frightened at first, more frightened than I had said. The feelings have been keeping me awake at night, but the Jester if I turn to him, can help me greatly. He not only calms me down, but we can have some important conversations – some wise discussions. I am feeling much more resourceful now and happier"

"You were looking to understand your emotions more fully and to find a way forward – where are you now?" – *repeating his initial intentions at the start.*

"Yes, it's been a very valuable new discovery. I feel stronger now and the churning in my stomach and chest has almost gone completely – I feel much more in control and resourceful, with my new Jester beside me. I am happy with what I have found." (we *smile together*)".

"One more question, if I may? – Does the emergence of your Jester offer insight into the organisation in which you are working?" – *I don't want to miss the chance for the client to consider the emergence of his Jester in the wider context of his work in the organisation – going beyond purely the personal to consider if there is relevance to the larger system.*

Client: "Yes, yes, my organisation needs a Jester! or certainly the person in charge does, there is so much overwhelm in the organisation" – *notice how the clients own sense of overwhelm may be a mirror of that in the organisation.*

"I wonder what role your Jester might play in service of your work in the organisation?".

Client: "He may become the King's Jester, and help guide me, when I am working with the person in charge?".

"Maybe so, I am intrigued to know how all three of you get on – that's you, your Jester and the person in charge" (*we smile together)*".

Session ends shortly after.

The lock is your key

This coaching conversation may illustrate an essential developmental principle vital to the work of the practitioner. What we fear and 'turn away from' appears to create a *lock* that can confine and limit our potential. However, as this conversation demonstrates, if we are able to 'face into', 'make conscious' and accept that which *locks*, therein we create the opportunity to discover 'the *key*' to our liberation.

The lock is your key.

(Machon, 2010, p. 204)

Notice when the client owned and explored their fear, how a new and novel inner character emerged that invited a new way of being for my client, and who was developmentally valued and important. What was synchronistic, shortly after completing this coaching conversation and whilst researching the mythology of the gods for this chapter, I discovered a reference to Hermes as the Jester, Trickster and/or Magician, where he was described as a mischievous character who may profoundly guide and who can forge communications spanning what is known and not yet known (Stein, 2006).

Owning vulnerability acknowledges vital resourcefulness

Brown (2012) defines vulnerability as what we attack in ourselves and others judge to be weak, rather than face the emotional exposure of what we fear. However, as we have illustrated, being able to 'face into', and to own and accept vulnerability, may be a vital developmental re-orientation.

This raises an important question: if we are able to recognise and more fully embrace the paradoxical nature of reality, then might acceptance of vulnerability, reveal vital strength and resourcefulness? Brown (2010) reminds how we need courage to risk being vulnerable and disappointed. And, Tolle (2005) recognises how we may need to learn how to say 'yes' to suffering, to be freed from its grip. Osbon (1991) invites us to accept *all* that we may encounter if we are to experience life to the full. It may be of note that developing the ability to 'face into' and accept apparent limitation and adversity, we may paradoxically experience liberation and development. Brown (2012) emphasises that if we can normalise discomfort, then we may discover new strength and resourcefulness.

Being able to 'face into' what we would have automatically rejected may build emotional awareness, agility and a consciousness of our deeper values and motivations (David & Congleton, 2013). This capacity to accept and, in some way, invite vulnerability may also foster the development of self-compassion (Ivtan et al., 2016). Turning inward to what we may have rejected, we can begin to listen for an emerging inner voice (Valliant, 1977) and respond to an inner calling, surrendering to the guidance of an innate actualising tendency (Rogers, 1980). We may conceive that this 'turning towards' vulnerability to be a responding to a call to adventure, a key stage of the Hero's Journey (Campbell, 1949/1988; Ivtan et al., 2016). In summary, when consciously and courageously we 'face' what we might judge to be weak, bad, wrong, negative, 'dark' and/or tragic, the opportunity emerges for the discovery of vital strength, 'light', hope, optimism and inner resourcefulness. Hope and meaning may be discovered through facing vulnerability and tragedy, permitting the discovery of a tragic optimism (Frankl, 1985; Wong, 2001). This may also point towards the nature of post-traumatic growth and how we may develop through the processing of trauma (Joseph, 2012). Seeing paradox appears to reveal secrets to our resilience.

> resilience
>> befriending suffering.

Machon (2018, p. 100)

Let's now consider how in 'seeing paradox', we may also elucidate the very means and process of how we develop.

Elucidating the process of self-transcendence

Worth and Smith (2021) have recently reviewed the process and function of self-transcendence (ST) from many 'angles', recognising this to be a ubiquitous process that underlies development. Self-transcendent experiences represent a spectrum of possible changes that may vary in intensity and frequency (Yaden et al., 2017). ST is a process of 'making whole', redeeming and re-uniting aspects once judged to be unwanted. This involves a 'bridging' of the conscious and unconscious divide and creating an expanded self-consciousness and growing sense of wholeness (Wilber, 2004). Csikszentmihalyi (1993) described the process of ST to involve two stages, namely, differentiation and integration. Here, we will include a further third stage that of synthesis.

Differentiation

As previously established, the self to which we may automatically revert perceives reality as duality. As a result, we see reality not as it is but as we have processed, differentiated and composed of conflictual pairs of which we make critical evaluations. The value of differentiation is that in selecting what we judge to be right, we affirm who we think we are, fostering difference and a sense of individuality. Such judging and selecting equally fosters inner division and a sense of separation. Alchemy accurately describes this phase as *separatio* – one of separating out (Miller, 2004).

Integration

We have also explored how we can learn to facilitate an inward transition from identifying with the self to which we default (the ego) to discover a new and emergent centre of awareness the 'I-Self' (Firman & Gila). The 'I' as we have previously established is inextricably interrelated with Self (Assagioli, 1965) and becoming conscious of this centre of awareness and innate interrelatedness may account for our perception of the paradoxical nature of reality.

The remarkable opportunity of seeing paradox permits us to see difference differently. Conflictual opposites can now be embraced, and their intimate dynamic interrelationship is revealed and studied (Ivtzan et al., 2016). This discovery informs the second phase of ST, integration, a 'holding together' of what we may have previously judged to be 'worlds apart'. In alchemical terms, this phase is referred to as *coniunctio*, the uniting of opposites (Miller, 2004). Ivtzan et al. (2016) reminds us that one of our greatest opportunities for development in the Hero's Journey emerges from learning how to embrace opposites in a third creative space which can accommodate the value of both and open to 'something more' still. This leads quite naturally to the third phase that of synthesis.

Synthesis

Synthesis essentially involves the creation of novelty. We have established how the interrelationship between the 'I' and 'Self' can provide a vital 'bridging' of the conscious and unconscious dimensions of existence, and this creates the possibility for 'divine intervention'. Consciousness may 'flow' between the 'I' and 'Self', allowing aspects once judged and rejected to be potentially reunited, creating novelty and potential healing (Stein, 2006). This vital 'bridging' and 'bringing together' of oppositely charged pairs appears to motivate and power the very 'engine' of development (Miller, 2004). In alchemical terms, this phase is described as *nigredo*, whereby our attention is directed towards the unconscious by surrendering to the irrational and the unknown by creatively encompassing both our height and depth. This potentially enables a remarkable expansion of awareness, a 'going beyond' the rational to encompass the irrational, the ordinary to encompass the extraordinary and the personal to encompass the transpersonal (Stein, 2006). Synthesis is commonly marked and accompanied by the emergence of symbols, metaphors, images and inner aspects or characters, which are manifest through a calling towards novelty and originality (Miller, 2004). Through the emergent symbol and metaphor, novelty finds form and creative expression. Recall from the case study, how the client discovered a new way of being through the emergence of 'the jester'.

Marrying of science and alchemy

In recognising how the 'bridging' of the conscious and unconscious, the rational and irrational are a vital aspect of development; we are left to contemplate if the scientific approach alone can comprehensively describe and elucidate the fundamental nature of development? Could the inclusion of alchemical thinking potentially move us beyond he science? The alchemical vision of reality considers, for example, that all opposites are joined together by a ubiquitous 'connective tissue' – a 'subtle body' and presence that has a remarkable capacity to mediate (Schwartz-Salent, 1998). Might we, in marrying the scientific and alchemical approaches more fully, illuminate our understanding of development and reveal how the seemingly irreconcilable, may relate?

Love – being 'at one with'

We have explored the restorative nature of ST and how this involves a continual 'making conscious' of an original way of being and wholeness. Might it be that through the transcendent 'bridge' and the process of continually 'making conscious', we can increasingly free ourselves from the unconscious grip of the self to which we revert until we may ultimately transcend the ego in its entirety?

Brown (2010) describes this becoming whole as an expression of wholehearted living. What might be a measure of our restoration and wholeness? The presence of the transpersonal quality (Firman & Gila, 1997) and the character strength and virtue (Peterson & Seligman, 2004) of love may be one measure.

Reflection

What is the value and your experience of working with love as a practitioner?

Take your time to respond before reading on. . .

We have explored how through ST we foster a growing sense of wholeness. We may expand our conceptual boundaries, deepen our connections and capacity to relate and foster our relatedness with the whole of existence (Tornstam, 2005; Reed, 2008). What this may, in turn, create is a deepening inner experience of 'being at one with'. Tolle (2005) expresses how the presence of love involves a shift in perception, a recognition of oneness in a world of duality.

> love
>   when two are at one.

Machon (2018, p. 86)

The capacity to be 'at one with' may mark the extent to which the practitioner can unconditionally hold and relate to the client, in their uniqueness (Fromm, 1957). Being 'at one with' invites self-acceptance in the client permitting the exploration of being and becoming authentic. Here, the client may 'borrow our eyes' to potentially see and discover more about themselves. If you wish, you can explore from Chapter 6, how the 'authentic mirror' is a vital aspect of the self-instrumentation of the practitioner. Fredrickson (2013) supports the important role of the practitioner in expanding and deepening self-awareness and especially in broadening the emotional experiences of the client, from which they can then respond. Worth (2017) describes how atonement – 'at-one-ment' – is an important phase of the Hero's Journey representing a period where the mind has been able to transcend pairs of opposites, fostering acceptance and constellating the qualities of compassion and above all, love.

Developing insight

To conclude this work, we have illustrated how our perception of reality and the world we see outside can remarkably change in parallel with our evolving self-consciousness cultivated from within. And how we can, with a dedication to practice, learn how to inwardly transition from perceiving reality as duality to paradox and ultimately to experience an 'at-one-ness'. Let's examine how these different perceptions of reality not only inform our understanding of endings and beginnings but also if and how we develop.

Perceiving reality as duality

We have illustrated how, in seeing reality in a binary way, beginnings and endings appear absolute and something to be feared. The result is that we appear to become caught in the conflict that we have unconsciously created and become developmentally dormant, unable to fully face death or live life.

Perceiving the paradoxical nature of reality

When our compulsion to analyse ends, we may be able to perceive reality less as we think and more as it is. What may present is a recognition of the paradoxical nature of reality. In perceiving paradox, we can embrace rather than judge difference. Instead of a compulsion to analyse, we realise an unconditional presence and being. This permits a remarkable developmental re-orientation whereby we can now be attentive to what we have previously judged and rejected, and 'face into' what we once 'turned away from'. As we can face into, accept and transcend our fear, the prospect of more fully experiencing endings and beginnings presents. In our acceptance of dying and death, we discover the opportunity to live and experience life more fully. Acceptance of ending creates the opportunity of a new beginning, 'the fruit of each ending is the seed of each beginning' (Machon, 2018, p. 138). And, the opportunity to develop replaces dormancy. The ability to turn attention inward and inwardly experience, not only primes 'self as an instrument' (see Chapter 6) but also activates and enables development. In embracing difference, we can reveal the dynamic interrelatedness of opposites (Ivtzan et al., 2016) and how this may power and provide the very 'engine' of development. The capacity to conceive of embracing difference also reveals our deeper motivation to resolve and mediate. We can now give our attention equally to conflictual opposites, inspiring mediation, in marked contrast to the compulsion to analyse, bringing novelty, creativity and originality to resolving difference. We have illustrated how the developmental re-orientation of being able to 'face into' what we would have rejected and 'turned away from' normalises weakness, broadening our emotional awareness, replacing a compulsion to react with the choice to respond. Paradoxically, what we may discover is that what we once judged to be weak, if 'faced', accepted and included, can through the process of transcendence, foster vital strength, creativity and resourcefulness.

It may be poignant at this point to return to one of the vital questions posed by Positive Psychology today when viewed from an existential perspective; How do we not only survive but learn how to thrive in a world of conflict and crisis? Rather than seeing this proposition as a vital problem that we must in some way solve, might we instead consciously consider a change of perception? In seeing reality as duality, we appear to become caught in the conflict that we unconsciously create the very conflict that we then perceive to be a threat to our survival.

However, if we can learn to recognise the paradoxical nature of reality and can conceive of embracing difference, then the presenting conflict transforms from being a threat to an opportunity. Developing such insight engages the potential prospect for transcendence, whereby, as we have explored, a normalising and accepting of apparent weakness can paradoxically reveal vital strength and resourcefulness. Threat may now invite opportunity and to dormancy the prospect of development. What we ultimately may come to realise is that without a conscious awareness of conflict and vulnerability, we would not develop. To facilitate this transformative step from threat to opportunity and, in turn, from surviving to thriving, we are invited to learn how to develop insight and evolve our perception of reality. Recently, Wong (2021b) expressed how seeing paradox may be vital to our growth in times of crisis. This work wholeheartedly supports the profound developmental opportunity that perceiving paradox offers. However, it is vital to note how such a change in perception is 'fashioned', as we have established, from the inside out. Developing insight necessitates the cultivation of a practice of re-focusing and directing our attention inward (see also Chapter 6), a conscious choice that we are invited to repeatedly make and an inner practice that we are invited to continually refine over the course of lifetime. If we are to learn how to thrive in conflict, then this requires a dedication to the conscious inner practice of developing insight.

Being 'at one with'

We have established how the presence of love in practice may be one measure of our capacity to be 'at one with' ourselves, others and the world around us. From this viewpoint, the finite nature of endings and beginnings appear to dissolve, pointing us towards the infinite and the awareness of an underlying source and continuity of being – a 'being in flow'. How does this awareness inform our understanding of development? There are moments in practice when we experience a being 'at one with' our client. Moments of such presence, unconditional 'holding' and bearing witness, in turn, invites the client to be fully 'at one with' themselves. In such moments, when our clients see reality as it is, we witness the development of the grace of self-acceptance, and then, quite remarkably, change appears to be both effortless and inevitable.

Summary – this chapter has

- Revealed how we may learn to develop insight and profoundly change how we perceive reality, from the inside out.
- Illustrated how the self to which we automatically revert perceives reality as duality.
- Shown how, in fearing endings and beginnings we become developmentally dormant, caught 'betwixt and between'.
  Shared guidance from the mythological gods Janus and Hermes to how we may evolve the way we see to initiate and facilitate developmental change.

- Demonstrated how the activation of development necessitates a vital re-orientation, an ability to 'turn towards' what we once judged and 'turned away from'.
- Illustrated how re-engaging with development parallels the emergence of a new inner centre of awareness the 'I–Self' and our role of mediator together with an ability to perceive the paradoxical nature of reality.
- Shown how paradox can illuminate our understanding of a vital transcendent principle that appears to underlie development:

  - That 'your *lock* is your *key*' – in making conscious that which *locks* and limits, you discover the *key* to your liberation.
  - Accepting vulnerability, gifts vital strength and resourcefulness.

- Illuminated and elucidated the function, mechanism and motivation of ST.
- Highlighted the nature of love as a 'fruit' of development and dedication to practice and how love gifts the remarkable growth opportunity of being 'at one with' ourselves, others and the world around us.

Existential perspective

Through the chapter, the attention of the reader is drawn inward to an experiential exploration of the nature of our existence and how we may evolve self-consciousness, changing our perception of reality and fostering development.

Research possibilities

- To determine the extent to which we can enable 'changes in perception' in ourselves and others facilitating development.
- To examine the nature and workings of the 'bridge' between the conscious and unconscious in the process of development and if and how the marrying of scientific and alchemical approaches can more fully inform this study.
- To further explore the nature of love and, indeed, other potential 'fruits' of a dedication to practice and developing a sense of wholeness, including the nature of wisdom and faith.

References and resources for further reading

Agnel, A. (1992). Another Degree of Complexity in the Transcendent Function: Individual and Collective Aspects. Proceedings of the Twelfth international Congress for Analytical Psychology. Daimon Verlag, August 23–28, pp. 38–51.

Assagioli, R. (1965). *Psychosynthesis: A Manual of Principles and Techniques.* Hobbs Dorman.

Brown, B. (2010). *The Gifts of Imperfection – Let Go of Who You Think You Are Supposed to Be and Embrace Who You Are.* Hazelden Publishing.

Brown, B. (2012). *Daring Greatly – How the Courage to Be Vulnerable Transforms the Way, We Live, Love, Parent and Lead*. London, Penguin Books Limited.

Campbell, J. (1949/1988). *The Hero with a Thousand Faces* (Paladin ed.). London, Grafton Publishing.

Csikszentmihalyi, M. (1993). *The Evolving Self*. London, Harper Collins.

David, S. and Congleton, C. (2013). Managing Yourself – Emotional Agility. *The Harvard Business Review*, November.

Downing, C. (1993). *Gods in Our Midst*. Chesnut Ridge, NY, Crossroad Publishing.

Frankl, V. (1985 / 2004). *Man's Search for Meaning – The Classic Tribute to Hope from the Holocaust*. London, Rider Classics, an imprint of Penguin Books.

Firman, J. and Gila, A. (1997). *The Primal Wound – A Transpersonal View of Trauma, Addiction and Growth*. New York, State University of New York Press.

Firman, J. and Gila, A. (2002). *The Psychology of the Spirit*. New York, State University of New York Press.

Fredrickson, B. (2013). *Love 2.0*. New York, Hudson Street Press.

Fromm, E. (1957). *The Art of Loving*. London, Thorsons Publishing Group.

Grimal, P. (1945). Le dieu Janus et les originies de Rome. *Lettres D'humanite*, 4, 15–121.

Holland, L.A. (1961). Janus and the Bridge. *Papers and Monographs of the American Academy in Rome*, 21, 231–233.

Iverach, L., Menzies, R.G. and Menzies, R.E. (2014). Death Anxiety and its Role in Psychopathology: Reviewing the Status of a Transdiagnostic Construct. *Clinical Psychology Review*, 34(2014), 580–593. DOI: 10.1016/j.cpr.2014.09.002

Ivtzan, I., Lomas, T., Hefferon, K. and Worth, P. (2016). *Second Wave Positive Psychology – Embracing the Dark Side of Life*. Abingdon, Oxon, Routledge.

Joseph, S. (2012). Trauma Can Be Good for You, Says Psychologist Who Helped Survivors of the Zeebrugge Disaster. *The Daily Mail*, January 30, 1

Lomas, T. (2020). Third Wave Positive Psychology – Broadening Towards Complexity. *The Journal of Positive Psychology*, *16*(5), 660–674. DOI: 10.1080/17439760.2020. 1805501

Machon, A. (2005). *Just Beyond the Visible – The Art of Being and Becoming*. Croyden, Arem Publishing Limited.

Machon, A. (2008). *A Difference of One – Rediscovering a Loving and Creative Originality* (11–20). Penarth, Wales, Oliver's Books.

Machon, A. (2010). *The Coaching Secret – How to Become an Exceptional Coach*. London, Pearson Education Limited.

Machon, A. (2018). *Guiding Lights*: *Images and Words Inspired by the Aurora Borealis*. Penarth, Wales, Oliver's Books.

May, R. (1983). *The Discovery of Being – Writings in Existential Psychology*. New York, W.W. Norton and Company.

Miller, J.C. (2004). *The Transcendent Function – Jung's Model of Psychological Growth through Dialogue with the Unconscious* (117). New York, State University of New York Press.

Osbon, D.K. (1991). *A Joseph Campbell Companion: Reflections on the Art of Living*. London, Harper Collins.

Palmer, R.E. (1969). *Hermeneutics: Interpretation Theory in Scheiermacher, Dilthey, Heidegger, and Gadamer*. Evanston, IL, Northwestern University Press.

Paris, G. (1990). *Pagan Grace*. Thompson, CN, Spring Publications, Inc.

Peterson, C. and Seligman, M.E.P. (2004). *Character Strengths and Virtues: A Handbook and Classification*. Oxford, Oxford University Press.

Reed, P.G. (2008). The Theory of Self-Transcendence. In P. R. Smith & M. J. Liehr (Eds.), *Middle Range Theory for Nursing* (2nd ed., 105–130). Cham, Switzerland, Springer Publishing.

Renard, M. (1953). Aspects anciens de Janus de Junon. *Revue belge de philologie et d'histoire*, 31(1), 6.

Rogers, C. (1980). *A Way of Being*. Boston, Houghton Mifflin Company.

Schwartz-Salent, N. (1998). *The Mystery of Human Relationship: Alchemy and the Transformation of Self*. Abingdon, Oxon, Routledge.

Stein, M. (2006). *The Principle of Individuation – Toward the Development of Human Consciousness*. Ashville, NC, Chiron Publications.

Tolle, E. (2005). *A New Earth – Awakening to Your Life's Purpose*. London, Penguin Group.

Tornstam, L. (2005). *Gerotranscendence. A Developmental Theory of Positive Ageing*. Cham, Switzerland, Springer Publishing Company.

Valliant, G. (1977). *Adaptation to Life*. Cambridge, MA, Harvard University Press.

Wilber, K. (2004). *The Simple Feeling of Being – Embracing Your True Nature* (19). Boston, Shambala Publications.

Williams, M. (1983). Deintegration and the Transcendent Function. *Journal of Analytical Psychology*, 28(1), 65–66.

Williamson, M. (1992). *Return of Love – Reflections on the Principles of a Course in Miracles*. London, Harper Collins. doi.org/10.1111/j.1465–5922.1983.00065.x

Wong, P.T.P. (2001). Tragic Optimism, Realist Pessimism and Mature Happiness: An Existential Model. Paper Presented at the Positive Psychology Summit, October.

Wong, P.T.P. (2004). Existential Psychology for the 21st Century. *International Journal of Existential Psychology and Psychotherapy*, 1(1), 1–2.

Wong, P.T.P. (2016). Existential Positive Psychology. *International Journal of Existential Psychology and Psychotherapy*, 6(1), February.

Wong, P.T.P. (2017). Meaning-Centred Approach to Research and Therapy, Positive Psychology and the Future of Humanistic Psychology. *The Humanistic Psychologist*, 45(3), 207–216. doi.org/10.1037/hum0000062

Wong, P.T.P. (2021a). Existential Positive Psychology (PP 2.0) ad Global Wellbeing: Why It Is Necessary During the Age of Covid-19. *International Journal of Existential Positive Psychology, 10*(1), 1–16.

Wong, P.T.P. (2021b). The Biggest Mental Health Breakthrough During the Pandemic: The Ancient Daoist Wisdom Can Save Millions of Lives. *Einpresswire*, April 28.

Worth, P. (2017). Positive Psychology Interventions: The First Intervention Is Our Self. In C. Proctor (Ed.), *Positive Psychology Interventions in Practice*. Cham, Switzerland, Springer International Publishing. AG.

Worth, P. and Smith, M.D. (2021). Clearing the Pathways to Self-Transcendence. *Frontiers in Psychology*, April. DOI: 10.3389/fpsyg.2021.648381

Yaden, D.B., Haidt, J., Hood, R.W. and Vago, D.R. (2017). The Varieties of Self-Transcendent Experiences. *Review of General Psychology*, 21(2). doi.org/10.1037/gpr0000102

Yalom, I.D. (2008). *Staring at the Sun: Overcoming the Dread of Death*. London, Piatkus Books.

Chapter 9

Existential positive psychology interventions in and over time

Piers Worth and Lesley Lyle

Learning objectives are: by the end of this chapter you will

- Understand the principles and practices on which current PPIs are planned and delivered.
- Recognise and explore how the characteristics of established PPIs may change when viewed from the 'existential' perspective.
- Appreciate a summary of developmental changes that occur over the adult lifespan and how selected EPP topics and interventions might respond to the needs of different ages.
- Realise and consider a range of possible subject areas appropriate for 'intervention' support through EPP.

Positive Psychology Interventions (PPIs) – definitions, categories and changes

The rationale and composition of PPIs have acquired several definitions during the years of the discipline's existence (Worth, 2020). For the purposes of this chapter, the context and definition chosen are more precise than others:

Parks and Biswas-Diener (2013) proposed a precise boundary over what can be considered a PPI – they need to be based on a positive psychology construct and have research-based evidence (Parks & Titova 2016). However, they nuance this definition of a PPI more directly as activities, promoting positive outcomes through the use of positive processes.

Schueller (2014) extended this definition further in proposing the activities develop or draw upon our strengths or counterbalance for our sources of unhappiness.

Seligman et al. (2006) previously moved the concept and application of interventions into populations that may be clinical or experiencing some form of difficulty. They argued that the PPI should support the individual in coping with either negative moods or events (Parks & Titova, 2016).

Parks and Biswas-Diener (2013) and Parks and Schueller (2014) undertook two milestone reviews to identify the type and content of PPIs existing at their time

DOI: 10.4324/9781003132530-9

of writing. Both reviews identified six core areas for PPIs (**strengths, gratitude, forgiveness, meaning, savouring and empathy**). Parks and Biswas-Diener (2013) also identified **social connections** as an additional core area.

However, there are two further interpretations of this list that offer a deeper understanding of PPI contributions available. First, that interventions have been created and used as individual subject exercises (strengths, gratitude and so on as listed earlier) (e.g. Lyubomirsky, 2008) *and also* as clusters of exercises (e.g. Rashid & Seligman, 2019). Second, which is of potentially stronger importance, the majority of the core areas identified appear to be what are called 'positive traits' or 'positive psychology character strengths' (Peterson & Seligman, 2004). These are individual differences that are stable, generalised and, in turn, shaped by culture and settings. Yet, while this infers that they may be inherited traits, Niemec (2018) implies these traits can also be learned. Positive traits are core to and **reflect our identity, our being and activity** (Niemec, 2018). Both choices, individual or clustered exercises, seek to **influence some aspect of individual experience and well-being** (Worth, 2021).

The experiential nature of PPIs is that they involve engaging us in some aspect of what PP pioneers considered 'the good life' or characteristics of a flourishing life (Seligman & Csikszentmihalyi, 2000). In the act of that engagement in a structured manner, they open us to new information and create potentially new experiences for us as individuals, which may, in turn, involve learning new behaviours. In their connection to positive aspects of life experience, they re-train our attention and broaden our focus to more positive aspects of life.

The authors of this chapter infer that the descriptions above are a benchmark standard adopted for 'PPIs' proposed and taught by leading academics in the discipline. In offering a definition as specific as this, Parks and Biswas-Diener acknowledged that some exercises that may contribute to positive experience would be excluded by it. As authors, we believe this exclusion and boundary must now be pushed or challenged and propose that to develop 'EPP interventions' the definition will need to become more flexible to identify and explore appropriate subject areas in this new development of a discipline.

An EPP intervention

The common characteristics and structure we propose for an EPPI used in exploration for this chapter are

- A structured use of a specific exercise or exercises for the purpose of promoting positive outcomes such as developing our sense of 'being' and personal unfolding, finding personal meaning in life and opening us to new information and behaviour.
- Chosen construct/s originate or are represented and researched within Positive Psychology, Existential or Humanistic Psychology.

- These interventions offer the scope for accumulated research evidence that can, in turn, be built upon in the development of this new discipline.
- Targeted on developing or improving an individual state of overall 'being', well-being or altering a negative state, introducing new perspectives, ideas and behaviours, increased awareness, altered attitudes and understanding of self. In the act of doing these, interventions may bring about an 'expansion' of perception and understanding, for example, reveal previously unconscious or unrealised thoughts, ideas, beliefs, change and bring them to awareness.

We accept that this proposal is a 'first step' and may be explored or added to by other writers and researchers.

How do PPIs typically work? A PPI involves the experiential application of a positive psychology construct, and via the experience and learning gained, personal perception and attention and state change. Our interpretation as authors is the PPI is focused on an aspect of life experience. An Existential PPI focus would be broader into our state of existence, being and expression as individuals.

Figure 9.1 is a precis of the process outlined by Layous and Lyubomirsky (2013). This suggests that the operation of the PPI has a systemic quality in that

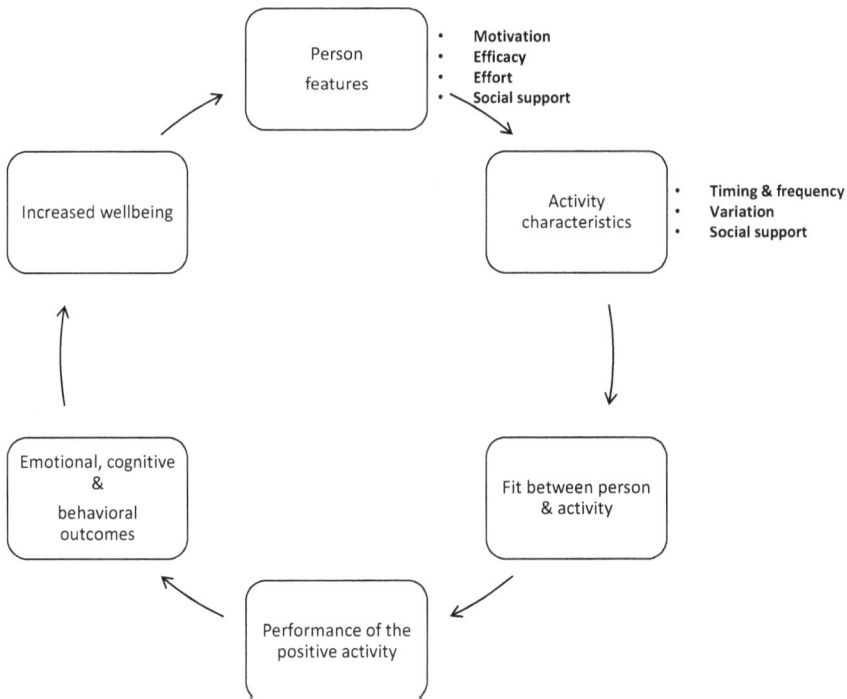

Figure 9.1 How does a PPI work?

the characteristics of the potential activity are matched to the needs and motivation of the individual with specific anticipated outcomes within the positive psychology construct involved. There is a period of time in which the activity is conducted which may result in cognitive, emotional and behavioural changes. Typically, within positive psychology constructs, this may result in a change to individual well-being.

It should be noted that one of the dynamics of exercises recognised by Lyubomirsky (2008) is what is termed 'the person-activity-fit'. This recognises that individuals are drawn to certain practices and not others. However, she more recently acknowledged that there can be a difference between what one imagines will be a 'person-activity-misfit' and the reality of a positive experience gained by putting aside pre-conceptions and participating in a PPI with an open mind (Lyubomirsky, 2008, p. 72). An EPPI may ask individuals to temporarily step outside of their comfort zone, so they can experience novel thoughts, situations and/ or environments. In contrast to exploring what is already known, this offers the possibility of gaining new information, understanding and awareness.

Schueller (2014) acknowledges that individuals gain fulfilment from many different aspects of their lives, such as personality, leisure and family lives. This being the case, it must be assumed that there will be a variation in what users of a PPI might seek or aspire to and, in turn, take and perceive as a gain or benefit. He proposes that research evidence indicates individuals will use part or a subset of the content of a PPI as their personal source of gain. Therefore, the fit of the PPI to the individual is critical on both of the earlier counts. This issue becomes more critical when one considers the culture within which the PPI and its user may sit. Pedrotti (2014) summarises facets of culture as including identity, race, ethnicity, gender, sexual orientation, religion, socio-economic status and disability. She proposes that individuals prioritise and define different aspects of the culture within which they exist and that these, in turn, contribute to the individual's worldview in personal and different ways. Yet, in the characteristics of 'existential psychology' and 'EPP', we might also seek to expand our awareness of aspects and experiences that shape our current context such as all the factors named earlier as well as going beyond our existing context. This is a further dynamic that must be considered in the design, development and application of an EPPI.

While the earlier descriptions represent a summary of established practice and perceptions in the application of PPIs, the change of attention to those with an 'EPP' perspective will deserve and need a new focus and application. Wong (2010) proposed that the discipline of EPP will take us back to our existential–humanistic roots. Chapter 1 outlines that this creates a revised attention to the quality of our existence and being, with particular focus on the commitment to the expression of our self, the polarities of our nature and experience and the unfolding development of our potentials. Implicit within the nature of existential or humanistic psychology or EPP is this process will expand our awareness of our nature, being and potential. The potential areas of focus are summarised in Figure 9.2 and 9.3.

Viktor Frankl Meaning-Centred Living Self-Transcendence	Rollo May 'Existence'; 'Being', '3 worlds'
Existential & Humanistic Psychology	
Carl Rogers Actualising tendency Core conditions for growth Fully Functioning Person	Abraham Maslow Self-Actualisation Peak Experiences Self-Transcendence

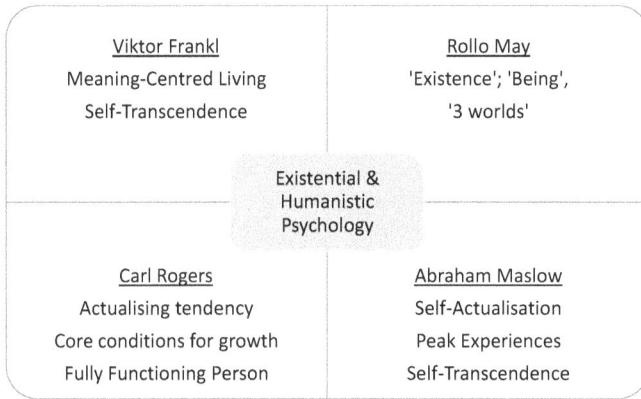

Figure 9.2 Areas of focus within existential psychology.

Existential Psychology: Key words

- Existence.   Being.
- Active committed living (passionate not passive).
- Response - ability
- Deeply aware and open in relating

Figure 9.3 Existential psychology 'keywords'.

Within Wong's (2010, 2016, 2021) papers, there are new areas of priority and focus that would not have been picked up in earlier work on positive psychology's attention on the aspects of a 'good life', well-being or flourishing that drove research-based choices of subject areas. New topics and subjects are needed for EPPI. Figures 9.2 and 9.3 illustrate areas to influence subject choice and development for these ideas.

Whereas many PPIs are generic in origin and offered as a 'one-size-fits-all' approach, an EPPI would potentially be designed and tailored or targeted to the needs of the individual. The focus of potential EPP interventions may have a focus of 'in time', relevant to a personal context in the present, or may also

Wong (2010 & 2016).

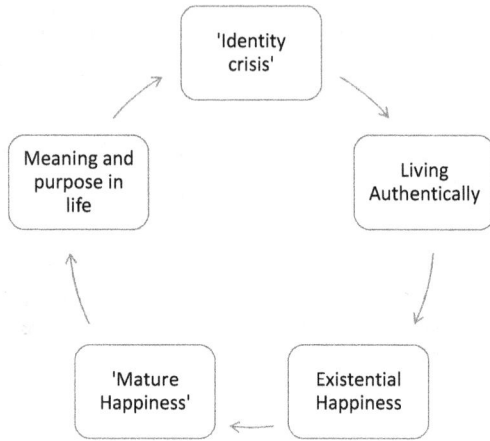

Figure 9.4 The structure and parts of existential positive psychology.

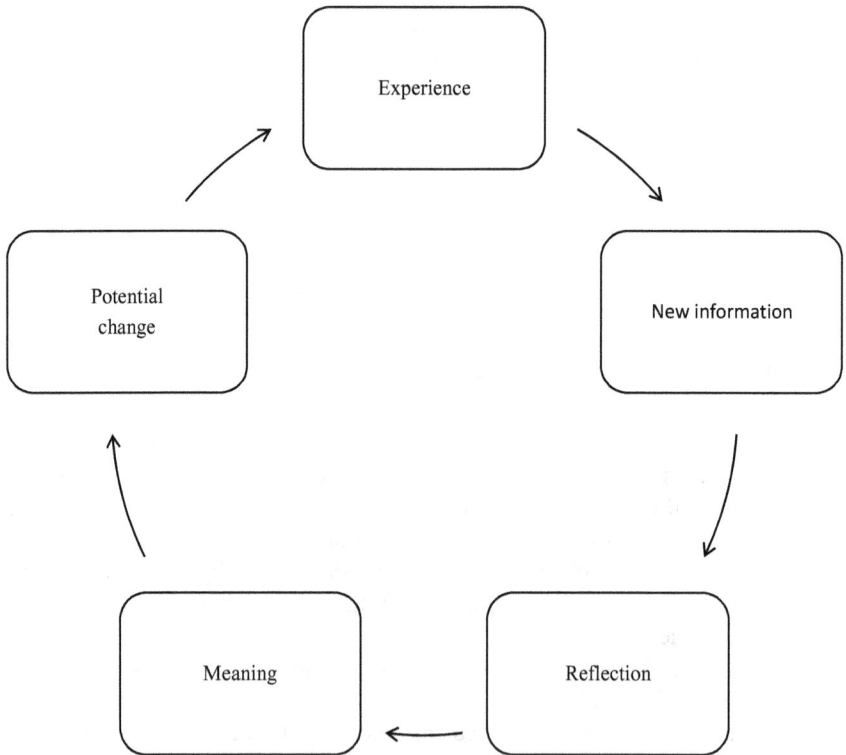

Figure 9.5 How an EPPI differs from a PPI.

involve explorations that will change and develop, particularly when the focus of unfolding time of our lifespan is involved. The five steps displayed in Figure 9.5 arguably represent a cycle through which we will travel in each developmental step of our nature.

EPPIs set out to provide experience and knowledge based on research but rather than focusing on a precise outcome 'to be happier', 'to be less anxious', the outcomes are broader: for example, 'to experience something new', develop our sense and experience of 'being', 'discover what this means to ME' and 'see some things from a different perspective'.

Whereas a PPI would generally focus on facilitating outcomes to support increased well-being, the intention of an EPPI may be directed more towards the elicitation of new information to increase self-awareness, life purpose and meaning. In this regard, the outome of an EPPI may be determined by the participant, that is, existentially based on there being no meaning to anything apart from the meaning we attribute to it. For example, a walk in the forest, a headache, spaghetti for dinner, a cat on your lap, a kiss on the lips, a haircut. In themselves, these experiences are meaningless, but we attach our own meaning when we experience them. So, the function of an EPPI would be to facilitate an experience, for the participant to evaluate the outcome, with steps taken within the structure to facilitate the reflection and understanding of the individual.

Maybe in approaching an EPPI, we will need an 'EPP attitude' – for example, the questions we ask ourselves about events? What can I learn from this? What else might it mean? Has something similar happened before? Does it matter? Will it matter in the future? Consider the situation/event from a third person perspective? What information might I be missing?

Prior to considering the detail of what this involves, the following section offers a summary of lifespan experiences over the decades, reflecting transitions and periods of stability. This will add a focus to the needs and contribution of EPP support and intervention over time. We propose that the EPP 'core' contribution is **managing, growing and developing our presence or attention, openness, insight or unfolding over time**.

Summary changes to life over time to which EPPIs may contribute?

Vaillant (2004) reminds us that in seeking to apply positive psychology to ageing, it is not only adding additional years to our lives but more life to those years. Health, and the life we lead, is bio-psycho-social, all three elements, and situated in the culture and history of our time. Nakamura et al. (2014) focus this further in saying each age phase in life reflects a culture of its own, framed by social contexts, class, ethnicity, gender, roles, beliefs, norms and expectations. The context in which the content of positive psychology is applied will have all of these influences, which ask of us a sensitivity and awareness to their experiences and meaning.

Table 9.1 Summary changes to life over time and potential existential positive psychology interventions

20s		30s		40s	
Transition	Stability	Transition	Stability	Transition	Stability
Exploring and experiencing relationships Choice of further or higher education Occupational exploration and experimentation Changed relationship with family of origin Patterns of adult behaviours 'Home' location, neighbourhood, culture Development of cognitive skills and personal values	Decisions explored and made Revisions and adjustments based on experience gained Gradual authorship of one's own identity and implied story Growth of fluid intelligence	A shift between exploring and experimenting with life choices and settled decisions Reviewing and possibly changing decisions of the 20s Commitment to expertise, work type and responsibility	Committing to gaining a form of expertise and knowledge Accepting increased responsibility Stability of occupational type (or coping with multiple work types implied in a 'gig' economy Narrowing and specialising our knowledge base An established personal relationship. Life style. Child rearing	Revisiting and adjusting life structure choices Contrasting the reality experienced with earlier aspirations Increased risk of health conditions	Relationships with partner and children Caring for ageing parents Growth of crystallised intelligence Prioritised strengths change as we age Entering the 'generativity' phase of life Being seen as and working as a more experienced workplace 'citizen' Readjusting our sense of life story

50s		60s		Older Age	
Transition	Stability	Transition	Stability	Transition	Stability
Adjustments to occupational choices Readjusting our sense of life story	Changing relationship to adult children Maintaining fitness and health Managing ill health Prioritised strengths change as we age Generativity phase of life	Readjusting our sense of life story Finding a balance between supporting and mentoring the next generation and learning from them Living the experience of polarities in ageing life (see later). As our bodies age, can we, in turn, stay connected to life, growth and engagement	Each of Erikson's developmental stage polarities (see Chapter 2) becomes part of life to encounter and live Reworking, resolving, reviewing, reexperiencing and refacing the balance of each developmental stage and emerging strength from this age onwards (Kivnick & Wells, 2013)	Readjusting our sense of life story Finding a balance between supporting and mentoring the next generation and learning from them Living the experience of polarities in ageing life (see later). As our bodies age, can we, in turn, stay connected to life, growth and engagement	As the time in front of us decreases, the focus moves to the experience and expression of the day. Meaningful engagement with the life around us Managing health. Being engaged with life while potentially also managing ill health? Managing experiences of the polarities – see later

EPPI Topics? Potentially all of the following. Re-storying the lifespan. Changes to the priorities given to strengths as we age. Development and adjustment to sense of purpose as we age. Creation of 'generativity'? Balancing the experience of polarities as we age, for example, Levinson highlights 'young/old', destruction/creation'. Plus considering how current PPIs need adjusting to different ages? Facilitating Erikson's final life stage? Living positive ageing?

2 The definition of older age is explored in more detail later in the next section of this chapter.
3 Kivnick and Wells (2013, p. 47).

The possible response to the question posed by the title of this section will be explored from two perspectives. First, Table 9.1 draws on the content of Chapter 2's exploration of the lifespan and thematically proposes what positive psychology content might be applicable, delivered in a manner that is responsive to the content of the age. Second, to draw on the review of positive ageing offered by Nakamura and Chen (2021) which suggest additional content for 'young old' and 'old old' ages.

EPPI Topics? Potentially all of the following: Re-storying the lifespan. Changes to the priorities given to strengths as we age. Development and adjustment to sense of purpose as we age. Creation of 'generativity'? Balancing the experience of polarities as we age, for example, Levinson highlights 'young/old', destruction/creation'. Plus considering how current PPIs need adjusting to different ages? Facilitating Erikson's final life stage? Living positive ageing?

Exploring the nature of positive ageing: Nakamura and Chen (2021)

The details contained in Table 9.1 have come from the content of Chapters 2 and 3 of this book, and earlier exploration in this chapter. In the weeks preceding the completion of this text, Nakamura and Chen (2021) published detailed insight and perspective on the nature of 'positive ageing' that expands the insight so far and points towards further possibility in older age. They pointed towards a combination of interpretation.

Baltes and Smith (2003) highlight that there is research evidence emerging from the Berlin Study of Ageing for two eras or phases in life occurring after the age of 70 that they call 'young old' and 'old old' age. They propose that the 'young old' are from 70 to approximately 80 years old, potentially later, and that 'old old' is from 80 years upwards. They suggest there are 'two faces' of ageing, gains and losses. While they propose possible gains occurring in the young old, they are blunt in their assessment that losses overtake and exceed opportunities for gain in 'old old' age. Further, that increases in longevity in these years are often years where living is under the strain of the losses occurring. They suggest that the increase in longevity raises the question of the challenge of physical and mental decline and the possibility of death with dignity in old old age, and what research and changes to practices may be possible to create positive change.

This interpretation put a spotlight on two aspects of how ageing is perceived and why. Tornstam (2005, 2011) summarised in Chapter 3 his view that younger researchers 'projected' their negative beliefs of the experience and consequence of ageing into their research evidence, particularly that of a limited scope for development. Gergen and Gergen (2001) added a concerning nuance to that view: that as we age, we live out, make real, the negative interpretations of the consequences of ageing held within society through the 'constructionist' perspective of development in which understanding is generated in relationship rather than purely factually. Despite that challenging and concerning possibility, Sheldon and

Kasser (2001) proposed that the Eriksonian phase of 'generativity', previously seen as 'mid-life', extended into the years of old age. Vaillant (2002) argued from the Grant Study of Adult Development that there is a dialectic that may express their view: generativity and care for the younger generation from the older, yet at the same time *to receive care* from the younger generation.

Gergen and Gergen (2001) observed many ways in which people may resist the assumed decline with age. They saw four interrelated resources: relational, physical well-being, mental states and engagement with life. Each resource is a doorway into 'positive ageing', one that has the scope to involve and interrelate with the others. They assert that the lens of 'appreciative inquiry' offered ample choices to emerge for the possibility of ageing well.

Nakamura and Chen (2021) point towards a spread of 'interventions' that have the potential to influence the trajectory and experience of ageing. They acknowledge that this is a new area of positive psychology work and advocate establishing a research base. Examples they propose include

- Mindfulness meditation
- Reminiscence, life review and life story interventions that may serve the development of 'ego integrity' proposed by Erikson et al. (1986) in this phase of life
- Exercise and activity focused on physical and cognitive well-being

A further potentially pivotal influence has emerged from research within the MIDUS study and based on Ryff's (1989) six-factor model of psychological well-being. Research is suggesting that 'purpose', coupled with 'positive relations with others', may have a powerful buffering effect on causes of mental deterioration in 'old old age' (Boyle, et al. 2010; Hill & Turiano, 2014; Lewis et al., 2016). These insights need to be incorporated into age-related future visions of PPIs or EPPIs.

Topic Areas and Characteristics of EPP 'Interventions'?

Driven and shaped by this review and reminder of the potential characteristics of EPP in and over time, the authors propose that there are distinct areas of potential contribution through which existential development and change may occur. These are summarised in Table 9.2.

We understand that this list is both new and, in different ways, invites additional clarification and definition. If we accept that EPP is a new disciplinary development, then it is a natural need to expand exploration over time. We propose that existing resources and additional resources will accompany the publication of this book through:

positivepsychologyonlinecourses.com/existential-positive-psychology website will offer the scope for expanding this area of practice.

This is a creative beginning for this new work and others may choose to explore and extend these ideas.

We also assert an additional step. Positive Psychology has developed as a discipline via its exploration of what has been called flourishing in life – aspects

Table 9.2 The table maps areas of 'existential positive psychology' with positive psychology interventions

EPPI Subject area	Examples of Current PPIs	New areas of focus and development in this context? EPP focus of attention	Age-related focus
Existential Psychology Key Words			
Existence/Being	[1] Mindfulness practices	Exercises which involve an increased mindfulness of our senses, particularly vision and breathing	Priorities and sense of purpose change with age
		Being in the moment with oneself; contemplation, exploration and self-awareness of inner thoughts, feelings and beliefs. Expressing and growing these characteristics	
Active committed passionate living	[2] Best Possible Selves exercise [3] VIA Strengths survey	Becoming one's potentialities, having a full realisation of one's potential	Noticing, exploring how Best Self may have changed over time and how we might choose it to change in future
		Be engaged in creative work	Prioritised strengths change as we age
		Link character strengths to the pursuit and actualisation of valuable life goals	Making choices aligned with values helps us live authentically
'Response-ability'	[3] VIA Strengths survey [4] Positive Emotion Intervention	Living in a way that is consistent with one's true nature and core values	Recognition we are who we are today because of our choices and the choices we make now will create the version of us that we become
			Perception and flexibility in our choices. Meaning attached to our choices

Awareness and openness in relating	5 Loving kindness Meditation	Relationships with self and others Holding others in positive regard, dignity, compassion, respect Self-compassion and self-acceptance	Relationships with others change throughout all life stages
Humanistic Psychology Key Topics			
'Self-Actualisation'	2 Best Possible Selves Exercise 3 VIA Strengths survey	Becoming aware of and realising one's current potentialities. The pursuit and actualisation of valuable life goals	Noticing and exploring how Best Self may have changed at different ages and how we might want it to change in future VIA survey for adolescents and adults
Self-Transcendence'	6 The Mindful Pause 7 Mindful living	Connection with something bigger than ourselves; improved engagement with the surrounding world; feelings of awe and reverence Exercises which evoke feelings of altruism, compassion, gratitude, interconnection with others	Strengths' priorities/expression will shift with age Commitment to a calling outside of one's self Increasing personal significance and self-worth
'Fully functioning person'	8 Life Summary 9 Building life perspective	Know and accept yourself – Be true to who you are (i.e., authentic) Discover one's own mission in life Creative values are based on what the person gives to the world, such as achievements and good deeds.	Integrate our sense of past and future that alters meaning in our present Meaning in life is a result of the meaning we attach to past and present events and circumstances We have to accept what we can't change and negative events We need to find a way to live with life's challenges
Core Conditions or Growth	5 Loving kindness mindfulness	Exercises to develop 'congruence', empathy and unconditional positive regard	

(Continued)

Table 9.2 (Continued)

EPPI Subject area	Examples of Current PPIs	New areas of focus and development in this context? EPP focus of attention	Age-related focus
Existential Psychology Key Words			
Phenomenological Field	[3] VIA Strengths survey	Distinguishing who actually are, from who we wish or think we are. The 'real' self is reflected in how we think, look and act	Research on ageing such as Tornstam's (2005, 2011) implies we may gravitate, move naturally to our 'real self' as we age; that we let go of external expectations and may relax into who we experience ourselves to be, and our shared humanity
Meaning-centred living	[8] Life narrative McAdams' Life Story Interview.	What sustains our being and makes life worth living? Pursue a life goal as a calling	Restorying life as we age and grow Priorities and sense of purpose changing with age Balancing the polarities in life as we age (Levinson et al. 1978)
Adjusting sense of identity	[3] VIA Strengths survey	Noticing, exploring changes to who we are over time and how we might choose it to change in future	An ongoing shift and adjustment at every life stage. A re-processing of our life experience occurs with each life stage, particularly in old age. We explore a long-term sense of who we are, and the balance of our life experience
Living Authentically	[3] VIA Strengths Survey	Awareness and application of signature strengths	Face the implications of old age
Authentic Happiness	[9] Character Strengths intervention	Exploration of pleasure and meaning gained from key aspects of our lives, social connection, relationships, spirituality	Understanding and accepting the true meaning of one's life situation

Mature Happiness	[8] Life review [3] VIA Strengths Survey	Finding balance between positive and negative experiences in life	Finding the capacity to overcome or live with suffering and stress. Achievement of mature happiness and flourishing despite the negative experience of human existence
Meaning and purpose in life	[10] PURE model	Purpose, understanding, responsible, evaluation Life questions us and in the act of finding meaning we take responsibility for our own lives	Drawing on MIDUS study findings of the buffering effect of purpose in life and positive relations with others on ill-health – interventions deserve exploration to propose these factors for older individuals and populations

Table References

1   Niemiec, R.M., (2012). Mindful living: Character strengths interventions as pathways for the five mindfulness trainings. April 2012 International Journal of Well-being 2(1) DOI:10.5502/ijw.v2i1.2

2   Sheldon, K. M., & Lyubomirsky, S. (2006). How to increase and sustain positive emotion: the effects of expressing gratitude and visualizing best possible selves. Journal of Positive Psychology, 1, 73–82.

3   www.viacharacter.org/ free character strengths survey

4   Falkman S, Moskowitz JT. Stress, Positive Emotion, and Coping. Current Directions in Psychological Science. 2000;9(4):115–118. doi:10.1111/1467-8721.00073

5   Fredrickson BL, Cohn MA, Coffey KA, Pek J, Finkel SM. Open hearts build lives: positive emotions, induced through loving-kindness meditation, build consequential personal resources. J Pers Soc Psychol. 2008;95(5):1045–1062. doi:10.1037/a0013262

6   www.viacharacter.org/topics/articles/a-mindful-pause-to-change-your-day

7   McAdams, D.P. (1993). The Stories We Live By: Personal Myths and the Making of the Self. London, The Guildford Press.

7   Niemiec, R.M., (2012). Mindful living: Character strengths interventions as pathways for the five mindfulness trainings

8   McAdams, D.P. (1993). The Stories We Live By: Personal Myths and the Making of the Self. London, The Guildford Press.

9   Niemiec, R. (2019). Six functions of character strengths for thriving at times of adversity and opportunity: A theoretical perspective. Applied Research in Quality of Life. DOI: doi:10.1007/s11482-018-9692-2

10   Wong, P.T.P. (2012). Toward a Dual-Systems Model of What Makes Life Worth Living. Chapter in: Wong, P.T.P. (Ed). (2012). The Human Quest for Meaning: Theories, Research and Applications: Second Edition. London, Routledge.

and qualities that support our development and expression. In the wish to ground this in research evidence, these have become 'interventions' with specific structures. Yet as illustrated in this book, and in this chapter, 'life' and our identity changes with time and age. EPP must be grounded in the nature of existence of the age of a person exploring and using it. This means 'one size does not fit all', and the expressions of these resources of psychology must be person-centred and age-centred.

Rather than measuring particular variables, we propose EPPI would focus more on the personal interpretation and meaning attributed by the participant and success would not be based or judged by any pre-determined hypothesis. Indeed, any observation or insight facilitated through an EPPI would be regarded as valuable and potentially useful information for the individual.

A PPI will often measure one variable and, as a consequence might ignore, fail to notice or overlook others. A gardening analogy for this would be growing plants. A PPI approach would be to select a specific seed, previously found to be reliable in producing a particular plant. Success would be judged solely on the quality of its health. Any random plants growing in the same pot would be regarded as weeds and ignored or removed. In contrast, an existentially oriented PPI could be likened to using a packet of mixed seeds with no expectation of what particular plant or plants would result but an interest in what and all that transpires. Even the non-appearance of plants would be considered interesting and informative.

The outcomes of EPPIs are not intended necessarily to be predicted as they rely solely on the experience and interpretation of each participant. The choice of intervention could be made on the basis of particular life stages, the transition and stability, or around a specific tenet of EPP such as identity, meaning, purpose and values.

It is likely that alost any PPI can be utilised and adapted to produce an EPPI as many positive psychology themes are shared in common with those of EPP. For example, flow, mindfulness, gratitude, love, awe, inspiration and peak experiences and others. The difference and outcome between the two approaches might be as simple as providing tailored questions for post-intervention reflection.

Creating EPPIs – Three examples

An EPPI would take into consideration the age and current life stage of the participant that would influence the choice of intervention and method used. For instance, a life review may not be as relevant to someone in their 20s who has limited life experience as it would to older participants. Individuals in their 30s might be more interested in how life choices affect their career; in their 40s, this may shift towards consideration of their personal relationships and during their 50s, they may consider how these relationships have changed/are changing and issues around health may appear. In their 60s, they may be interpreted past events with new perspectives, and during later life stages of the 70s and beyond, there may be increased challenges to health and the desire to leave behind a legacy after death.

The age might also be taken into consideration when choosing the design of an intervention. A younger person may typically be more interested to participate in an action-based intervention and comfortable with using personal technology, keeping online records and using mobile phone cameras and Apps. Whereas those in advancing years may prefer to participate in reflective exercises and those that involve a narrative approach.

Simply 'being'

Perhaps, a most effective EPPI would be one where the participant was required to do nothing – quite literally! Making time to just 'be' may be an intervention in itself. Time for reflection and introspection may seem an obvious opportunity for individuals to consider existential questions regarding all aspects of living a meaningful and purposeful life. However, in an age where many people report they have little time to themselves and feel overly busy with family and work commitments, free time might be scarce. Even when people do have moments of free time, it is likely to be filled with social media and using personal technology. Indeed, in studies involving more than 700 participants, the majority reported they found it unpleasant to spend 6–15 minutes alone with their just their thoughts (Wilson et al., 2014). This appeared to affect men more than women, and in one experiment, 64% of men and 15% of women chose to administer a mild electric shock to themselves rather than spend time doing nothing.

This is concerning from an existential perspective, as contemplation and exploration of inner thoughts and self-awareness are central to understanding who we are (Erikson & Erikson, 1997). Whether people have simply grown accustomed to always having something to do or deliberately avoid the possibility of confronting challenging thoughts is unclear but an EPPI to encourage reflective practice may be a useful way to start a meaningful conversation with oneself.

This may be as simple as asking people to just sit and be for 10 minutes. For some, this would be uncomfortable and an example of when an EPPI would require individuals to temporarily step out of their comfort zone to discover something new. With no instructions on what to think about any information gained from the experiment would be considered useful. Even the realisation of how uncomfortable it can feel to be a human 'being', rather than a 'human-always-doing-something', would be knowledge worthy of examination. Providing individuals with the opportunity to reflect on aspects of themselves or their past/present/future life might be a first step in developing the EPPI attitude referred to earlier in this text.

In other variations, participants could be asked to reflect on questions relevant to their age and stage of adult development. Mindfulness practice and somatic-based exercises, such as breathwork, could also be useful.

Intervention on narrative identity?

Identity is a central theme in existential psychology and a key component in EPP. Having a strong sense of who we are allows us to live life authentically.

In daily life not only are we *being*, which reflects who we are, but we are also in the process of discovering who we are *becoming*. We are constantly evolving because our physical and psychological state is never static or complete. Although individuals of all ages have been found to easily recall ways in which their tastes, values and behaviours have changed over the years until the present time, it appears that it is harder to envisage further changes in the future. In a phenomenon referred to as 'the end of history illusion' (Quoidbach et al. 2013), individuals imagine the person they are in the present moment will remain relatively constant without changes to their values and current interests. However, evidence shows we will all continue to change throughout our lifetime. Even though people change less when they are older, they still underestimate their capacity to change to the same extent as younger individuals (Quoidbach et al. 2013).

Our identity is an essential part of our development throughout life. PPIs around character strengths can help us recognise and utilise our values. Our character strengths are said to be a reflection of who we are and expressing our signature strengths has been found to lead to a number of benefits, including increased physical health, self-acceptance and autonomy. The free VIA character strengths online survey has been taken by more than 15 million people, offering both an adult version and one for children aged 10–17 years. Dr. Ryan Niemiec, Education Director of the VIA Institute, has also produced a number of character strengths interventions (Niemiec, 2018) many of them reflecting existential themes such as Meaning and Engagement, Positive Relationships, Goal-Setting, Achievement and Mindfulness.

In what he describes as narrative, identity, Dan McAdams (1993, 2018) explains how we have an internalised story about ourselves. It is the story of how I became the person I am today and the person I am becoming. Our individual story is based on the most memorable or extraordinary experiences we have encountered. Whether these are viewed as positive or negative depends on the meaning we attach to them. However, our opinions and interpretations of life events are subject to change, especially with the benefit of new understanding and a mature outlook that often evolves over time. For instance, in childhood, we may consider our parents to be strict and unreasonable about the amount of freedom they allow us, but later as an adult and/or a parent ourselves, we are able to see things with a different perspective and attach a different meaning. Narrative exercises such as a life review can help individuals make sense of their past and get a better understanding of who they are which may support their transition into a stable stage of adult development.

If we were to use a life review to help people explore their identity, we might consider adapting for different life stages, for instance. The questions 'Who am I?'

and 'What matters?' will focus on different issues at different ages and life stages. Examples might be in relation to family education choices (20s), work and personal relationships (30s), intimate relationships and generativity (40s), changes to work and health (50s), making adjustments for health and ageing (60s), readjusting a sense of life story (older age).

At any time in life, individuals may experience an 'existential crisis' when they will feel their identity is challenged, for instance, if one's sense of identity is bound to a role, such as a particular occupation, a role as parent or partner and is altered or removed through circumstances such as redundancy, divorce, bereavement or children leaving home. Although these events may cause upheaval and anxiety, this discomfort is described as being necessary for initiating a quest for authenticity and can be an opportunity for personal growth (Wong, 2010).

Intervention in our sense of spirituality?

Spirituality, a sense of being connected to something bigger than ourselves is an important element of existentialism. Positive psychology research has shown spirituality to be related to well-being and the self-transcendent positive emotions of awe, gratitude, love and peace (Van Cappellen et al., 2016). The Collins dictionary describes 'spiritual' as, relating to people's thoughts and beliefs rather than their bodies and physical surroundings ('spiritual', Collins Dictionary, 2021). For many, this will come from a specific set of organised religious beliefs, whilst for others, spirituality will be expressed as an individual practice that provides a sense of meaning. Exploration of spirituality will be pertinent across all age groups. What they are likely to have in common is an understanding of and connection to, 'something bigger than ourselves'. For example, being in nature provides the opportunity to connect with a sense of the spiritual by evoking feelings of awe and reverence (Niemiec, 2017).

As has been explained in previous chapters, there are many ways we can explore our sense of being and how to connect to the world and ourselves. For example, through the practice of creativity, meditation, mindfulness and contemplation, all of which could be utilised as methods for participants to explore some aspect of the world of nature.

Mindful photography has been found to be an effective way of increasing positive mood, savouring and appreciation of one's physical environment and one's life, in general (Bryant et al., 2005). Nowadays, the majority of people have access to a camera feature on their phone. (In 2020, Internet statistics indicated 84% of adults in the United Kingdom owned a smartphone and 95% of those under the age of 50.)[1] The expectation is that most people, particularly the young, would find this method of exploration easy to participate in and less formal than a classroom-based environment or an intervention that requires written notes or records to be kept.

Summary of this chapter

This chapter has
- Summarised the definitions of PPIs.
- Proposed the characteristics of an 'EPP intervention'.
- Indicated how our needs may change over the decades of our lives, in periods of stability and transition.
- Summarised implications of social expectations on the implications of ageing.
- Suggested possible areas of focus for interventions associated with ageing.
- Tabulated a range of 'existentially' focused subjects may be represented or served in PPIs and EPPIs.
- Discussed the potential and implications for two EPPIs – based on identity and spirituality.

Reflective questions

When you consider your 'being' or 'existence', what aspect of your life immediately comes to mind?

When you look at the table of possible EPP interventions in this chapter, which might come closest to supporting the exploration of your 'being' or 'existence'?

Existential perspectives on this subject area

This chapter seeks to take the content and direction of existential perspectives in this book closest to new ways of thinking, exploring and acting within existing positive psychology resources adjusted to this new context.

Resources

Consider turning to positivepsychologyonlinecourses.com/existential-positive-psychology website to further explore your interests and questions.

Note

1 www.finder.com/uk/mobile-internet-statistics#:~:text=In%202020%2C%2084%25%20of%20UK,is%20spent%20on%20social%20media.

References

Baltes, P.B. and Smith, J. (2003). New Frontiers in the Future of Aging: From Successful Aging of the Young Old, to the Dilemmas of the Fourth Age. *Gerontology*, 49, 123–135. doi.org/ 10.1159/000067946

Boyle, P.A., Buchman, A.S., Barnes, L.L. and Bennett, D.A. (2010, March). Effect of a Purpose in Life on Risk of Incident Alzheimer Disease and Mild Cognitive Impairment in Community-Dwelling Older Persons. *Archive of General Psychiatry*, 67(3), 304–310.

Bryant, F.B., Smart, C.M. and King, S.P. (2005). Using the Past to Enhance the Present: Boosting Happiness Through Positive Reminiscence. *Journal of Happiness Studies*, 6, 227–260.

Erikson, E.H., Erikson, J.H. and Kivnick, H.Q. (1986). *Vital Involvement in Old Age*. New York, W.W. Norton.

Erikson, E.H. and Erikson, J.M. (1997). *The Life Cycle Completed: Extended Version*. New York, W.W. Norton.

Gergen, M.M. and Gergen, K.J. (2001). Positive Aging: New Images for a New Age. *Ageing International*, 27, 3–23.

Hill, P.L. and Turiano, N.A. (2014). Purpose in Life as a Predictor of Mortality Across Adulthood. *Psychological Science*, 25, 1482–1486.

Kivnick, H.Q. and Wells, K.W. (2013). Untapped Richness in Erik H. Erikson's Rootstock. *The Gerontologist*, 54(1), 40–50. doi.org/10.1093/geront/gnt123

Layous, K. and Lyubomirsky, S. (2013). How Do Simple Positive Activities Increase Well-Being? *Current Directions in Psychological Science*, 22, 57–62.

Levinson, D.J., Darrow, C.N., Klein, E.B., Levinson, M.H. and McKee, B. (1978). *The Seasons of a Man's Life*. New York, Ballantine Books.

Lewis, N.A., Turiano, N.A., Payne, B.R. and Hill, P.L. (2016). Purpose in Life and Cognitive Functioning in Adulthood. *Ageing, Neuropsychology and Cognition*, 1–10. doi.org/10.1080/13825585.2016.1251549

Lyubomirsky, S. (2008). *The How of Happiness: A Scientific Approach to Getting the Life You Want*. New York, Penguin Press.

McAdams, D.P. (1993). *The Stories We Live By: Personal Myths and the Making of the Self*. London, Guildford Press.

McAdams, D. P. (2018). Narrative Identity: What Is It? What Does It do? How Do You Measure It? *Imagination, Cognition and Personality: Consciousness in Theory, Research and Clinical Practice*, 37(3), 359–372. doi.org/10.1177/0276236618756704

Nakamura, J. and Chen, T. (2021). Positive Aging from a Lifespan Perspective. Chapter in: Snyder, C.R., Lopez, S.J., Edwards, L.M. and Marques, S.C. (Eds.), *The Oxford Handbook of Positive Psychology*. Oxford, Oxford University Press.

Nakamura, J., Warren, M., Branand, B., Liu, P.-J., Wheeler, B. and Chan, T. (2014). Positive Psychology Across the Lifespan. In Teramoto Pedrotti, J. and Edwards, L.M. (Eds.), *Perspectives on the Intersection of Multiculturalism and Positive Psychology* (pp. 109–124). Springer Science+Business Media. https://doi.org/10.1007/978-94-017-8654-6_8

Niemiec, R.M. (2017). *Character Strengths Interventions: A Field Guide for Practitioners*. Boston, Hogrefe Publishing Corporation.

Parks, A.C. and Biswas-Diener, R. (2013). Positive Interventions: Past, Present and Future. Chapter in: Kashdan, T. et al. (Eds.). *Mindfulness, Acceptance and Positive Psychology*. Oakland, Context Press.

Parks, A.C. and Titova, L. (2016). Positive Psychology Interventions: An Overview. Chapter in: Wood, A.M. and Johnson, J. (Eds.). *The Wiley Handbook of Positive Clinical Psychology*. Chichester, John Wiley & Sons.

Parks, A.C. and Schueller, S.M. (Eds.). (2014). *The Wiley Handbook of Positive Psychology Interventions*. Chichester, John Wiley & Sons Ltd.

Pedrotti, J.T. (2014). Taking Culture into Account with Positive Psychology Interventions. Chapter in: Parks, A.C. and Schueller, S.M. (Eds.). *The Wiley Handbook of Positive Psychology Interventions*. Chichester, John Wiley & Sons Ltd.

Peterson, C. and Seligman, M.E.P. (2004). *Character Strengths and Virtues*. Oxford, Oxford University Press.

Quoidbach, J., Gilbert, D.T. and Wilson, T.D. (2013). End of History Illusion. *Science*, 339, 96–98. https://doi.org/10.1126/science.1229294

Rashid, T. and Seligman, M.E.P. (2019). *Positive Psychotherapy: Clinicians Manual*. Oxford, Oxford University Press.

Ryff, C.D. (1989). Happiness Is Everything, or Is It? Explorations on the Meaning of Psychological Well-Being. *Journal of Personality and Social Psychology*, 57(6), 1069–1081. https://doi.org/10.1037/0022-3514.57.6.1069

Schueller, S.M. (2014). Person-Activity Fit in Positive Psychology Interventions. Chapter in: Parks, A.C. and Schueller, S.M. (Eds.). *The Wiley Handbook of Positive Psychology Interventions*. Chichester, John Wiley & Sons Ltd.

Seligman, M.E.P. and Csikszentmihalyi, M. (2000). Positive Psychology: An Introduction. *American Psychologist*, 55(1), 5–14. https://doi.org/10.1037/0003-066X.55.1.5

Seligman, M.E.P., Rashid, T. and Parks, A.C. (2006). Positive Psychotherapy. *American Psychologist*. doi.org/10.1037/0003–066X.61.8.774

Sheldon, K.M. and Kasser, T. (2001). Getting Older, Getting Better? Personal Strivings and Psychological Maturity Across the Life Span. *Developmental Psychology*, 37(4), 491–501. doi.org/10.1037/0012–1649.37.4.491

Tornstam, L. (2005). *Gerotranscendence: A Developmental Theory of Positive Aging*. New York, Springer Publishing Company.

Tornstam, L. (2011). Maturing into Gerotranscendence. *The Journal of Transpersonal Psychology*, 43(2), 169 to 180.

Vaillant, G.E. (2002). *Aging Well*. Boston, Little Brown.

Vaillant, G.E. (2004). Positive Aging. Chapter in: Linley, P.A. and Joseph, S. (Eds.). *Positive Psychology in Practice*. Chichester, John Wiley & Sons Inc.

Van Cappellen, P., Toth-Gauthier, M., Saroglou, V. et al. (2016). Religion and Well-Being: The Mediating Role of Positive Emotions. *Journal of Happiness Studies*, 17, 485–505. https://doi.org/10.1007/s10902-014-9605-5

Wilson, T.D., Reinhard, D.A., Westgate, E.C., Gilbert, D.T., Ellerbeck, N., Hahn, C., Brown, C.L. and Shaked, A. (2014). Social Psychology. Just Think: The Challenges of the Disengaged Mind. *Science (New York, N.Y.)*, 345(6192), 75–77. https://doi.org/10.1126/science.1250830

Wong, P.T.P. (2010, July). What Is Existential Positive Psychology? *International Journal of Existential Psychology and Psychotherapy*, 3(1).

Wong, P.T.P. (2016, February). Existential Positive Psychology. *International Journal of Existential Psychology and Psychotherapy*, 6(1).

Wong, P.T.P. (2021). Existential Positive Psychology (PP 2.0) and Global Wellbeing: Why It Is Necessary During the Age of Covid-19. Posted by Paul Wong | Jan 5, 2021 | Existential Psychology, Positive Psychology, Writing. Available online at: http://www.drpaulwong.com

Worth, P. (2020). The Potential Use of 'Positive Psychology Interventions' as a Means of Affecting Individual Senses of Identity and Coping Capacity Impacted by 4IR Job and Employment Changes. *International Review of Psychiatry*, 32(7–8), 606–615. DOI: 10.1080/09540261.2020.1814222

Chapter 10

Revisiting positive psychology across the lifespan

An existential perspective

Piers Worth, Andrew Machon and Lesley Lyle

Learning objectives:

*   Before you read further, please consider your own learning objectives, what you would like to achieve and learn from this final over-arching chapter?
*   This chapter will consider the book in its entirety and draw out key insights, conclusions and learning that have emerged for the authors and the editor.
*   What will be highlighted is how this book both informs and moves forward the discipline.

Introduction

The original idea and proposal for this book were to place in print a teaching process we knew had a profound understanding for many post-graduate students and practitioners – an orientation to the lifespan that their training and experience to date had not offered. In the teaching and the original idea for the book, the subjects and chapters were individual, discrete subjects. We knew the impact and contribution from offering different forms of life 'context' to practitioners as they developed their application of positive psychology. The experience of that teaching shaped this chapter in the goal to highlight key aspects of this content that we saw most influencing those we taught, and some theories and research that students and readers at times overlooked.

Yet in the act of writing this book, we started to experience what we hope you as readers would – new understanding that we hadn't achieved before. We also made a choice to share our shifts and changes of understanding, a mosaic of insights gained, in writing this chapter to mirror or perhaps prompt changes you may experience as readers.

These insights have become part of the uniqueness of this book. In sharing how we came to make sense of the whole, we hope we support readers in their own sense-making process.

The uniqueness of the book is found in its title in three places.

Psychology as a professional discipline tends towards specialist areas of research and practice, which by implication are focused or narrow. For us to

DOI: 10.4324/9781003132530-10

choose to take a 'lifespan' perspective is unusual in its size, breadth of vision and the implication of 'wholeness' (Vaillant, 2012). It offers an opportunity to see life as a whole.

Positive psychology originated in, and has evolved from, specific subject areas that are associated with flourishing or well-being (Seligman & Csikszentmihalyi, 2000). To look at the lifespan *and* the potential positioning of PP across it is ambitious and a creative challenge to enter and create a new ground of vision, theory and practice in our specialist area.

And to do this with an 'existential perspective' enters areas of theory and application that are not yet seen as positive psychology and may be more associated with disciplines such as humanistic psychology, and psychotherapy – a significant step away from research-oriented psychology that is often drawn to aspects of life that can be counted and measured.

Therefore, this book represents new ground, new ideas – the 'bridge' described in Chapter 1 and pictured on the cover of the book.

We have made our best efforts to articulate these possibilities for the reader. We believe that we offer a sound and articulate 'start' of new application from which others can test, research and follow. This book is a beginning.

Yet, in offering these possibilities and perspectives, we want to acknowledge a further key step. You as a reader will be drawn to aspects of these ideas that matter most to you. You will put together and make sense of these ideas and combinations of ideas in a way that you choose and need. We are working with an openness, reflecting Carl Rogers' (1969) concepts of 'Freedom to Learn' that commits to supporting how you create something you wish out of these ideas.

Preparing this chapter – having written the book – introduced a new understanding: the sequence of the chapters as they now represent a connected unfolding of the overall intention to offer insight on the lifespan. This will be explained further in this chapter.

This chapter endeavours to draw key aspects of the book into one place. All reflect perspectives that draw on or are grounded in the 'existential', and lure us into our existence and being, and exploring that in its fullness.

The numbering sequence that follows mirrors the chapter numbers of the book.

1 Introduction to positive psychology across the lifespan: an existential perspective

The initial milestone change in the focus of the book, beyond our previous experience of teaching this material, was the incorporation of an 'EPP' perspective and grounding this in the theories of Paul Wong (2004, 2010, 2011, 2016, 2021). We looked at the form and shape this perspective would take in the experiences of our lives.

When one goes into the term and discipline of the 'existential', things change. I (PW) wanted to recognise this simply and clearly, so we had language for how it may relate to PP. The origins of existentialism in philosophy and psychology bring us to a spotlight, or 'reckoning', on what this term means. Hartman and Zimberoff (2015: pp. 62–65) offer the most concise and focused summary in our exploration of literature of where this would take our intention and goal of practice:

> Existentialism is a sensibility and perspective on life.
>
> Reflecting the writings of Neitzsche, the purpose of life is to really exist, not just 'live'.
>
> This involves a commitment to our talents and virtues.
>
> And through this, becoming the person we really are.
>
> This involves an energy, a passionate commitment. Living life to the fullest.
>
> Accept we have the freedom to make choices, and to do so responsibly.
>
> Take that responsibility: for who we are, how we face the world and what we do.
>
> Through this, we live authentically.
>
> All of this accepts life is shaped, socially, culturally and spiritually.
>
> There are no right answers to these questions, only our own answers.
>
> Meaning in life is found in living each moment.
>
> Commit passionately to one's life, purpose and relationships.
>
> In the act of facing death, we commit to life.
>
> 'Existence' is mirrored and expressed in our 'Being'.
>
> 'Being' is a state of presence, of open awareness, attention and awe.
>
> 'Being' is a presence of emotions, thoughts and relating.

If we allow ourselves to pause for a moment, and sense and feel what this perspective might mean if incorporated in our 'living', an intensity emerges, an experience or presence of being and living here, right now. This has a quality of life in the present moment. By implication, this might mean the need for awareness of the habits of our consciousness that define patterns of attention and perception, in turn, supporting or potentially blocking an openness to the present moment and those we meet (Worth, 2017). Echoing a term used in Chapter 1, this existential shift of focus would extend the reach of positive psychology and involve new areas of focus and exploration in human lives, and an energetic commitment to them, an energy from within us in daily life. This would draw out new ways of practising positive psychology, and for the methods of understanding its influence and effect.

Adopting Wong's (2010, 2016, 2021) exploration of EPP gives a focus and structure, a 'map' through which this may be expressed and explored.

We have been drawn to realise, to real-ise, make real, that an existential perspective is key. Without an existential perspective and the invitation to turn our attention inward towards the nature of our being, and outward to the nature of our existence – we may see development in a very partial way with a single outward mission – to gain the 'something more' that we want to have that we 'make believe' will make us feel complete and whole – the bigger house, better job etc.

Wong (2010 & 2016).

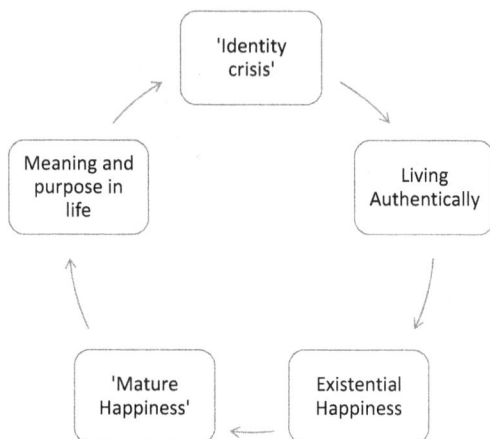

Figure 10.1 Wong's five-part model of Existential Positive Psychology.

But this is the wish of a 'partial self' (that may be blind to its partiality) and so will never be satisfied by such a compulsion. But as we evolve inwardly, this perspective may profoundly change to realise that the 'something more' we seek may be the person that we long to become (Machon, 2018). So, we initiate development by giving attention to the source of our development – being and becoming.

2 Change in and over time: our journey of development

Key to us teaching lifespan perspectives is the experience that many of us lose a sense of the unfolding of life and time around us. The first step in gaining a wider perspective of our lives in which the existential may be expressed is to see the form and shape that time and the phases of development may take, highlighted by key researchers, 'story tellers' of how our life experience may unfold. There is a goal and a gift for any of us to find a way of seeing the pattern, rhythm and nature of life changes we will encounter over time, not just in our past, yet in the future.

If we accept the research of Quoidbach et al. (2013), the implication is we may see retrospectively the extent of change we have experienced, yet be left with the sense that in the present we have become who we are, and the change that will come in the future is less. If this is the case, there is the risk or likelihood that we lose our 'bearings' and anticipation of what future life phases may bring to us and ask of us. This lack of anticipation or awareness does suggest that the process of ageing for us as a result may involve stresses, challenges and surprises. We might call this a form of existential 'blindness' towards what may be coming. Or as Erikson and Erikson (1997) implied – we might guess at the changes coming in later years, yet we do not know an 'age' until we have lived it.

Chapter 2 summarises five research-based theories individually; yet, the move to weave together their characteristics into an integrated backdrop was a revealing and moving perspective and more detailed than we had achieved previously. It allows us to understand patterns of change we will experience, and is a description and compass bearing of time now, and what may be coming.

These researchers all convey a pattern of eras, phases and stages within our lives.

An ancient text (Ecclesiastes 3) has words for what this might mean: it highlights 'to everything there is a season'. This is shown in the eras, phases and stages.

Each of these eras, phases and stages have a time-related content in the development of our lives. All will be culturally and historically situated. Each calls on us to explore and make decisions on what and how we will express in our lives. Each will also involve an alternating pattern of periods of building and maintaining an age-related and culturally based expression of our lives, and periods of transition in which we move towards a new one reflecting shifting changes in our life content, the process of ageing and becoming more mature.

Within these phases, we seek and adjust a 'life structure' that reflects our choices, decisions and identity (Levinson et al., 1978; Levinson & Levinson, 1996) within the stages and phases being described here.

It is important to consider the dynamics of these stages together. Erikson saw each stage as emerging from and dependent on its predecessor. Each stage is seen as 'grounded' in all the ones preceding it, and the achievement of an emerging developmental strength is expected to give new connotations or experiences to all the ones that had been experienced to date (Erikson et al., 1986). Nakamura et al. (2014) interpret the strengths in Erikson's life cycle stages, and the re-interpretation of them in time as reflections of positive psychology in practice.

This suggests a process that is evident in Vaillant's (1977, 1993, 2002) findings: we continue to process and re-understand our experiences over time – this adds to and changes our sense of awareness and who we are.

Vaillant identified within the Harvard Grant Study data empirical evidence for 'adaptive defence mechanisms' in the individual stories that acted as an unconscious adjustment to, and coping with, the experiences of life over time. These represented a process of adaptation to life (the title of Vaillant's 1977 text) and a maturation of the individual ego (1977, 1993, 2002). Vaillant (2004) was clear that their presence in research participants was associated with positive ageing.

He movingly defined the ego we develop as a precipitate of benign and positive role models experienced over time that become a form of identification for us (1977). As the study progressed and Vaillant reported further (1993, 2002, 2012), he expressed a defining perspective on ageing: that we become a 'sum' of all those we have loved and that as we lose others through life changes, illness or death, we must seek new people to love. This is a defining quality of our growth and capacity to grow.

Implicitly, this making-sense-of-self task never stops and becomes revised through life.

McAdams (1985, 1993, 2001, 2013, 2015) proposes that stories we perceive and make of our lives have multiple functions, including explanation, sense-making, entertainment, learning about morals and virtue and how to live what would be called a good life, as well as creating autobiographical memory.

Having established via research the presence of stories and their contribution to the understanding of self, McAdams has given us the gift of extending the ideas much further. He defines 'identity' as an integrative configuration of the self in the world (2001). The configuration brings together in the present time roles and relationships in a culturally situated world. Further, that the stories allow us to understand and adjust to changes we have experienced, to changes of stories, over time. The life story is internalised and evolving, focusing on reconstructed perspectives of the past and an imagined future which, combined, give qualities of focus and purpose in the present time (McAdams & McLean 2013).

Our cultural context will be a powerful influence on the content and shape of personal narratives (Erikson, 1958/1980,1963) and well-being.

Arnett portrayed for us how existing demographic and social changes created a shift in the late teens and 20s dynamic of development. He reports how early and emerging adulthood are a period of exploration and experimentation ahead of life decision-making.

Arnett (2000, 2004, 2020) suggests that the young person moves from emerging adulthood to what is now being named as 'established adulthood' at the age 30. If demographic and social changes are altering this age range in life, we must assume other changes are also influencing later years.

Each of the earlier research examples is based on perceived generalised patterns displayed in research populations. While these are a gift and a story of seeking understanding of the human life, they are generalisations, and they are also representative of an era in time, a point in history and a cultural context (Nakamura et al., 2014). There is another genre or discipline of research focused on drawing out the 'voices' of those from whom theories emerge (e.g. Freeman, 1993). In a time in our society where more focus and priority are occurring for those previously marginalised in our culture, the shift to exploring 'voices' is an important development and worthy of exploration. Suggestions, sources and resources are listed in Chapter 2.

If this offers us a sense of the 'what' and 'how' of our lives, an orientation on the pattern and rhythms over time, where is the 'why' of our lives, the growth over time?

3 Our unfolding journey of growth

This section offers a 'mosaic' of psychological theories reflecting how this unfolding growth may occur. Writing the chapter was a moving experience that highlighted what we felt were the potentially infinite number of ways in which we might grow in and across our lives. Yet, there are aspects, possibilities which are core that are summarised here.

Norton (1976), in a classic text exploring this perspective, offered insight. He proposed that the imperatives emerging from Greek philosophers were that we should know ourselves, and commit to who we are, as our destiny, and who we are to become. The inner self we were to discover was described as our inner 'Daimon', an aspect of ourselves that was inborn, from birth, our innate potential, there to be discovered.

Norton's words imply something not readily addressed by mainstream psychology: that we each contain a unique expression of ourselves that we are drawn to express and grow. Other psychological disciplines, such as the transpersonal, and the psychotherapeutic seem to recognise this readily, called by various names, such as the Self. Those of us who work 1:1 with others, clients, know the frequency with which individuals feel and need to find the uniqueness in themselves, a calling embodied in them. We need to name and acknowledge that presence.

Rogers' (1951) concept of the 'actualising tendency' implies that all biological nature has a unique growth to express in the best conditions. Again, this implies a uniqueness in us and that specific characteristics in the environment and those we relate to will bring out this best expression.

Perhaps, Positive Psychology, through the Values in Action literature, research and psychometric questionnaire come closest in mainstream psychology in proposing research-based character virtues and strengths that are cross cultural and an indication of the best in us; the idea that as individuals our most prioritised strengths represent an expression of our 'signature' displayed our way in our context (Peterson & Seligman, 2004; Niemec, 2018). What this research also highlights is the virtues and strengths we prioritise shift over time, so the changes in strengths we learn to express will need to be also adjusted in new time periods.

May (1983) describes a process which is both simple and profound: he saw a transcendent perspective to be a normal aspect of our consciousness through which we might 'stand to one side' of our experiences and reflect on what is happening. Perhaps, this is the simplest definition of how we learn and change through ongoing reflection and go beyond an earlier conception of ourselves. Yaden et al. (2017) identified a spectrum of activities that take us out of ourselves and brought about a sense or experience of self-transcendence, such as mindfulness practice and listening to or playing music.

Csikszentmihalyi (1993), based on his research on 'flow', proposes that each time we accept a challenge to extend our skills while working on the edge of our ability, then we also grow in awareness and consciousness. He is implying that each time we choose to move beyond what we previously knew into something more, we are changing, growing and evolving. While his description is localised to an occasion of learning through extending ourselves, he also proposes this is the ongoing cycle in which we choose to let go and go beyond what we previously knew to extend our capabilities and grow.

Kanigel (1986/, Worth (2000) and Vaillant (1977, 2002) each propose in different ways that a fundamental pattern in our growth in life is the influence of the mentor, role model, or caring adult who mirrors to us some aspect of who we are and supports perhaps in a context or point in time our growth and internalisation of ability and/or our positive qualities. Vaillant (2002) says we often internalise qualities of these figures to become part of who we are, and these relationships may often have qualities of love. My own (PW) doctoral research (Worth, 2000) confirmed the sense of presence of love and that the more influences of this nature we have in our lives, the more we seem to grow and perform.

Frankl (1946, 1959, 1966, 1969) highlights a primary drive and motive of humankind to seek and find meaning in life. 'Situational' meaning might be considered as here and now, 'small picture'. Finding a calling or seeing beyond the present world to a sense of the ultimate would each have a deeper and longer-term identity level perspective.

Yet, the movement within and across the phases and eras of our lives point to an active and cumulative process. Each phase of life has a localised experiential and cultural component that we learn from and becomes part of our overall self. However, each age and era have a relevant contribution to life overall, a time, a contribution in our development (Nakamura & Chen, 2021). As highlighted earlier, Erikson, Vaillant and Tornstam all point towards a reprocessing of current and earlier experience as we move into a new type of life content and experience – a reprocessing that becomes a transcendence of our 'former' self. This aspect of life is ongoing. We transcend earlier life experience, perceive it differently, leading to a change in a sense of time and self. Reed (e.g., 2008) and Hartman and Zimberoff (2015) suggest the transcendence of self is intra-personal, inter-personal, in time (Tornstam, 2005, 2011) and creates the transpersonal and brings out our sense of unity with others.

This passage of development takes us from a dialectical perspective of life, where we see and are shaped by polarities, that we seek or resist, to one where polarities may be encountered as 'both and', and the linking or unifying perspective that supports this happening becomes part of our perceptual process (Tornstam, 2005, 2011).

4 The journey's hero and 5. Our symbolic journey

The earlier chapters in the text have focused on relatively conventional psychology research and theories of development and growth. These two chapters, 4 and 5, move into a different form of exploration that of culturally based myths, stories, metaphors and 'archetypal' patterns of growth and life experience expressing the energy and symbolism of life. Their symbolism and metaphors give us organic feeling-oriented ways of perceiving change. We are drawn to aetypal stories expressing the energy and symbolism of life. The symbolism and metaphors give us organic feeling-oriented ways of perceiving change. These are stories over time that teach and shape us (Campbell & Moyers, 1988). These were recurring patterns of change and growth that occurred in our lives which were a pathway to encountering and accepting our strengths and uniqueness. Campbell (1949) and Campbell and Moyers (1988) had asserted that each of us, in our development, experience and live lives that are unique, that there had never been someone like us before and would never be again. If we could congruently accept that interpretation, some of our inner struggle stops; there is no need to be different or better than others if we are 'unique'. We can seek and support our own development and that of others.

Chapter 4 explores and extends these views by offering a perspective of the Hero's Journey as a journey of experienced transformation and maturation within our lives. Newitt writes in detail of how this journey is part of 'breaking out', 'breaking through' and 'breaking in' to new insights, perceptions and relationship within our lives. The calling to an individual path is an often slow and challenging route, sometimes involving living someone else's life, a compromise prospect for many. Drawn from ancient wisdom, the Hero's Journey still symbolically signposts the journey ahead if we accept the 'call' that keeps calling from within (Worth, 2016).

Chapter 5 is a powerful and moving extension and challenge to earlier views of the hero's journey. Herbert challenges views she sees as culturally and historically dated in asserting their failure to recognise the experience of women. She sets out to assert women's experience, hear and bring out their voices in psychological theorising and encourage anyone who does not identify with psychology as it is now to bring out their voices and experiences so that psychology can be more representative. Her work is timely, brave and creative, providing language and perspectives on women's experiences that will support insight and inclusivity.

Chapters 6–8 move to highlight and develop perspectives on practice.

6 The relational context of change

We exist and learn in the 'mirror' of the world around us. Echoing Erikson's assertion that we are bio-psycho-social beings, (1958/1980, 1963) our understanding of who we are is fundamentally influenced by our experiences of the world around us.

May (1983) questioned whether we, as psychology practitioners, and implicitly as any human being, ever truly 'met' and 'saw' the other person with which we interact and relate. His question came from the understanding that we all 'see' through the lens of our historical experience, our capacity for perception and the qualities of our attention. In posing this question, he was seeking to take us to a perspective of exploring whether we could find a place of openness and 'being' in which we could truly encounter another person and who they are in that moment of time.

Chapter 6, mirroring the work of Rogers (1957), highlights when we can find and offer this state of openness and authenticity within us it profoundly supports growth in another person. By proposing a framework through which our perception and being can be relaxed and opened, and through which the capacity to show who we authentically are at that moment in time, accepting and seeing the other person, can, in turn, enable their own change and development. Machon has offered this from the perspective of the practitioner/researcher and the development of a model he has shared and tested in his own coaching, mentoring and teaching of others.

The model is illustrated in Figure 10.2 and described fully in Chapter 6.

Machon's writing echoes the views of Rogers (1957) and Worth (2017) which illustrates what for many of us is a startling paradox: in the world in which we might feel pressed to 'do' and 'act', when we can be quiet, open, receptive, congruent and an authentic mirror to those we work with, we and they, in turn, learn those qualities from the experience. Machon further advances thinking by highlighting the innate relational nature of our source of being and how in evolving self-consciousness we cultivate our capacity to relate.

As we relax, let go and accept who and where we are and encounter the environment and person with openness, Worth (2017) and Machon in his chapter here propose these are qualities of love. Other 'fruits' of change

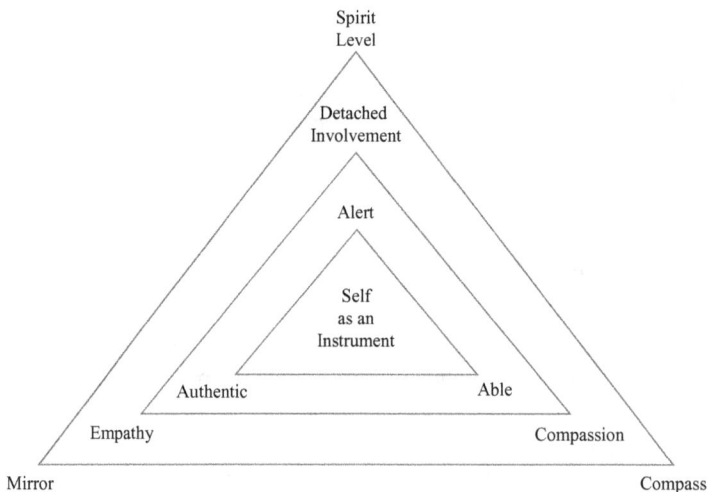

Figure 10.2 Three essential attitudes, qualities and innate instruments of the self.

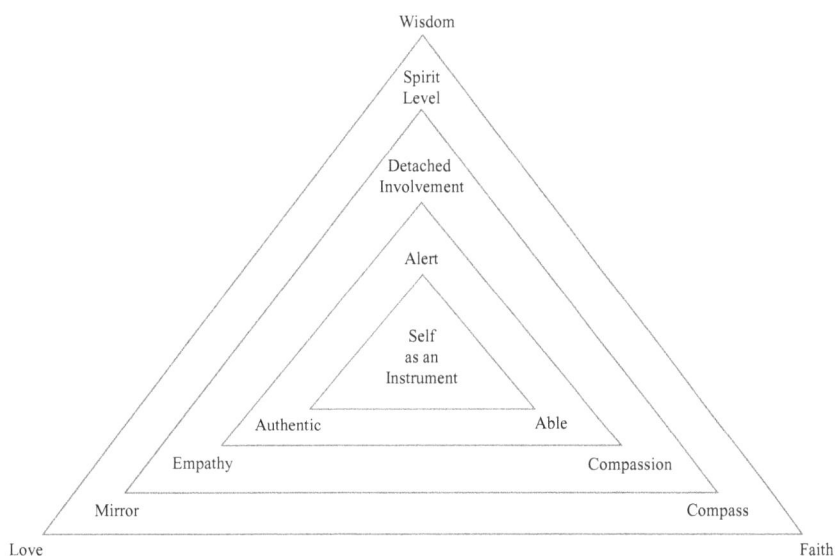

Figure 10.3 Three essential attitudes, qualities and innate instruments of the self and fruits of practice.

emerge, fruits deserving of future research. We speculate from experience that these fruits are:

Wisdom – as we become alert and can balance the 'I' and work with detached involvement – our thinking can move beyond the rational and open to wisdom – here wisdom is seen as a reflective and receptive knowledge of the whole.

Faith – emerges as a belief in a source and innate directionality to life and work. The practitioner becomes increasingly aware of an innate directionality to their life and work and in working with others. Something in which they can trust in terms of their own unfolding and the developmental unfolding of others – this is a growing consciousness of source – a faith in something larger than ourselves, a source of innate directionality.

Future work could show how the model Machon proposes is continually open to evolution. We anticipate we will be dedicating more time and research to bring forth these vital 'fruits' of a dedicated practice that further inform the nature of 'self as an instrument' and our remarkable potential instrumentality as individuals and practitioners.

7 Introduction to the TTM of change

The motive of this chapter and subject in the context of the book is to offer a model of a process of personal change given that in our experience of PG teaching, many PP practitioners do not have that training. This model is one example. This chapter intentionally chose one method of change amongst many to orientate practitioners and readers generally to the stages and processes of change from a 'face validity'. Based on over 40 years of research on psychotherapy and successful 'self-changers', the chapter is an introductory summary of very detailed work.

The reason for this choice is the two core elements of the model.

The stages of change represent researched experiences of successful self-changers.

The processes of change emerge from an extraordinary integration and synthesis of psychotherapeutic methods found through nine editions of Prochaska's milestone text 'Systems of Psychotherapy' (Prochaska & Norcross, 2018).

Combined, these are two unique resources brought to the nature of human change. Both are identified and defined from the researched inner experiences of individuals who change.

Chapter 7 summarises the background, research and structure associated with the TTM and, in turn, proposes how positive psychology may contribute to its practice.

8 Developing insight

The insight and capacity for any of us to see the dialectical nature of reality emerge is one of the deepest and most challenging aspects of the journey embraced in this book. Wong (2011), Ivtzan et al. (2016) and others highlight that life experience is rooted in opposites, polarities and paradox. Our early life is deeply shaped by the socialisation that life is 'one thing *or* another', for example, that we should find and experience positive aspects of life and resist their opposites. Levinson et al. (1978) and Vaillant (1977, 1993, 2002) found that ageing, which included living the implications of our age, frailty and mortality, brought the polarities of experience into awareness. Levinson et al. (1978) was explicit this involved finding ways to accept *both* aspects of a polarity.

Machon has undertaken something brave and bold in articulating how we may perceive, relate to, and live with the dialectical nature of reality and that in doing so our way of being will change.

If we then look at change through seeing the paradoxical nature of reality, not resisting one aspect, but accepting both, something profound happens. We find the ability to turn towards what we may have previously judged and rejected, and through this, we may remarkably discover vital strength and resourcefulness, a perspective that can bridge and unify the polarity, and the confidence to be authentically who we are. When we have compassion for this dynamic in ourselves, we can, in turn, see and offer this to others.

When we operate in this manner as practitioners and learn how to be 'at one with' our clients, in such an unconditional presence, the client discovers the rare chance of what it means to be true to themselves, see themselves without condition in their entirety, and recall who they long to be and were born to become. In such developmental relationships, there is a patience embedded in a belief and unwavering faith that the client will discover their own way.

What then happens, in unexpected moments as Machon affirms, is that the 'grace' of acceptance enters the relational space, and when we are able to witness what is, just as it is, we then change (Worth, 2017; Rogers, 1957).

We note how our understanding of change profoundly shifts in line with our evolving perceptions of reality. Do we discover a deeper motivation for change and resolution that emerges from embracing our uniqueness which, in turn, accepts the difference in another person? Worth (2017) inferred that these ways of perceiving, acting and being present with another person are a form of love. Do we, with presence, patience and love await the insight that permits us to fully see and accept what is, for then this way of working suggests change is both effortless and inevitable.

9 Existential PPIs in and over time

The chapter proposes the common characteristics and structure for an EPPI are

- A structured use of a specific exercise or exercises for the purpose of promoting positive outcomes, such as developing our sense of 'being' and personal unfolding; finding personal meaning in life and opening us to new information and behaviour.
- Chosen construct/s originate or are represented and researched within PP, Existential or Humanistic Psychology.
- These interventions offer the scope for accumulated research evidence that can, in turn, be built upon in the development of this new discipline.
- Targeted on developing or improving an individual state of overall 'being', well-being or altering a negative state, introducing new perspectives, ideas and behaviours, increased awareness, altered attitudes and understanding of self. In the act of doing these, interventions may bring about an 'expansion' of perception and understanding, for example, reveal previously unconscious or unrealised thoughts, ideas, beliefs, change and bring them to awareness.

The chapter has tabulated the decades of the life cycle of stability and change to indicate what types of intervention might be appropriate to support the experiences of ageing with an existential quality.

The chapter analysis suggests potentially all the following interventions developed in positive psychology have an age-related contribution to make: Re-storying the lifespan; Changes to the priorities given to strengths as we age; Development and adjustment to sense of purpose as we age; Creation of 'generativity' (ways of supporting a younger generation); Balancing the experience of polarities as we age; (for example, Levinson highlights 'young/old', destruction/creation'). Plus we consider how current PPIs may need adjusting to different ages (Facilitating Erikson's final life stage? Living positive ageing?).

In a further contribution of seeking to define potential EPPI, the chapter tabulates different existential perspectives and characteristics and draws out in detail how existing PPIs may serve a double purpose when viewed and used from an adjusted existential framework. Using a term from Chapter 1, this extends the 'reach' of positive psychology as a discipline.

Where does this book 'end'?

The intention of this chapter was to summarise an essence of the preceding chapters of the book. Seen cumulatively, they point towards characteristics of our 'existence' through our lifetime (e.g. Yalom, 2008), the processes through which we grow and can open to growth, the stories that can be symbolic of how we change and finding the strength of our voice in both existence, being and change. All of this is experienced relationally in the world around us and confronts us in an experience of the dialectic nature of life. When we can experience and accept both aspects of the dialectic, a polarity as 'both and', it introduces a relaxed and accepting energy towards ourselves and others.

The existential approach is inviting us to turn inward as well as outward. A scientific and sometimes over-rational approach is preoccupied with objectivity and the outward view of things. One of the key shifts through the existential is a turning inwards to respect and place value on the subjective and experiential – in other words, the value of our experiences as well as facts and data.

Our view as writers is an existential viewpoint invites us to look within – and is one that initiates development – through developing self-consciousness and insight. But of what do we become aware? The answer is the source and expression of our being – whether we refer to our source as an actualising tendency or some other words does not matter – what matters is that when we turn inwards, we discover both our source of being and becoming (May, 1983; Yalom, 2008). This alignment and activation of source is a profoundly different experience to the self to which we habitually revert – which is on a form of 'autopilot' – this dimension of self, offers a chance to re-set our vital coordinates – to remember what is truly important and valued and to activate or re-activate our journey of development.

Positive psychology, when explored from an existential perspective, can be turned to highlight and bring out the vibrancy, uniqueness and originality of our being. In positive psychology as a discipline, this invites us to extend our reach in both vision of our experience of being, and how we may explore and research what this means. This book is intended as a 'bridge' to new possibilities. Its contents are a beginning not an ending or definitive. Any reader is invited to extend these ideas further.

As we return to the metaphor of the bridge, it may be that there is no 'bridge' that we cannot build and no 'bridge' that we cannot ultimately cross. In this way, the 'bridge' is both an aspiration and inspiration. It reminds that at the heart of development is both a being and becoming. Maybe a bridge underlies our current metaphor of waves of positive psychology such that our approach is more integrative. What the 'bridge' respects is that development is an aspiration towards wholeness and the making conscious of a vital source that continually inspires our journey. In this way, the existential finds its place within the integrative process of making whole.

Further support for the contents of this book

The spirit of this book is intended as a primer and introduction to the possible nature and development of EPP and is 'free standing' in the content it offers. There are more ideas and possible developments of EPP than can be included in this book. Our intention is to offer support and additional material for the book on:

  positivepsychologyonlinecourses.com/existential-positive-psychology website

The nature of the website content will evolve and change over time. We anticipate this including:

– Suggestions for 'EPP interventions'
– Podcasts, vlogs and interviews based on selected book content
– Recommended and suggested additional reading
– Updates on chapter content when they occur

Some of this content will be free for download and also shared on another sister website thepositivepsychologypeople.com and YouTube channel. Other more detailed aspects may involve a payment.

  www.positivepsychologyonlinecourses.com is a relatively new website that is mainly of interest to those studying positive psychology academically.

  thepositivepsychologypeople.com currently has a larger audience and attracts people new to the concept of positive psychology.

References

Campbell, J. (1949). *The Hero with a Thousand Faces*. Princeton, NJ, Princeton University Press.
Campbell, J. and Moyers, B. (1988). *The Power of Myth*. New York, Doubleday.
Csikszentmihalyi, M. (1993). *The Evolving Self*. New York, Harper Collins.
Erikson, E.H. (1958 / 1980). *Identity and the Life Cycle*. New York, Norton.
Erikson, E.H. (1963). *Childhood and Society* (2nd Edition). New York, Norton.
Erikson, E.H., Erikson, J.M. and Kivnick, H.Q. (1986). *Vital Involvement in Old Age*. New York, Norton.
Erikson, E.H. and Erikson, J.M. (1997). *The Life Cycle Completed: Extended Version*. New York, W.W. Norton.

Frankl, V. (1946 / 2020). *Yes to Life, Inspite of Everything*. London, Random House.

Frankl, V. (1959 / 1992). *Man's Search for Meaning*. London, Random House.

Frankl, V. (1966). Self-Transcendence as a Human Phenomenon. *Journal of Existential Psychiatry*, 97–106. doi.org/10.1177/002216786600600201

Frankl, V. (1969 / 2004). *The Doctor and the Soul: From Psychotherapy to Logotherapy*. Revised from the original edition. London, Souvenir Press.

Freeman, M. (1993). *Finding the Muse: A Sociopsychological Inquiry into the Conditions of Artistic Creativity*. Cambridge, Cambridge University Press.

Hartman, D. and Zimberoff, D. (2015). *Self-Transcendence and Ego Surrender*. Issaquah, WA, The Wellness Press. ISBN: 9780962272899

Ivtzan, I., Lomas, T., Hefferon, K. and Worth, P. (2016). *Second Wave Positive Psychology – Embracing the Dark Side of Life*. Abingdon, Oxon, Routledge.

Kanigel, R. (1986 / 1993). *Apprentice to Genius: The Making of a Scientific Dynasty*. Baltimore, The John Hopkins University Press.

Levinson, D.J., Darrow, C.N., Klein, E.B., Levinson, M.H. and McKee, B. (1978). *The Seasons of a Man's Life*. New York, Ballantine Books.

Levinson, D.J. and Levinson, J. (1996). *The Season's of a Woman's Life*. New York, Alfred Knopf.

Machon, A. (2018). *Guiding Lights: Images and Words Inspired by the Aurora Borealis*. Penarth, Wales, Oliver's Books.

May, R. (1983). *The Discovery of Being*. New York, W. Norton.

McAdams, D.P. (1985). *Power, Intimacy and the Live Story: Personological Inquiries into Identity*. London, Guildford Press.

McAdams, D.P. (1993). *The Stories We Live By: Personal Myths and the Making of the Self*. London, Guildford Press.

McAdams, D.P. (2001). The Psychology of Life Stories. *Review of General Psychology*, 5(2), 100–122. doi.org/10.1037/1089–2680.5.2.100

McAdams, D.P. (2013). The Psychological Self as Actor, Agent, and Author. *Perspectives on Psychological Science*, 8(3), 272–295. doi.org/10.1177/1745691612464657

McAdams, D.P. (2015). *The Art and Science of Personality Development*. London, Guildford Press.

McAdams, D.P. and McLean, K.C. (2013). Narrative Identity. *Current Directions in Psychological Science*, 22(3), 233–238. doi.org/10.1177/0963721413475622

Nakamura, J. and Chen, T. (2021). Positive Aging from a Lifespan Perspective. Chapter in: Snyder, C.R., Lopez, S.J., Edwards, L.M. and Marques, S.C. (Eds.), *The Oxford Handbook of Positive Psychology*. Oxford, Oxford University Press.

Nakamura, J., Warren, M., Branand, B., Liu, P.-J., Wheeler, B. and Chan, T. (2014). Positive Psychology Across the Lifespan. Chapter in: Teramoto Pedrotti, J. and Edwards, L.M. (Eds.), *Perspectives on the Intersection of Multiculturalism and Positive Psychology* (pp. 109–124). Springer Science + Business Media. https://doi.org/10.1007/978-94-017-8654-6_8

Niemiec, R.M. (2018). *Character Strengths Interventions: A Field Guide for Practitioners*. Boston, Hogrefe Publishing Corporation.

Norton, D.L. (1976). *Personal Destinies: A Philosophy of Ethical Individualism*. Princeton, Princeton University Press.

Peterson, C. and Seligman, M.E.P. (2004). *Character Strengths and Virtues*. Oxford, Oxford University Press.

Prochaska, J. and Norcross, J. (2018). *Systems of Psychotherapy* (9th Edition). Oxford, Oxford University Press.

Quoidbach, J., Gilbert, D.T. and Wilson, T.D. (2013). End of History Illusion. *Science*, 339, 96–98. doi: 10.1126/science.1229294

Reed, P.G. (2008). Theory of Self-Transcendence. Chapter in: Smith, M.J. and Liehr, P.R. (Eds.), *Middle Range Theory for Nursing* (2nd Edition). Cham, Switzerland, Springer Publishing.

Rogers, C.R. (1951). *Client-Centred Therapy*. London, Robinson.

Rogers, C.R. (1957). The Necessary and Sufficient Conditions of Therapeutic Personality Change. *Journal of Consulting Psychology*, 21, 95–103. https://doi.org/10.1037/h0045357

Rogers, C.R. (1969). *Freedom to Learn*. Columbus, OH, Charles E. Merril Publishing Company.

Seligman, M.E.P. and Csikszentmihalyi, M. (2000). Positive Psychology: An Introduction. *American Psychologist*, 55(1), 5–14. https://doi.org/10.1037/0003-066X.55.1.5

Tornstam, L. (2005). *Gerotranscendence: A Developmental Theory of Positive Aging*. New York, Springer Publishing Company.

Tornstam, L. (2011). Maturing into Gerotranscendence. *The Journal of Transpersonal Psychology*, 43(2), 169–180.

Vaillant, G.E. (1977). *Adaptation to Life*. Boston, Little, Brown.

Vaillant, G.E. (1993). *The Wisdom of the Ego*. Cambridge, Harvard University Press.

Vaillant, G.E. (2002). *Aging Well*. Boston, Little Brown.

Vaillant, G.E. (2004). Positive Aging. Chapter in: Linley, P.A. and Joseph, S. (Eds.), *Positive Psychology in Practice*. Chichester, John Wiley & Sons Inc.

Vaillant, G.E. (2012). *Triumphs of Experience: The Men of the Harvard Grant Study*. Cambridge, The Belknap Press of Harvard University Press.

Worth, P. (2000). Localised Creativity: A Life Span Perspective. Unpublished Ph.D. thesis – The Open University.

Worth, P. (2016). The Hero's Journey. Chapter in: Ivtzan, I., Lomas, T., Hefferon, K. and Worth, P. (Eds.), *Second Wave Positive Psychology – Embracing the Dark Side of Life*. Abingdon, Oxon, Routledge.

Worth, P. (2017). Positive Psychology Interventions: The First Intervention Is Our Self. Chapter in: Proctor, C. (Ed.), *Positive Psychology Interventions in Practice*. Cham, Switzerland, Springer Publishing.

Wong, P.T.P. (2004). Existential Psychology for the 21st Century. *International Journal of Existential Psychology and Psychotherapy*, 1(1), 1–2.

Wong, P.T.P. (2010). What Is Existential Positive Psychology? *International Journal of Existential Psychology and Psychotherapy*, 3(1), July.

Wong, P.T.P. (2011). Positive Psychology 2.0: Towards a Balanced Interactive Model of the Good Life. *Canadian Psychology/Psychologie Canadienne*, 52(2), 69–81. https://doi.org/10.1037/a0022511

Wong, P.T.P. (2016). Existential Positive Psychology. *International Journal of Existential Psychology and Psychotherapy*, 6(1), February.

Wong, P.T.P. (2021). Existential Positive Psychology (PP 2.0) ad Global Wellbeing: Why It Is Necessary During the Age of Covid-19. Posted by Paul Wong | Jan 5, 2021 | Existential Psychology, Positive Psychology.

Yaden, D.B., Haidt, J., Hood, R.W. Jr., Vago, D.R. and Newberg, A.B. (2017). The Varieties of Self-Transcendent Experience. *The Review of General Psychology*, May 1–18. doi.org/10.1037/gpr0000102

Yalom, I.D. (2008). *Staring at the Sun: Overcoming the Dread of Death*. London, Piatkus Books.bmhw

Index

Note: Page numbers in *italics* indicate a figure and page numbers in **bold** indicate a table on the corresponding page.

For Product Safety Concerns and Information please contact our EU
representative GPSR@taylorandfrancis.com
Taylor & Francis Verlag GmbH, Kaufingerstraße 24, 80331 München, Germany